Charters and Charter Scholarship in Britain and Ireland

Charters and Charter Scholarship in Britain and Ireland

Edited by

Marie Therese Flanagan and Judith A. Green

First published 2005 by
PALGRAVE MACMILLAN
Houndmills, Basingstoke, Hampshire RG21 6XS and
175 Fifth Avenue, New York, N.Y. 10010
Companies and representatives throughout the world

PALGRAVE MACMILLAN is the global academic imprint of the Palgrave
Macmillan division of St. Martin's Press, LLC and of Palgrave Macmillan Ltd.
Macmillan® is a registered trademark in the United States, United Kingdom
and other countries. Palgrave is a registered trademark in the European
Union and other countries.

ISBN-13: 978–1–4039–3217–4 hardback
ISBN-10: 1–4039–3217–4 hardback

This book is printed on paper suitable for recycling and made from fully
managed and sustained forest sources.

A catalogue record for this book is available from the British Library.

Library of Congress Cataloging-in-Publication Data
Charters and charter scholarship in Britain and Ireland / edited by Marie Therese
    Flanagan and Judith A. Green.
        p.   cm.
    Includes bibliographical references (p.) and index.
    ISBN 1–4039–3217–4 (cloth)
    1. Great Britain—History—Medieval period, 1066–1485—Historiography.
    2. Great Britain—History—Anglo-Saxon period, 449–1066—Historiography.
    3. Great Britain—Charters, grants, privileges—Historiography.   4. Ireland—
    Charters, grants, privileges—Historiography.   5. Ireland—History—To 1603—
    Historiography.   6. Historiography—Great Britain.   7. Historiography—
    Ireland.   I. Flanagan, Marie Therese.   II. Green, Judith A.

    DA129.5.C47 2005
    941.03—dc22

                                                                2005043035

10   9   8   7   6   5   4   3   2   1
14   13   12   11   10   09   08   07   06   05

Printed and bound in Great Britain by
Antony Rowe Ltd, Chippenham and Eastbourne

Contents

Contents

Abbreviations

Aelred, *Genealogia*	Aelred of Rievaulx, 'Genealogia Regum Anglorum', in *PL*, 195, cols 711–38
AFM	*Annála Ríoghachta Éireann: Annals of the Kingdom of Ireland by the Four Masters from the Earliest Period to the Year 1616*, ed. and trans. J. O'Donovan, 7 vols (Dublin, 1845–51)
AI	*The Annals of Inisfallen*, ed. S. Mac Airt (Dublin, 1951)
ATig	'The Annals of Tigernach', ed. W. Stokes, *Revue Celtique*, 16 (1895), 374–419; 17 (1896), 6–33, 119–263, 337–420; 18 (1897), 9–59, 150–97, 267–303; reprinted in two vols (Felinfach, 1993)
ANS	*Anglo-Norman Studies*
ASC	*The Anglo-Saxon Chronicle: A Revised Translation*, ed. D. Whitelock, D. C. Douglas and S. I. Tucker (London, 1961)
AU	*Annála Uladh: Annals of Ulster*, ed. W. M. Hennessy and B. MacCarthy, 4 vols (Dublin, 1887–1901)
AU^2	Annals of Ulster, ed. S. Mac Airt and G. Mac Niocaill (Dublin, 1983)
AWR	*The Acts of Welsh Rulers, 1120–1283*, ed. H. Pryce with the assistance of C. Insley (Cardiff, 2005)
BL	British Library, London
CS	*Chronicon Scotorum*, ed. W. M. Hennessy (London, 1886)
Dunfermline Registrum	*Registrum de Dunfermelyn: Liber Cartarum Abbatie Benedictine S. S. Trinitatis et B. Margarete Regine de Dunfermlyn*, ed. C. Innes, Bannatyne Club (Edinburgh, 1842)
ESC	Lawrie, A. C., *Early Scottish Charters prior to A. D. 1153* (Glasgow, 1905)
Holyrood Liber	*Liber Cartarum Sancte Crucis: Munimenta Ecclesie Sancte Crucis de Edwinesburg*, ed. C. Innes, Bannatyne Club (Edinburgh, 1840)

JW	*The Chronicle of John of Worcester*, ii, ed. R. R. Darlington and P. McGurk (Oxford, 1995); iii, ed. P. McGurk (Oxford, 1998)
Melrose Liber	*Liber Sancte Marie de Melros: Munimenta Vetustiora Monasterii Cisterciensis de Melros*, ed. C. Innes, Bannatyne Club (Edinburgh, 1837)
Mon. Ang.	Dugdale, W., *Monasticon Anglicanum*, ed. J. Caley, H. Ellis and B. Bandinel, 6 vols in 8 (London, 1817–30)
NAS	National Archives of Scotland, Edinburgh (formerly the Scottish Record Office)
NLS	National Library of Scotland, Edinburgh
NLWJ	*National Library of Wales Journal*
OV	*The Ecclesiastical History of Orderic Vitalis*, ed. M. Chibnall, 6 vols (Oxford, 1969–80)
PL	*Patrologiae Cursus Completus. Series Latina, Patrologia Latina*, ed. J.-P. Migne, 221 vols (Paris, 1844–64)
PRO	Public Record Office, London (National Archives)
RH	*Recueil des actes de Henri II roi d'Angleterre et duc de Normandie concernant les provinces françaises et les affaires de France*, ed. L. Delisle and E. Berger, 4 vols (Paris, 1909–27)
RRAN	*Regesta Regum Anglo-Normannorum*, 4 vols, i, ed. H. W. C. Davis; ii, ed. C. Johnson and H. A. Cronne; iii and iv, ed. H. A. Cronne and R. H. C. Davis (Oxford, 1913–69)
RRAN, ed. Bates	*Regesta Regum Anglo-Normannorum: The Acta of William I (1066–1087)*, ed. D. Bates (Oxford, 1998)
RRS, i	*Regesta Regum Scottorum*, i, *The Acts of Malcolm IV, King of Scots 1153–65*, ed. G. W. S. Barrow (Edinburgh, 1960)
RRS, ii	*Regesta Regum Scottorum*, ii, *The Acts of William I, King of Scots 1165–1214*, ed. G. W. S. Barrow, in collaboration with W. W. Scott (Edinburgh, 1971)
RS	Rolls Series
S	P. H. Sawyer, *Anglo-Saxon Charters: An Annotated List and Bibliography* (London, 1968)

Note on references

All works, apart from those listed above, are referred to in the endnotes by author and short title; full bibliographical details are given in the Works Cited.

Acknowledgements

This book contains papers presented at a colloquium held under the auspices of the Wiles Trust at the Queen's University of Belfast on 26–28 September 2003. The colloquium brought together scholars working on charters of different areas of the British Isles and enabled a fruitful exchange of ideas and exploration of the comparative dimensions of both charter production and charter use. The papers highlight the crucial importance of charters as sources for the history of royal administration and more broadly for perceptions and portrayals of kingly power, as well as general aspects of political and religious history and developments in written culture. It is a pleasure to thank the individual contributors for their participation, the School of History in Queen's which hosted the colloquium, and most especially the Wiles Trust whose generous financial support made the event possible. Thanks for administrative assistance are due to the senior Secretary in the School of History, Mrs Siobhán Gunn, Mr Steve Flanders, and Professors Ian Green and Peter Jupp.

Marie Therese Flanagan
Judith A. Green

Notes on the Contributors

David Bates is Professor of History and Director of the Institute of Historical Research at the University of London. He is editor of *Regesta Regum Anglo-Normannorum: The Acta of William I, 1066–1087* (Oxford, 1999). His publications include *Normandy before 1066* (London, 1982). He is currently preparing a new biography of William the Conqueror.

Dauvit Broun is Senior Lecturer in the Department of History (Scottish) at Glasgow University. He is the author of *The Charters of Gaelic Scotland and Ireland in the Early and Central Middle Ages* (Cambridge, 1995), *The Irish Identity of the Kingdom of the Scots in the Twelfth and Thirteenth Centuries* (Woodbridge, 1999) and co-editor (with Thomas Owen Clancy) of *Spes Scotorum: Hope of Scots – Saint Columba, Iona and Scotland* (Edinburgh, 1999).

Marie Therese Flanagan is Senior Lecturer in the School of History, Queen's University, Belfast. Her publications include *Irish Society, Anglo-Norman Settlers, Angevin Kingship: Interactions in Ireland in the Late Twelfth Century* (Oxford, 1989) and *Irish Royal Charters: Texts and Contexts* (Oxford, 2005).

Judith A. Green is Professor of Medieval History in the School of History, Queen's University, Belfast. Her publications include *The Government of England under Henry I* (Cambridge, 1986), *The Aristocracy of Norman England* (Cambridge, 1997) and *Henry I* (Cambridge, 2005).

Michael Haren is the editor of the calendars of Papal Registers for the Irish Manuscripts Commission. His publications include *Medieval Thought: The Western Intellectual Tradition from Antiquity to the Thirteenth Century*, 2nd edn (London, 1992) and *Sin and Society in Fourteenth-Century England: A Study of the Memoriale Presbiterorum* (Oxford, 2000), and articles on ecclesiastical and intellectual history.

Máire Herbert is Associate Professor in the Department of Early and Medieval Irish, University College, Cork. She is the author of *Iona, Kells and Derry: The History and Hagiography of the Monastic Familia of Columba*

(Oxford, 1988), editor (with Pádraig Ó Riain) of *Betha Adamnáin: The Irish Life of Adamnán*, Irish Texts Society, 54 (London, 1988), and (with John Carey) *Studies in Irish Hagiography: Saints and Scholars* (Dublin, 2001) and numerous articles on Irish literature and hagiography.

Charles Insley is Senior Lecturer in the Department of History, Canterbury Christ Church University College. He was assistant editor of *The Victoria History of the County of Northampton*, 5 (Woodbridge, 2002), and assisted Huw Pryce with *The Acts of Welsh Rulers, 1120–1283* (Cardiff, 2005). He is currently preparing an edition of the Anglo-Saxon charters of Exeter cathedral.

Huw Pryce is Reader in History at the Department of History and Welsh History, University of Wales, Bangor. He is the author of *Native Law and the Church in Medieval Wales* (Oxford, 1993), and editor of *Literacy in Medieval Celtic Societies* (Cambridge, 1998) and (with the assistance of Charles Insley) *The Acts of Welsh Rulers, 1120–1283* (Cardiff, 2005).

Richard Sharpe is Professor of Diplomatic at the University of Oxford. His publications include *Medieval Irish Saints' Lives: An Introduction to Vitae Sanctorum Hiberniae* (Oxford, 1991), *Adomnán of Iona, Life of St Columba* (London, 1995), and (with J. P. Carley, R. M. Thomson, A. G. Watson) *English Benedictine Libraries: The Shorter Catalogues*, 4 (London, 1996), *A Handlist of the Latin Writers of Great Britain and Ireland before 1540* (Turnhout, 1997), and *Titulus. Identifying Medieval Latin Texts: An Evidence-Based Approach* (Turnhout, 2003). He is currently supervising projects to edit British medieval library catalogues and Anglo-Norman royal acta.

Nicholas Vincent is Professor of Medieval History in the School of History, University of East Anglia. His publications include *English Episcopal Acta IX: Winchester 1205–1238* (Oxford, 1994), *Peter des Roches: An Alien in English Politics* (Cambridge, 1996), and *The Holy Blood: King Henry III and the Westminster Blood Relic* (Cambridge, 2001). He is currently completing an edition of the letters and charters of Henry II, King of England, and is director of the British Academy's Angevin acta project.

1

Charters and Historians of Britain and Ireland: Problems and Possibilities

David Bates

For many historical subjects up until at least the middle of the thirteenth century, charters are so important that the topic concerned could not feasibly be studied without them. In general, the vast majority are short documents which appear at first sight to be written in limited language and constricting form. The appearance of limitation is, however, utterly deceptive; this simplicity can, and usually does, conceal an enormous variety of transactions, conflicts and, at a deeper level still, emotions. With significant methodological changes now taking place in their study, recent work needs to be brought into focus and suggestions made for the future. It is important that these changes are assessed in relation to the British Isles and Ireland as a whole since, differences notwithstanding, their cultural interdependence in matters of documentary form creates both an appearance of uniformity and an illusion of sameness which need to be probed. For most of the period which I am writing about Normandy must also be brought into the discussion and reference made to wider regions of northern France.

While the publication of editions of charters has been a steadily productive industry since the second half of the nineteenth century, recent years have seen something of a boom. Many charters have been edited, great series such as *English Episcopal Acta* and *Anglo-Saxon Charters* are moving closer to completion, and major new projects are under way.[1] B. R. Kemp has produced an outstanding edition of the *acta* of twelfth- and early thirteenth-century English archdeacons, G. W. S. Barrow has edited the *acta* of King David I, and K. L. Maund has published a handlist of the *acta* of twelfth- and thirteenth-century Welsh rulers.[2] The contributors to this book have made, and are making, many outstanding contributions.

The study of charters as documents has traditionally, and very respect-ably, been associated with something called diplomatic. To suggest that we need to think about how we define the study of diplomatic is not new; the point has, for example, recently been eloquently made by K. Heidecker in a book which is part of the large project on medieval literacy based at the University of Utrecht.[3] In fact, while we do need to examine critically a discipline whose basic methodology goes back to Mabillon, the central issue is surely how we define the link between dip-lomatic and source criticism, the one, broadly speaking, dealing with what is there in the text, and the other with how we should read that text. For all that almost all medievalists use charters, I do wonder whether we really know how to value them. Specifically, do we think about form, content, production and language in relation to purpose, audience and context as much as we should? Some might wish to contest these assertions. The brilliant pioneering work of M. T. Clanchy is an immediate exception. Nonetheless, it is beyond question that until recently, there has not existed in English any equivalent to the theoretical studies of different types of document which have appeared in France over the last decade, associated above all with M. Parisse, O. Guyotjeannin and several others. These scholars have used conferences to suggest general conclusions about the production and interpretation of cartularies and *pancartes*. They have also tackled a theme much more familiar to the Anglophone world, the charter as a written record, and one which is much less familiar, the charter as an expression of power.[4]

Clanchy's *From Memory to Written Record*, with a powerful glance back to the influence of V. H. Galbraith, marks an unquestioned turning point in the study of English charters. The way in which it related the production and use of charters to issues such as literacy, orality, memory and ritual has produced currents which have been felt far beyond these islands.[5] The way in which the interpretative use of charters has broadened in recent decades is illustrated by—some examples from many— D. Crouch's study of the image of aristocracy in Wales, England and Scotland,[6] J. Hudson's work on charters as a source for law and land tenure in England and, more recently, for Scotland,[7] D. Broun's many contri-butions, which include a recent comparative analysis of the diplomatic of Scottish, English and Welsh rulers' charters as the basis for some very perceptive comments on Scottish self-identity,[8] and S. M. Johns's book which has brought women and gender in charters in the Anglo-Norman period into the foreground for the first time.[9]

There is, if I am not mistaken, a strong tide flowing in the direction of treating charters in the same way as what are broadly termed literary sources, if you like to 'read' them as 'texts'. It is probable even that the tide has reached the shore. Certainly the old dichotomy between the supposedly reliable and objective administrative record and the opinionated and untrustworthy chronicle or hagiography which predominated until some time around the middle of the twentieth century has long since broken down. The traditional and indeed eternally valid objectives of diplomatic, namely to establish authenticity and to discover the rules by which documents of a particular kind were written in a specific epoch, have been absorbed into wider concerns about context, discourse and the construction of text. Charters are now every bit as much the subject of deconstruction as any literary text. While some of the chapters in this book show splendidly how they still fulfil their long-established role as a source for administration and the personnel of government and aristocratic society, they are now also the bedrock of enquiries into a host of other topics.

A recent article by J. Crick, for example, ostensibly devoted to twelfth-century forged charters from the abbeys of Westminster and St Albans has to range over the six previous centuries to draw out the monks' memory of their past and how they constructed it.[10] Among its many achievements are to shift the focus away from the supposed big bang which was once thought to have initiated this creative activity, namely the Norman Conquest, and to show that the process of writing and rewriting was a much longer one, sparked by a recurrent sense of crisis. And if we do stay with the Norman Conquest for a moment, I too have drawn attention in different ways to how the many-layered strata of memory and straightforward inventiveness either mined or made up the past to negotiate the present. At Canterbury and Winchester, for example, the point of departure for all legal claims was not 'the day on which King Edward was alive and dead', but the days before the pontificate of Stigand.[11] As sources for the history of ideas, the politics of the moment and a great deal else, charters can seize the imagination because they are made in the midst of events. And where they are more considered creations, they can show quite brilliantly how contemporaries brought all kinds of perceptions to bear on the present.

The widening of horizons and the great awareness of form and context must have consequences for the language we use in discussing charters. 'Forgery' has always been a difficult term. It can, for example, imply a document created *de novo* to claim what in fact had never been held. It may, however, be used in the case of a document created to meet contemporary norms, which in fact does no more than couch long-held rights and possessions in language acceptable to contemporaries. A phrase like 'diplomatic pollution', although used with a precise meaning in the example I have in mind, must be used carefully when critical methods being employed can arguably owe as much to critical theory as to traditional diplomatic.[12] Is it acceptable to use the oft-repeated phrase that a charter was 'issued'? The statement is arguably acceptable from the late twelfth century at the highest levels of society when organized writing-offices had proliferated, but it must become problematic lower down the social scale both at that date and for decades thereafter. All depends on how we define the word 'issued'—as a description of an act by which a public authority turned out a formal and legally binding document, or more vaguely as the production of a document to record a transaction? In specific terms, is the verb 'issued' appropriate in a case such as the story of how William the Conqueror, having brought a plea to a conclusion at Caen, ordered that a charter be written? The victorious monks, seemingly without any embarrassment, announced that they did not have the text with them and retreated to one of their priories at Briouze, collected the document, and caught up with William again a month later on the river Seine at Boscherville where the charter was confirmed.[13] The use of 'issued' to describe such a procedure may well be appropriate, but it simplifies hugely, as it must surely always do in relation to the very widespread practice of writing a charter in advance and then presenting it for confirmation.

To turn now to the British Isles, Hudson has recently reminded us that F. W. Maitland, in correspondence with G. Neilson, commented that 'I have long had the dream that Scotland is the link between England and Normandy', also that 'If I had another life I would spend much of it among your Scotch documents, and this for the sake of England.'[14] In truth, Maitland had neither cultural dissemination nor charter diplomatic in mind when he wrote his typically elegant phrases. What struck him was that lordship, meaning aristocratic power as opposed to royal, seemed relatively stronger in France and Scotland, and indeed in the northern counties of England, than in that supposedly typical part of the world, the South-east of England. While his opinions, which were after all expressed in private correspondence, have sadly failed over the course of a century to provoke a mass exodus of charter scholars from the great Scottish universities to such places as the Archives départementales of Seine-Maritime in Rouen, his general sentiment that we must look outside our own worlds is of fundamental importance. With so much work now in progress on Norman charters, the present is very much the time for fruitful comparative work.

While charters had been an aspect of British and Irish society since the seventh century, in recent times their proliferation has legitimately been seen as a facet of the European diaspora of the long twelfth century. As such, their spread must be viewed as an assimilation to forms of power and culture which were increasingly becoming the norms of the twelfth- and thirteenth-century West by societies already highly literate in various distinctive ways. R. Bartlett has made the general point very well.[15] Historians of Britain and Ireland have long been aware of this and have treated extensively of the subject.[16] This book (with one exception)[17], and therefore this chapter, is mostly concerned with the charters of the twelfth and thirteenth centuries. The debates about Celtic charters are therefore regretfully left on one side.[18] Mention must, however, be made of the monumental contribution of S. Keynes to the study of Anglo-Saxon charters. Throughout his work runs consistently the theme of seeking to relate charters to the circumstances which produced them and to use them to reconstruct otherwise hidden narratives.[19] C. L. G. Insley's chapter, in this book, on the submission of the Cornish to King Athelstan is a fine example of this type of scholarship.[20] Mention must also be made of important arguments which suggest a pan-British charter culture from the eighth century onwards.[21] The responsiveness of charter production to specific circumstances and to broader cultural and social change, which is very much a theme of this present chapter, is also central to modern discussion of Anglo-Saxon charters.[22]

For historians of Scotland and Wales, the general conclusion that English or Anglo-Norman influence on their charters was very important is a self-evident and unshakeable one. Continental influence is more evident in Ireland than elsewhere,[23] but everywhere the view is that the basic diplomatic matrices transmitted from either England or elsewhere were shaped by local conditions.[24] M. T. Flanagan's demonstration that one of the earliest surviving charters of an Irish ruler drew on German imperial models is an astonishing illustration of long-distance cultural dissemination, but it is an exceptional case.[25] Her chapter in this book discusses another supposed generalized influence on Irish twelfth-century charter production, that of the Cistercians.[26] The identification of similarities and differences in charter form and language across Britain and Ireland usually requires attention to detail within much less exciting parameters than German imperial diplomas. Local influence was always crucial and needs constantly to be identified.

The big problem with the analysis of the charter diaspora is England. A secondary one is Irish, Scottish and Welsh responses to it. When, for example, that great charter scholar Barrow can write 'Only the Dunfermline examples keep strictly to the conventions of the (Anglo-Norman) diploma', it begs the question of what 'the conventions of the Anglo-Norman diploma' exactly were.[27] M. Fauroux was after all stressing the diplomatic diversity of Norman ducal diplomas before 1066 in her edition which was published over 40 years ago. It is now clear that the Anglo-Norman derivative is just, if not more, complex.[28] What exactly 'the conventions' might have been strikes me as a fairly open question. Certainly, without any book having ever been written on English, Norman or Anglo-Norman charters, the task of identifying either English or Anglo-Norman influence is not entirely straightforward. Change within English and Anglo-Norman charters is also a crucial issue. J. A. Green's discussion, in this book, of Henry I's Coronation Charter illuminates how the form could be adapted in a new way to perform a traditional kingly role.[29] R. Sharpe's chapter is also concerned with change within the Anglo-Norman world.[30] The analysis of cultural dissemination may well become an easier one in the centralizing chancery world which developed from the second half of the twelfth century. In earlier times, diplomatic fluidity of a kind which awaits a great deal more serious work makes the task much more difficult.

One of the most urgent tasks facing charter scholarship in the British Isles is without doubt the production of editions of the charters of the twelfth-century kings of the English. N. Vincent and now R. Sharpe are running with this particular baton to great effect. It will be a wonderful day—and one which is not that far off—when we have excellent modern editions of the charters of every king who ruled 'the English' from the earliest times until 1199. If we stay with the racing metaphor, and immediately acknowledge that Scottish charter scholarship is well in the lead, it is even more wondrous to contemplate the day when H. Pryce and M. T. Flanagan will also bring their projects to completion. Then we can really reflect on the charter diaspora. It truly will be a time for celebration when all this has happened. Yet thinking about it now is surely a clarion call to consider also the computer technology which will make for fast and efficient collaboration.

The edition of the *acta* of rulers is an indispensable foundation, although they are only part of the story and they may not be as dominant a part as has often been assumed. Having written some 20 years ago about the earliest writs to survive from the duchy of Normandy and become very aware of the distinctive features that the structure of Norman society placed on their use, I was still surprised some five years ago when I returned to the topic and discovered how small the wider diplomatic influence of the writ was in the duchy in the first half of the twelfth century.[31] Outwith the diplomatic world of the kings/dukes, Normandy was a land of *notitiae, conventiones* and chirographs with the occasional diploma thrown in—just like most other parts of northern France, in other words. The phrase 'horses for courses' comes to mind. England, it should be said, is not without its oddities too; the long-term survival of features of the Anglo-Saxon diploma being one.

In a socio-legal world in which ritual, symbolism and custom are now seen as centrally important, the introduction and/or increased usage of the charter was a delicate process. In the British Isles and Ireland, which for this subject has again to include Normandy, the speed of change and inclusiveness is as interesting for what did happen as well as for what did not. A. Adamska's suggestion of a parallel twelfth-century development between Ireland and Poland is an interesting one, although she is surely wrong to include Scotland in the comparison.[32] Within the British Isles, Ireland and Normandy, the two extremes are Ireland, a society in which charters were rare in the twelfth century, and England and Normandy, where documents are overwhelmingly numerous. Yet as my twenty-year-old comparison between Normandy and England suggests, even where societies are under the same ruler for most of the time and where assimilation is evident, difference can be profound and enduring. Vincent's chapter, in this book, illustrates further this point across the much larger geographical range of the so-called Angevin Empire.[33]

Irish and Welsh charter scholarship place monastic *scriptoria* at the centre of documentary writing and dissemination well on into the thirteenth century. Kings and rulers unquestionably exercised a direct and consistent influence on the content of charters, but production was mostly the responsibility of monastic scribes.[34] The English and Scottish kingdoms were undoubtedly in a different league when it comes to bureaucracy, that is in terms of the predominant role of a chancery, and certainly were by the last decades of the twelfth century. Yet even in Scotland, the beneficiary's role in the creation of texts and documents remained considerable.[35] The same may well be true in England, although we must await Vincent's edition of Henry II's *acta* before the topic can be fully explored. When a wider perspective is taken, I do wonder whether, for all the massive differences in the quantity of documents from elsewhere, England really was as dissimilar to other parts of the British Isles and Ireland in terms of centralized documentary production as is sometimes thought. Magnate and episcopal writing-offices are not much in evidence there until well on into the second half of the twelfth century.[36] The striking feature of any large collection of original charters from England—Durham is a superb example—is the diversity of their size, form and script. Book hands of various kinds hugely outnumber business hands. A period during the episcopate of Ranulf Flambard, when the diplomatic of the bishop's *acta* was heavily influenced by the royal chancery, was followed after his death by one when documentary forms became much more miscellaneous.[37] It is a paradoxical argument, yet one which may well be sustainable, that the crucial next stage in the analysis of the charters of the British Isles and Ireland is a much more systematic understanding of all forms and kinds of English charters. The logical way forward is the creation of an electronic archive of twelfth-century English charters.

The widespread adoption of Guyotjeannin's and his colleagues' definition of an eleventh-century chancery and its application to twelfth- and even thirteenth-century Britain has been immensely productive.[38] To dissolve the barriers between the work of royal *clerici* and beneficiaries' *scriptoria* allows us to see royal documents as the products of negotiation. Similar interaction is now argued for Anglo-Saxon England, surely rendering older arguments about the existence, or otherwise, of a tenth-century chancery somewhat sterile.[39] The way in which some English religious houses moved in on William the Conqueror soon after his coronation to confirm documents manifestly based on pre-1066 exemplars illustrates something similar.[40] Sharpe's contribution to this book represents a huge advance in terms of the Anglo-Norman period; a royal writ might well be imbued with immense inherent authority, but it was dialogue and awareness of local power and interests which informed the creation of a text.[41] At one level, namely that of script, these developments probably have little impact on the received history of the Anglo-Norman royal writing-office.[42] But in terms of documentary production and under-standing the way in which documents were used and ideas disseminated, they have a profound significance which is only starting to be explored. They open up discussion about the processes whereby language and phraseology evolved across the board. Regional diversity and decentralized change within England come on to the agenda.

There are other ways in which it can be profitable to seek stimulus from colleagues across the Channel. D. Barthélemy's phrase *la mutation documentaire* has been vaguely formulated on its author's own admission.[43] But it does focus attention on the inter-relationship of documentary and social change and whether the former must, of necessity, imply the latter. Formulated perhaps in reaction to the conclusions which seemed very evident to an earlier generation of French medievalists who drew on older traditions of diplomatic scholarship, it sets out to argue against the idea that the proliferation of new types of document and the partial dissolution of the distinction between royal and 'private' charters must mean, of necessity, the collapse of traditional forms of authority. In England the manifestations of change are differently expressed. Nonetheless, whatever the reason for the dearth of surviving non-royal English charters from between 1066 and c.1090 in comparison to the previous and subsequent periods, the explosion in numbers and types thereafter is dramatic and undeniable. It is far greater than any statistical analysis based solely on royal *acta* would suggest. The source of the charter forms and practices was unquestionably northern France.

This English *mutation* cannot, however, possibly reflect a weakening of royal authority. In some ways, it may well have been a stimulus to the kings to strengthen control over the production of their own charters and to differentiate them from others, hence the considerable development of an organized writing-office from the early twelfth century; an argument which seems particularly applicable to Normandy. The huge increase in the surviving number of documents may also be in some considerable measure a resumption of normal service after the disruption of the Conquest generation; since the imperative to preserve post-Conquest, as opposed to pre-Conquest charters, was unquestionably greater and as the start of regular production of cartularies meant that more documents were preserved, any direct statistical comparison is fundamentally flawed. It undeniably illustrates an expanding adoption of literate procedures.[44] The idea of a *mutation* is applicable too to Ireland, Scotland and Wales. Here the framework is different in that we are dealing with a development seemingly in complete conflict with existing practices. Yet again all conclusions stress that it must have integrated into existing structures and tended, if anything, to reinforce rulers' authority.[45]

Another invaluable borrowing from French scholarship would be to take full account of Parisse's work on the construction of the texts known conventionally as *pancartes* and confirmation charters.[46] It can be applied to almost any document which falls into this diplomatic category. As it happens, it is the Dunfermline diplomas which came to mind as I was assembling this chapter. In them, as in so many other texts of this kind, we unquestionably see the old assimilated to the more modern and the contemporary.[47] To disentangle the layers rather than to resort to blanket condemnation is crucial.

P. R. Hyams's statement to the effect that charters often hide the circumstances which produced them is now well known. It ought to become, if it is not already, a truism of charter scholarship.[48] It is most easily illustrated when a narrative exists of the transaction to which the charter relates, or when two or more distinct documents describe the same transaction. The so-called charter-chronicles of twelfth-century England show the point very well. So too, for example, as I have observed before, do the surviving writ and chirograph recording the grant of lands in Blyborough (Lincs.) to the monks of Durham in 1148. The imaginative step which needs to be taken is to visualize how we would interpret the event if only one of the two documents survived. If the writ, we would presumably deduce a world where lordship, seigneurial consent to a grant and the authority of the written word were paramount. If the chirograph, then it would be kindred consent, symbolism and ritual.[49] The fact that the knife, once inserted through a parchment tongue and, presumably, also placed on the altar, survives only heightens further the second impression. Translated into the realm of social history, the contrast has immense significance. It is a warning that almost no document can be taken as describing fully the context which brought it into existence. Another example of a contrast of this kind is provided by the brieve and chirograph dealing with settlement of the dispute between Durham and the abbey of Crowland about Edrom in Berwickshire. William the Lion's confirmation is a brief statement that the matter has been settled in Durham's favour in William's court. The chirograph gives a longer list of those present, includes procedural details and records that Durham agreed to make an annual payment to Crowland.[50]

The issue for the future is to move forward from recognizing that a narrative and a context lie behind each and every document to trying to see whether there are any interpretative rules, or at the least guidelines, we can apply when there is no obvious contextual material. One area where there has certainly been progress is in the development of more sophisticated methods of analyzing patterns of attestation and witnessing. While the link between regular appearances among the *testes* or the *signa* unquestionably remains an index of political influence, both the type and form of a document and the relationship between content and witnessing must be taken into account. Where possible, corroborative external checks must be brought into play.[51] Observations of a similar kind have been made about the use of attestation and witnessing patterns to suggest the development of affinities beyond the framework of the honour during the civil war between King Stephen and the Angevins.[52] The charter evidence for the place of women in Anglo-Norman aristocratic society has also undergone significant re-evaluation. In general, women's role within the kindred is identified as very important because their role was often a hidden one.[53] It would be interesting to see how assessments based on different documentary forms impact on topics which Hudson has very much made his own, such as the consent of heirs to grants.[54]

These observations prompt me to suggest that the history of the chirograph in Normandy and Britain from 1066 to 1200 deserves more attention than it has so far been given. Crucial to analysis of the lay-religious inter-face, they have been much more studied for the Anglo-Saxon period, but not much for the Anglo-Norman. Their spread into Wales and Scotland has not been systematically examined at all.[55] The more I look, the more numerous these documents appear to have been from the late eleventh century onwards. Recent editions of charters from Burton abbey and St Peter's Gloucester, by R. Bartlett and R. B. Patterson, suggest this very strongly.[56] My own work on collections of original charters from Durham and Jumièges suggests the same.[57] Consistently more detailed than confirmations, they often include narrative and put a stronger emphasis on witness. They are surely the best route that charters can provide into lay literacy, pragmatic or otherwise. If *conventiones*, preserved either as originals or in cartularies, are added to the picture, my general impression is that form and content vary somewhat from beneficiary to beneficiary. The *conventiones* in the early twelfth-century *Textus Roffensis*, for example, tend to have more continental features, notably *laudatio* clauses, whereas later ones do not.[58]

Another area of enquiry which would benefit from further work is the construction of cartularies. The celebrated Worcester cartulary known as Hemming's cartulary has been given a lot of attention; it is particularly valuable because it actually tells us why it was written and why specific texts were copied.[59] So too have *Liber Landavensis* and a late eleventh-century cartulary from Christ Church, Canterbury. Other early cartularies, such as *Textus Roffensis*, the recently rediscovered cartulary of St-Etienne of Caen and the lost but reconstructable cartulary of Fécamp, deserve the same attention. The central task would be to analyze their author's selection of material, which continental parallels suggest must have been deliberate and purposeful. The inquest need not be restricted to cartularies which are early in date, but should also include those which are known to contain a lot of early material; here those of Burton, Dunfermline, St-Pierre of Préaux and St-Martin of Sées immediately come to mind, while a cartulary-chronicle such as Abingdon can provide invaluable material on selection of texts and narrative context. From this work a clearer picture would emerge of the archival culture of our period and of the significance that contemporaries attached to particular types of charter. The theoretical framework for this type of analysis is already very much in place.[60] The compilers of cartularies were not mere copiers of existing texts. They selected, and sometimes paraphrased or extended, and the memory of the past, as well as of rights, determined what was written. It is too often facilely assumed by an excessively insular scholarly community that the start of regular cartulary production was a consequence of the Norman Conquest, whereas simple chronology indicates that it was part of a broader European trend.

The overall objective must be to reach a position in which large numbers of charters from the British Isles and Ireland for the period from the late eleventh to the thirteenth century are available on line and are readily searchable in an efficient way. In terms of the country with which I am most familiar, France, the great ARTEM project at the University of Nancy which includes all original charters in French archives for the period before 1120 is close to completion. In Britain and Ireland, with the honourable exception of Anglo-Saxon charters, we trail a long way behind. Given the inter-relationships involved, it seems to me axiomatic that a great project should cover the whole British Isles and Ireland. It should also include Normandy, for obvious reasons. There a large project is already under way at the University of Caen under the direction of P. Bauduin to computerize all Norman charters which date from before 1100. I ought, nonetheless, to end by pointing out that the aspiration to master the subject of the charter in Britain in what we can for convenience call the long twelfth century is not in fact a new one. Although his immediate concerns were only with England, around 90 years ago Sir Frank Stenton did set his future wife the task of copying all the non-Danelaw charters.[61] They, along with the other masters of charter scholarship among our predecessors, attempted by systematic transcription and compilation what our generation has an obligation to accomplish collectively.

Notes

1. It would take too much space to list recent publications, especially as many of the important publications of recent years are listed in the chapters which follow.
2. *Twelfth-Century English Archidiaconal and Vice-Archidiaconal Acta; Charters of King David I; Handlist of the Acts of Native Welsh Rulers.*
3. See, for example, the remarks by Heidecker in *Charters and the Use of the Written Word*, 2–4.
4. Guyotjeannin *et al.* (ed.), *Cartulaires;* Parisse *et al.* (ed.), *Pancartes monastiques;* Gasse-Grandjean and Tock (ed.), *Les actes comme expression du pouvoir.*
5. Clanchy, *From Memory to Written Record.* The book edited by Heidecker, n. 3, provides an obvious example which tackles the issues across much of Europe.
6. Crouch, *Image of Aristocracy.*
7. Hudson, *Land, Law and Lordship; idem*, 'Legal Aspects of Scottish Charter Diplomatic'.
8. Broun, 'Absence of Regnal Years'.

9. Johns, *Noblewomen, Aristocracy and Power*.
10. Crick, 'St Albans, Westminster and Some Twelfth-Century Views'.
11. Bates, *Re-ordering the Past*, 8–9.
12. The phrase is used in Hudson, 'Legal Aspects of Scottish Charter Diplomatic', 122.
13. *RRAN*, ed. Bates, no. 267(I).
14. Hudson, 'Legal Aspects of Scottish Charter Diplomatic', 121.
15. Bartlett, *Making of Europe*, 283–6.
16. For a convenient bibliographical guide, Pryce, 'Welsh Rulers and the Written Word'. It is, of course, one aspect of the debate about what R. R. Davies has termed 'the Anglicization of the British Isles', Davies, *First English Empire*, 142–71.
17. See pp. 107–19.
18. Davies, 'Latin Charter-Tradition', 258–80; cf. Broun, 'Writing of Charters', 114–19.
19. See for example, Keynes, 'West Saxon Charters of King Æthelwulf'.
20. See pp. 15–31.
21. Howlett, *Sealed from Within*.
22. See in particular, Insley, 'Where Did All the Charters Go?'; Stafford, 'Political Ideas in Late Tenth-Century England'.
23. Flanagan, 'Context and Uses of the Latin Charter', 120–4.
24. Pryce, 'Welsh Rulers and the Written Word', 75–6, supplies many relevant references.
25. Flanagan, 'Context and Uses of the Latin Charter', 121–2.
26. See pp. 120–39.
27. Barrow, *Charters of David I*, 4.
28. See now, Mortimer, 'Anglo-Norman Lay Charters'.
29. See pp. 53–69.
30. See pp. 30–52.
31. Bates 'Earliest Norman Writs'; *Re-ordering the Past*, 11–12.
32. Adamska, 'From Memory to Written Record'.
33. See pp. 70–106.
34. Pryce, 'Welsh Rulers and the Written Word', 86–7; Flanagan, 'Context and Uses of the Latin Charter', 120–3.
35. Broun, 'Writing of Charters', 122–4.
36. For a general statement on this theme see, Webber, 'Scribes and Handwriting of the Original Charters', 138–40; Clanchy, *From Memory to Written Record*, 56.
37. The exceptionally rich Durham archive deserves a much fuller discussion than can be given here. For some comment and references, Bates, *Re-ordering the Past*, 15–16.
38. Guyotjeannin *et al.* (eds), *La diplomatique médiévale*, 223–4. See *RRAN*, ed. Bates, 96–8, 104–9; Broun, 'Writing of Charters', 122–3.
39. The cultural context of Anglo-Saxon charter production is also important to the subject. See Kelly, 'Anglo-Saxon Lay Society', 43–52.
40. *RRAN*, ed. Bates, 49.
41. See pp. 32–52.
42. For this, see the classic works, *Facsimiles of English Royal Writs*, ed. Bishop and Chaplais; *Scriptores Regis*, ed. Bishop; Chaplais, 'Une charte originale de Guillaume le Conquérant'; 'Original Charters of Herbert and Gervase'; and 'Seals and Original Charters of Henry I'.

43. Note especially the comments in Barthélemy, 'Une crise de l'écrit?', 99, n. 24.
44. Clanchy, *From Memory to Written Record*, 44–80; Bates, *Re-ordering the Past*, 12–16; see further, *idem*, 'La "mutation documentaire" et le royaume Anglo-Normand'.
45. Broun, 'Writing of Charters', 119–24; Pryce, 'Welsh Rulers and the Written Word', 83–8; Flanagan, 'Context and Uses of the Latin Charter', 117–22. See also the contributions by Broun and Pryce, see pp. 164–202.
46. Parisse, 'Écriture et réécriture'; *idem*, 'Les Pancartes: étude d'un type d'acte diplomatique'.
47. Barrow, *Charters of David I*, nos 33, 172.
48. Hyams, 'The Charter as a Source for the Early Common Law', 176.
49. Major, 'Blyborough Charters', nos 1 and 2; *Charters of the Honour of Mowbray*, ed. Greenway, no. 89; Bates, *Re-ordering the Past*, 5, with further comment there.
50. *RRS*, i, no. 105; Raine, *History and Antiquities of North Durham*, no. 642 (Durham, Dean and Chapter Muniments, 1.4. Ebor. 9).
51. Bates, 'Prosopographical Study of Anglo-Norman Royal Charters'; Marritt, 'King Stephen and the Bishops', 132–7; Vincent, 'Les Normands de l'entourage d'Henri II Plantagenêt'.
52. Green, *Aristocracy of Norman England*, 217–18; cf. Crouch, 'Debate: Bastard Feudalism Revised', 173.
53. Johns, *Noblewomen*, 53–121.
54. Hudson, *Land, Law and Lordship*, 173–207.
55. Lowe, 'Lay Literacy in Anglo-Saxon England', 161–203.
56. Geoffrey of Burton, *Life and Miracles of St Modwenna*, pp. xlv–lxxi, with original chirographs at nos 10, 16, 17, 18, 19, 24, 27; *Original Acta of St Peter's Abbey, Gloucester*, p. xlix. The same general point about chirographs is made in Chaplais, 'Original Charters of Herbert and Gervase', 90.
57. Much of this work remains unpublished.
58. *Textus Roffensis*, fos 191v–202r.
59. See most recently, Tinti, 'From Episcopal Conception to Monastic Compilation'.
60. For recent discussions, see Declercq, 'Originals and Cartularies'; Morelle, 'Metamorphosis of Three Monastic Charter Collections'; Bouchard, 'Organising Eternity'. See also Iogna-Prat, 'Confection des cartulaires'.
61. D. M. Stenton, 'Frank Merry Stenton, 1880–1967', 375.

2

Athelstan, Charters and the English in Cornwall

Charles Insley

Illos quoque impigre ab Execestra, quam ad id temporis aequo cum anglis iure inhabitarant, cedere compulit terminum prouintiae suae citra Tambram fluuium constituens, sicut Aquilonalibus Britannis amnem Waiam limitem posuerat. Urbem igitur illam, quam contaminatae gentis repurgio defaecauerat, turribus muniuit, muro ex quadratis lapidibus cinxit.[1]

(They [the Cornish] too were attacked vigorously and forced to leave Exeter, where they had lived until then on an equal footing with the English; and he fixed the boundary of their territory at the River Tamar, just as he had fixed the boundary of the northern British at the River Wye. Having thus purged that city [Exeter] by sweeping out an infected race he [Athelstan] fortified it with towers and surrounded it with a wall of square cut stone.)

This is William of Malmesbury's description of Athelstan and his campaigns against the *Occidentales Britones*, the British of the south-western peninsula in the late 920s and early 930s. William's description of the cleansing of Exeter and the expulsion of the Cornish (*Cornualenses*) from Devon has been seized upon by modern writers, in particular Peter Berresford Ellis, who have seen this as early evidence of 'ethnic cleansing'—words used by Berresford Ellis—by the English of their British neighbours in the south-west.[2] Berresford Ellis was writing in the early 1990s and by implication was inviting comparisons between the expulsion of the British beyond the River Tamar and the expulsion of Bosnian Muslims from Srebrenica, Mostar or Novi Travnik, or the attempts by the Serb leadership to create a 'Greater Serbia' and Athelstan's 'English Empire'. Berresford Ellis goes on to suggest that only the submission of the Cornish to Athelstan prevented similar campaigning in Cornwall itself.[3]

Berresford Ellis's comparisons between the horrors of our own century and those visited on the British of the south-west have been echoed by other Cornish writers, notably Pol Hodge who has used place-name evidence to reinforce the idea of ethnic cleansing in Devon and Cornwall during the Anglo-Saxon period. The problems of using modern terminology and modern ideas of 'ethnicity' and applying them to the tenth century are readily apparent and do not need spelling out here. To an extent, it is a little disingenuous to level this critique at Berresford Ellis, who is somewhat of a straw man in this context: it is unlikely that many, if any, other historians of the south-west would recognize Berresford Ellis's reading of their evidence. Nevertheless, it is worth moving beyond this very superficial approach to looking at Cornwall in the tenth century and to briefly survey the evidence—in particular the charter evidence—for the Anglo-Saxon impact on Cornwall in the tenth century and to provide a context for the relationship between the English kings and their Cornish subjects.[4]

The creation of the kingdom of England in the tenth century, the 'English Empire' as some would have it, is often seen as having happened exclusively at the point of the sword. This is the image fostered by the Anglo-Saxon Chronicle's descriptions of the campaigns of Edward the Elder, the meeting at Eamont Bridge, Edgar's Dee-rowing episode and above all the verse account of the Battle of Brunanburh later inserted into the Chronicle.[5] Undoubtedly, West Saxon military power played an important role in the creation of the English kingdom, especially in the early years of the tenth century, but we must look beyond the battlefield prowess of its kings to uncover the basis of the *modus vivendi* between the English and their British neighbours. This fits into wider questions about the extent of the power of the English kingdom, especially at its margins. How did the English kingdom of the tenth century, with which we are all so familiar, appear to its south-western subjects: what was the view from the periphery?

William of Malmesbury's description of an aggressive, imperialist Athelstan throwing the British out of Exeter is one of the few pieces of evidence for the relationship between the English and the West-Welsh and, as already noted, has been duly seized upon by historians. The fact that William perhaps had access to a now lost Latin account of Athelstan's reign, found in an 'ancient book', seems to lend weight to his account.[6] As Bartlett has discussed, specifically in relation to Gerald of Wales, but also to twelfth-century historical writing in northern

Europe, there are, however, major problems involved in taking twelfth-century writers at face value.[7] As he has convincingly shown with Gerald of Wales's works on Ireland and Wales, Gerald's view of the Irish and Welsh was informed by twelfth-century ethnography and a desire to draw a distinction between the civilized Anglo-Norman world and a semi-barbarous periphery, in turn based in part on Classical ethnography.[8] It seems likely that the same concerns were also present in William of Malmesbury's work, convinced as William was in the vitality of 'English History'. Indeed, William could be quite hostile to the Celtic neighbours of the English, on one occasion belittling a 'rural, dirty crowd of Irishmen'.[9] When William's predilection for editing his sources is also taken into account, then doubts must be raised about whether the Exeter episode happened at all, and certainly in the way described: whilst William may have been using lost material from the tenth century, what we are getting may be as much spin as authoritative truth.

Undoubtedly, the early tenth century was an important phase in the evolving relationship between the English and the Cornish, since it saw the more or less complete incorporation of Cornwall into the English kingdom and its administrative and ecclesiastical structures. We do, however, need to look further back, to the ninth century, in looking at the changing relationship between the English and the Cornish. Needless to say, the history of early medieval Cornwall is almost entirely obscure and, for that matter, the early history of Devon is not much clearer.[10] Beyond the limited archaeological evidence, there are a handful of fragmentary written sources, perhaps the most important of which is a tenth-century list of Cornish parochial saints copied into a Breton manuscript.[11] In this respect, the few pre-Conquest Cornish charters represent a major concentration of evidence.

St Aldhelm apparently visited Cornwall during the early seventh century: his *Carmen Rhythmicum* describes a terrific storm which was endured by Aldhelm on his way to Devon and travelling through Cornwall. Aldhelm's only comment about Cornwall, other than the implication of its stormy climate, was that is was 'devoid of any flowering vegetation or grasses in any abundance'.[12] Our evidence for the political relationship between the English and the Cornish really begins with the Anglo-Saxon Chronicle's entries for the early ninth century. As one might expect, the Cornish material in the Anglo-Saxon Chronicle is extremely exiguous. In 825, there was a battle between the 'Britons' and the men of Devon at Galford.[13] Five years later, Ecgberht led an army against the Welsh and reduced them to 'humble submission'.[14] We run here into a major terminological problem, however, since the Anglo-Saxon

Chronicle (and, indeed, other Anglo-Saxon sources) are not consistent in how they describe the British of the south-west. Generally, the term 'West-Welsh' (*west wealas*) was used of the south-western British, while 'Welsh' seems to have been applied to the inhabitants of modern Wales. However, in the Anglo-Saxon Chronicle entry for 927, which famously records the 'submission' of British and Scandinavian rulers to Athelstan at Eamont Bridge, near Carlisle, there is a reference to a Howel, king of the West-Welsh. Berresford Ellis took this at face value and suggested that this was a hitherto unrecorded king of Cornwall who submitted to Athelstan.[15] It is clear, however, from the context of the annal that 'West-Welsh' refers to the Welsh beyond, that is, west of, Gwent and that the Howel referred to is in fact Hywel Dda, king of Deheubarth, which brings us back to the 830 entry for the Anglo-Saxon Chronicle, that could, therefore, refer to Ecgberht campaigning either in Wales or in Cornwall. That this might have been Cornwall is suggested by the fact that eight years later, Ecgberht was recorded as having defeated a combined force of Cornishmen and Vikings at Hingston Down.[16]

At some point between 833 and 870 (probably not long after Ecgberht's victory at Hingston Down) a man called Kenstec, 'elected to an episcopal see among the Cornish in the *monasterium* which is called in the British language *Dinuurrin*', made a profession of obedience to Archbishop Ceolnoth of Canterbury.[17] It is otherwise unclear who Kenstec was or where the *monasterium* of *Dinuurrin* was located, although Lynette Olson suggested that *Dinuurrin*, possibly a site based around the cult of St Uuron, was a fortified site near Bodmin.[18] Ecgberht is also recorded in two different sources as giving land in Cornwall to the bishop of Sherborne, whose vast diocese theoretically included Cornwall. In a letter supposedly written by Dunstan in the 980s, Ecgberht gave three estates, *Polltun* (Pawton), *Landwithan* (Lawhitton) and *Caellincg* (unidentified) to the bishop of Sherborne.[19] The Sherborne Missal, a fourteenth-century manuscript, states that Ecgberht gave three estates at *Ros* (Rame), *Kelk* (Kilkhampton and *Macor* (Maker) to the bishopric.[20] When these gifts are considered alongside the seven Cornish estates left by Alfred, then it seems that West Saxon kings enjoyed some form of hegemony, however ill-defined, over the Cornish during the ninth century.[21] That this may have been the case by the late ninth and early tenth century is suggested by two further scraps of evidence, both extremely slight. In 891 the Anglo-Saxon Chronicle recorded the curious episode of the three 'Scots' (i.e. Irishmen) who arrived in Cornwall, from Ireland, in a boat with no oars. Having landed, they went immediately to King Alfred.[22] What one is to make of this story is unclear: there is just enough there, perhaps, to suggest that the linkage between the Irishmen landing in Cornwall and the sub-sequent visit to King Alfred was not coincidental—that in some way the Irishmen felt they had entered Alfred's land as soon as they had landed in Cornwall, or at least, the very near contemporary compiler of the Chronicle felt that this was the case. One might even suggest that, given that Alfred bequeathed land in Cornwall in his will and that Asser records the king as having hunted in Cornwall, the Irishmen visited Alfred in Cornwall: this however, is almost certainly going too far with the evidence.

Twenty or so years later, the Anglo-Saxon Chronicle refers to the attack on south-west Britain by the Vikings and their capture of Cyfeiliog, bishop of Archenfield.[23] The annal then states that King Edward organized forces against them on the south side of the Bristol Channel, from Cornwall as far as Avonmouth.[24] What is suggestive here is that Edward may have had some ability to call on Cornish military support. Nevertheless, despite these fragmentary, if suggestive, pieces of evidence about West Saxon lord-ship over the West-Welsh, it is also clear that there were native Cornish kings through most of the century—the *Annales Cambriae*, for instance, records the death of a Cornish king called Dumngarth in the 870s.[25]

Further light on the relationship between the Cornish and their West Saxon neighbours in the ninth century is shed by Asser's Life of King Alfred or, more correctly, by considering one of the possible audiences for the life. One of the most notable elements in Asser's work is the use of Welsh glosses for 12 English place-names.[26] This has been interpreted in a variety of ways. For Simon Keynes and Michael Lapidge, it was proof of Asser's intended Welsh audience, while for Alfred Smyth it was further evidence of the bogus nature of the Life, showing what he considered to be a rather facile attempt at creating a Welsh dimension to the work.[27] However, Paul Kershaw has recently suggested that a coherent pattern can be seen in Asser's use of Welsh glosses.[28] Of the 12 places glossed, 9 fall within the diocese of Sherborne and only Nottingham (*Tig Ghuocbauc*), Thanet (*Ruim*) and Cirencester (*Cairceri*) fall outside this area. It is clear, then, for the majority of these places, that Asser was using the Brittonic name to refer to places under his control, either at Exeter or at Sherborne. The only people for whom this could have any meaning, surely, were the British within the diocese of Sherborne. Is it going too far, perhaps, to suggest that one of the functions of Asser's work was to legitimize West Saxon and Alfred's lordship over the *Wealcynne*?

This is the background against which we must set the events of the tenth century and the charter evidence for it. Once we consider some of the charter evidence for the 'conquest' of Cornwall, then a very different picture from that provided by William of Malmesbury begins to emerge. Although there are only a handful of surviving Cornish charters from the tenth century, they shed valuable light on various aspects of the relationship between the English 'state' and the Cornish.

The first charter to consider is a document now in the archives of Athelney Abbey, concerning a grant of land at *Lanlovern*, by a *comes* Maenchi, son of Pretnigor.[29] Padel suggested, very plausibly, that *Lanlovern* is probably Lanlawren in the modern Cornish parish of Lanteglos.[30] The grant is to St *Heldenus*, which had been interpreted by previous commentators as St Æthelwin, but is more likely, as Padel has suggested, to have been St Hyldren, a local Cornish saint.[31] The charter is dateable to the period 924×939, since, critically, it contains a confirmation by Athelstan of Maenchi's grant: Bates, in his edition of the Athelney cartulary suggested a date of 937.[32] There seems to be no reason to doubt the authenticity of this charter, although Athelstan's involvement may well be an interpolation. Indeed, a number of diplomatic features lend weight to the charter's overall authenticity. The dedication to the saint, rather than the institution, and the use of the third person in the dispositive section fit into the broad 'Celtic Latin charter tradition' model articulated by Wendy Davies.[33] Whether or not Davies's model works, the Lanlovern charter certainly stands well outside the diplomatic tradition of Anglo-Saxon charters. That reason alone makes it very unlikely that the charter is, for instance, a forgery made by a monk at Athelney. This charter then is the only surviving example of a charter granted by a native Cornishman, drafted in a native Cornish diplomatic tradition and its content suggests that native Cornish lords were still in existence towards the middle of the tenth century and still able to grant land, albeit perhaps with the permission of the English king. The evidence is very sketchy, but one can see here a measurable increase in West Saxon power in Cornwall in the early tenth century, as also, perhaps, suggested by the Anglo-Saxon Chronicle's entry for 914 discussed above. There is no evidence that ninth-century Cornish lords needed West Saxon royal permission to grant land: not only does Maenchi seek Athelstan's confirmation, but Athelstan's reign also marks the earliest surviving English royal grants of land in Cornwall. Maenchi's charter also highlights the precarious nature of such survivals, his charter only surviving because it was copied into the Athelney cartulary. We must consider the possibility, therefore, that there were other grants by native Cornish lords from the same period which no longer survive.

We now turn to the charter evidence for the creation of the Anglo-Saxon bishopric of St Germans. Both Devon and Cornwall had in theory been part of the diocese of Sherborne until c.909/10, when a separate bishopric for Devon and Cornwall was established at Crediton.[34] The vernacular account of the West Saxon sees supposedly sent by Archbishop Dunstan to Æthelred II (S 1296) contains a contemporary interlineation describing the appointment by Athelstan of Conan as the first bishop across the Tamar (*Þa gelamp hit Þ æÞestan cing. sealde cunune bisceoprice eal swa tamur scæt*), dating this event to the period between 925 and 931, Conan's first appearance among the witnesses to a reputable charter. A slight spanner is thrown into the works by the ghost of John Leland, who recorded, during his peregrination around the churches and monasteries of England, a charter dating from 936 granting St Germans to Conan. Since Conan had been witnessing otherwise reputable charters since 931 this poses a problem. A further charter has more recently come to light in the register of Plympton Priory, again thanks to the detective work of Picken and Padel.[35] This charter restored the liberties to the see of the blessed St Germans: 'restituo et in diocesim perpetuam libenter offero'. It seems plausible, although ultimately dismissed by Olson, that Leland's charter and the Plympton charter are in fact the same document, in that Leland may have misread the restoration of liberties as the granting of the see.[36] We should also remember that there is a strong likelihood that St Germans was already an existing centre of ecclesiastical power, perhaps one of a number in Cornwall, along with the *Dinuurrin* of Kenstec's profession. An excommunication formula added in the late tenth or early eleventh century to the Lanalet Pontifical (Rouen, Bibliothèque municipale, MS A. 27) describes the bishop of Cornwall as the bishop of the *monasterium* of Lanalet. The pontifical has a St Germans provenance and, indeed, belonged to Lifing, bishop of St Germans between c.1019 and 1046. It seems likely, therefore, that Lanalet was an older or alternative name for St Germans. What seems to have happened in Cornwall was the reconstitution of an existing native Cornish see at St Germans as an Anglo-Saxon '*scirebisceoprice*' and perhaps the transferral of wider episcopal powers to that site.

The first three bishops of St Germans were also quite possibly native Cornishmen. Conan seems to have been, and it is possible that his successor Daniel was as well, given the predilection within the Welsh and Cornish clergy for Old Testament names.[37] Daniel's successor, Wulfsige, also seems to have been a native, if we can accept his identification with the Bishop Cemoyre who appears in some of the Bodmin manumissions. We must be wary of making too much of this; both Daniel and Wulfsige were recorded in the *De Antiquitate Glastonie Ecclesie* as having been members of the community of Glastonbury.[38] Then again, Glastonbury seems to have had strong links with Cornish churches during the late Anglo-Saxon period.[39] If Daniel and Wulfsige truly were Cornishmen, they were Cornishmen who had been members of one of the leading Anglo-Saxon religious institutions of the tenth century. Even so, the location of the Anglo-Saxon bishopric of Cornwall at an existing native episcopal site, with Cornish personnel, reveals a sensitivity to regional identity that is not so readily paralleled in Anglo-Saxon ecclesiastical appointments elsewhere.

The exact status of this new bishopric and its possession of the estates in Cornwall granted by Ecgberht to the bishop of Sherborne seems initially to have been unclear. There seems to have been an ongoing wrangle between the bishoprics of Crediton and St Germans for much of the tenth century over these estates, which almost certainly masks a wider struggle over the precise authority of the Cornish bishop, since one of the two accounts circulating in Wessex towards the end of the tenth century of the history of the south-western sees explicitly links possession of the estates to the bishop's pastoral responsibilities (S 1451a). These two accounts, one in Latin and one in Old English, outline the respective claims of Crediton and St Germans to these estates and both make use of a largely fictional account of the involvement of Pope Formosus in the creation of the sees of Crediton, Wells and Ramsbury in c.909/10, including an account of an occasion at which Archbishop Plegmund consecrated five new bishops in one day.[40] Both Formosus's involvement (he died in 896) and the mass-consecration story are complete fabrications.[41] What is interesting, however, is that the Crediton text, in Latin, seems to have enjoyed a wide circulation, with versions surviving amongst the muniments of Winchester and Christ Church Canterbury as well as edited versions copied by William of Malmesbury and the Worcester Chronicler.[42] This wrangle between the two south-western bishoprics was resolved in 994 by the grant of a charter (S 880) which made the full status of the Cornish bishopric unequivocal. The content of the 994 charter makes it also clear that the status of the bishop of St Germans had been unclear within Cornwall as well as outside it: a further part of the disposition places the *regimen* of St Petroc under the bishop of St Germans's authority. This has been seen as signifying the physical transfer of the bishopric to Bodmin, the site of the Petroc community, but it seems much more likely, as Olson has suggested, that it was transferring the episcopal authority wielded by the Petroc community, perhaps successors to Kenstec's *Dinuurrin*, to the bishop of St Germans.[43] What we have here, then, is a process that occupies much of the tenth century, in which one of a number of Cornish episcopal centres is effectively recognized and legitimized by the English king as the 'bishopric over the Tamar', but which then takes a further 60 years to have that authority fully recognized both by its neighbours and within Cornwall.

There is one further point to raise in relation to the charter in the Plympton register. The diplomatic of this charter is largely unexceptional except for two elements of odd diplomatic phrasing which may hint at the survival of older traditions of charter drafting. Like *Comes* Maenchi's charter, the charter, in the Plympton Register uses the phrase *in diocesim perpetuam* to describe the grant. This does not appear to be an element of Anglo-Saxon diplomatic practice. The Plympton charter also contains a reference in the reservation clause to the duty of coast watch (*vigiliis marinis*). This is a very unusual reservation and is found in only one other Anglo-Saxon charter, which also has a Cornish context. The charter is a late tenth-century grant to Ealdorman Æthelweard of land at Traboe, Trevallack, Trethewey and Grugwith, in north Cornwall.[44] Its diplomatic, too, is entirely in keeping with the mainstream, if it existed, of Anglo-Saxon diplomatic, except for a reference to *vigiliis marinis*? One could make the point that in an area with a large coastline and one which was vulnerable to the depredations of pirates, both Norse and Irish, it would have made sense to add maritime watch to the other military reservations. That said, such a duty may have been an existing obligation on Cornish land and one which crept into later Anglo-Saxon diplomatic practice in the south-west. It is worth mentioning at this stage the grant of Athelstan to the church of St Buryan (S 450) and the later grant by Edgar to the church of Sts Dawe and Kew (S 810). While both these charters are not without their textual problems, it is perhaps significant that both are expressed as grants to the saint, rather than to the church or to a particular individual. Again, this falls outside the norm for Anglo-Saxon diplomatic and may represent the survival of a fragment of older Cornish diplomatic practice.[45]

Four other Cornish charters also shed light on both the relationship between the English and the Cornish and the impact that the English 'conquest' of Cornwall had on the Cornish church. So far it has been suggested that the Anglo-Saxon impact on Cornwall was in some respects surprisingly limited and certainly less negative than might otherwise be thought, especially bearing in mind the sentiments expressed by William of Malmesbury. However, we now turn to the evidence for Anglo-Saxon despoliation and usurpation of Cornish ecclesiastical land. At least two charters from the period 930–1000 definitely concern the fragmentation of an ecclesiastical estate: S 755 and S 832. In the case of S 755, the ecclesiastical origin of the land granted is unambiguous, since the name 'Lesneage', or *Les Manaoc* as it is in the charter, is a form of the Old Cornish *Lys Menaghek*, or the court of the meneage, the meneage being an area of land subject to the monastery.[46] Two more charters, S 684 and S 770, may also concern secular encroachment of ecclesiastical land. In the case of S 755 and S 832, the lands concerned probably belonged to the canons of St Achebran, whilst the community of St Piran may have been the losers in the case of S 684. There are also several references in Domesday Book to the usurpation of estates belonging to the community of St Petroc at Bodmin by Harold Godwineson.

Two observations can be made at this point. Usurpation of ecclesiastical land was not a phenomenon confined to Cornwall, and despoliation of Cornish ecclesiastical property does not seem excessive when compared with the rest of England: one might also argue that wrangles over ecclesiastical landholding were part and parcel of the world of Anglo-Saxon conveyancing. The Godwine family in general were noted for their acquisitive attitude towards ecclesiastical property, and Harold Godwineson, for instance, was also the main usurper of ecclesiastical property in Devon in Domesday Book.[47] The second observation to be drawn is that the beneficiaries of two of these grants were men with partly Cornish names, Wulfnoth Rumuncant and Ælfheah Gerent. Whilst one might maintain that the usurpation of Cornish ecclesiastical land may be evidence of Anglo-Saxon disregard for the lands of the Cornish church, it is hard to do so when at least two of the beneficiaries of this asset-stripping were probably Cornish themselves. While the relationship between naming patterns, identity and ethnicity is a complex one, it seems unlikely that an individual with an English and a Cornish name was anything other, or felt himself to be anything other, than Cornish. It is likely, therefore, that both Wulfnoth Rumoncant and Ælfheah Gerent were members of a native landholding class clearly still flourishing in the later tenth century. A question that must be asked, although probably unanswerable, is to what extent such 'usurpation' of monastic estates took place prior to the tenth century? It is possible that Wulfnoth Rumuncant and Ælfheah Gerent were merely continuing a tradition that had existed for centuries.

Before turning to my conclusion, it is worth moving, briefly, beyond the charters to think about another key body of evidence, the Bodmin manumissions. These are a much underused and neglected source: the only modern edition, that by Max Förster, was produced as long ago as 1930.[48] The manumissions consist of 51 texts copied into the first and last four folios of British Library, Additional MS 9381, a tenth-century set of gospels possibly produced in Brittany. They are undated, but can be assigned to between c.930 and c.1050. Individual manumissions can be dated more closely: a number of manumissions were by, or for the soul of, a particular king or bishop.[49] In a couple of cases the manumission can be dated from the presence of certain witnesses: for instance, a manumission by Ealdorman Æthelweard and his wife, Æthelflæd, can be dated by Æthelweard's presence to before 1019, when he was exiled, and after 1002, the last appearance of the predecessor of one of the witnesses, Bishop Burhwold.[50] The majority are in Latin, with a handful in Old English. Generally, they are in the form of either '*x* freed *y* for his soul and the soul of king *z* on the altar of St Petroc' or 'these are the names of *x* and *y* freed by *z* on the altar of St Petroc'. There are two documents which are not manumissions as such, but deal with claims to free status.[51] Another text records a two-stage manumission in which a slave is freed in the vill in which, presumably, she lived, and then again on the altar of St Petroc at Bodmin.[52] In all cases, the common theme is St Petroc, in the form of either his altar at Bodmin or, in the case referred to above, his bell, along with the presence of members of the Bodmin community among the witnesses to the manumission.

These texts have not been thoroughly explored and only the tip of the iceberg can be touched here.[53] As well as the list of slaves and those freeing them, the witnesses of the manumissions would repay further detailed study, although space precludes it here. What follows is a crude use of the names of the slave-owners in the manumissions to provide a very rough index of the property-owning elite in Bodmin's hinterland during the later tenth and early eleventh centuries, based on the admittedly risky assumption that slave ownership can be equated with the ownership of other forms of property, especially land. At first glance, the manumissions seem to suggest that the majority of slave-owners who manumitted their slaves at Padstow or Bodmin had English names (a ratio of 17:12/13). Simply using personal names as a guide to identity is deeply problematic: naming patterns and customs were complex social and cultural organisms. Nevertheless, it seems rather unlikely that those of English extraction would have Cornish names. This does not, of course, discount the possibility that Cornishmen had Anglo-Saxon names—indeed, there are, as we have seen, a number of examples of individuals with both Cornish and English names. Four English kings freed slaves at St Petroc's on six occasions. Once the crown is removed from the equation, then we have a ratio of 13:13 slave-owners with English and Cornish names. By far and away the largest manumitter of slaves, in terms of both the number of occasions and the total number of slaves freed, was Wulfsige, bishop of Cornwall c.963–c.90, who freed slaves on eight occasions during his episcopate, including sixteen on one occasion. As I have argued above, Bishop Wulfsige was probably a Cornishman himself, appearing in one of the manumissions as Bishop Cemoyre.[54] It is also extremely likely that the bishopric of St Germans as constituted by Athelstan c.930 was the successor to a native bishopric at the same location and which also probably owned a relatively large number of slaves. Once the English king and the bishop of Cornwall are removed from the equation, then there are a larger number of slave-owners among the Cornish names in the Bodmin Gospels. This, of course, takes no account of the possibility that some of the individuals with English names may have been, like Ælfheah Gerent and Wulfnoth Rumuncant, native Cornishmen. The manumissions also reveal at least one servant of the English state with a Cornish name: Maccos, the *centurion*, which we can probably translate, as Hooke has, as the 'hundred-reeve'.[55] There is no doubt that this evidence is frustratingly intangible, but at the very least the manumissions hint at the survival of a native Cornish property-owning class well into the eleventh century and, in the person of Maccos, the presence of Cornishmen within the Anglo-Saxon adminis-tration of Cornwall.

This has been a very rough and ready preliminary investigation of what the Bodmin manumissions might tell us, and it only raises more questions than it answers. The above analysis takes no account of chrono-logical progression through the period covered by the manumissions: are there, for instance, more Cornish slave-owners recorded in the earlier manumissions than later? A second question, yet to be explored, is what these manumissions might tell us about relationships between ecclesiastical institutions in Cornwall? Why, for instance, does the bishop of St Germans free slaves on the altar of St Petroc, rather than St Germanus? The witness lists for the manumissions also raise intriguing questions. The bulk of the witnesses are either explicitly or by implica-tion members of the Bodmin community and have a mixture of Cornish and English names, with a smattering of Old and New Testament names. Occasionally, there are also lay witnesses to the transactions, again with a mixture of Cornish and English names. What we are to make of Ylcaerthon, the *prepositus*, and Tethion, the *consul*, is unclear![56]

How do we then locate the charter and manumission evidence in a wider consideration of the relationship between the English state and the Cornish in the late Anglo-Saxon period? In some respects, the impact of the absorption of Cornwall into the English state seems to have been remarkably muted. Both Athelstan and Edgar were active patrons of

Cornish churches and Cornish saints. In addition to the grant of the bishopric of St Germans to Bishop Conan, Athelstan also granted land to the church of St Buryan as well as confirming Maenchi's grant to St Hyldren, whilst Edgar granted land to the foundations of St Dochou (quite probably the *Docco* referred to in the *Vita Sancti Samsoni* and therefore a very old foundation indeed) and St Cywa (modern St Daw and St Kew).[57] Patronage of such saints' cults and, indeed, Athelstan's avid collection of the relics of Cornish and Breton saints might be seen as acts of cynical *realpolitik*, as a way for the English state to control the *foci* of local sentiment and identity and to ensure, perhaps, that these cults did not become the focus of opposition to English rule.[58] This was almost certainly the case with English royal patronage of the cult of St Cuthbert and may be true of the transfer of relics of Sts Kea, Rumon, Indract and Petroc to Glastonbury.[59] Nevertheless, there may also be in the patronage of such cults a genuine sensitivity to local sentiment and Glastonbury seems to have long-established links with the church in Cornwall.

Olson has noted that in Domesday Book the estates of the Cornish collegiate churches were almost entirely exempt from geld liability, whereas the estates of ecclesiastical landowners from outside Cornwall (the bishop of Exeter and the abbot of Tavistock) were not.[60] Whilst most Cornish churches were not extensive landowners, the bulk of St Petroc's 26 estates in 1066 were exempt from geld.[61] Olson suggested that this was an ecclesiastical privilege accorded to Cornish churches and one which may have pre-dated the absorption of Cornwall into the English kingdom. If it is indeed the case that this privilege was then continued after the 930s it reveals an interesting philanthropy on behalf of the English kings of the tenth century, given that very few churches elsewhere in England had such an important immunity.

There seems to have been a genuine interest in Celtic saints' cults, especially from Brittany and Cornwall, among the English kings of the late ninth and early tenth century. Athelstan's gift of relics to the community at Exeter contained a number of Breton relics and the early tenth century saw the feast days of such saints, especially the Breton ones, introduced into English liturgical calendars.[62] Such patronage may have had very real and worldly motives, but it is also likely that there was a genuine interest in these cults.

Alfred, Edward the Elder and Athelstan all maintained links with Brittany. According to Asser, Alfred gave gifts to Breton churches whilst William of Malmesbury referred to a letter requesting aid sent to Athelstan by Radbod, prior to the community of St Samson at Dol.[63] The letter states that Athelstan is continually in the community's prayers and reminds Athelstan of his father's good favour towards Dol. We know from other sources that Athelstan sheltered Breton exiles at his court, most notably Matuedoi, son of the count of Poher, and even gave active military support to Matuedoi's son, Alan 'Barbetorte'.[64] Rollason saw Athelstan's acquisition of Breton relics and patronage of cults as an exercise in prestige building at the expense of his less fortunate neighbours, but it is interesting that Breton cults were of such interest to Athelstan at the very period he was attempting to incorporate Cornwall into the English kingdom.[65] The links between Alfred, Edward, Athelstan and Brittany may reveal something of the attitude of these kings to their Celtic neighbours.

Despite the frustratingly fragmentary evidence briefly surveyed here, we can perhaps arrive at some tentative conclusions about the processes by which Cornwall was made part of the English kingdom and how the relationship between Cornwall and England evolved. To return to the sentiments of William of Malmesbury and the 'ethnic cleansing' of the south-west, it is clear that such an analysis is flawed. Nothing that the English kings of the tenth century did was entirely altruistic, and certainly Cornish ecclesiastical property was stolen but perhaps no more than elsewhere in the English kingdom. The charter evidence suggests that, in many respects, Cornish ecclesiastical establishments fared rather well. In parallel with the continued flourishing of existing churches, including, perhaps, their geld-free status, we can glimpse the survival of a native landowning elite through the tenth and into the eleventh centuries and, in the case of Maccos, the hundred-reeve, the survival of Cornishmen in positions of administration. One cannot really think in terms of ethnic cleansing, but possibly, to borrow a phrase from Rees Davies, of 'conquest and coexistence' with perhaps a little bit of change.

Notes

1. William of Malmesbury, *Gesta Regum Anglorum*, i, 216.
2. Berresford Ellis, *Celt and Saxon*, 203.
3. Ibid., 203–4.
4. See for instance the works of Padel, 'Two New Pre-Conquest Charters'; *idem*, 'Cornish Background to the Tristan Stories'; *idem*, *Cornish Place-Name Elements*; *idem*, 'Some South-Western Sites with Arthurian Associations'; Pearce, *Early Church in Western Britain and Ireland*; Olson, *Early Monasteries*; *eadem*, with Padel, 'Tenth-Century List of Cornish Parochial Saints'; Jankulak, *Medieval Cult and Relics of St Petroc*; Orme, *Unity and Variety*; *idem*, *Saints of Cornwall*.

5. *ASC*, D, s.a. 910, 912, 914–17, 927, 973; C, s.a. 937. The reference to Edgar being rowed on the see by British 'sub-kings' does not occur in the contemporary sources; the earliest mention is in the twelfth-century: JW, ii, 422–4. For a discussion of the events of 973, see Thornton, 'Edgar and the Eight Kings' and Barrow, 'Chester's Earliest Regatta?'.

6. The issue of the origin of the material incorporated by William into his history is a complex one. Lapidge has expressed scepticism about the material used by William and regards it as having been derived from a much later Latin poem, 'Some Latin Poems as Evidence for the Reign of Athelstan', 62–71. Wood, however, has articulated the view that William did indeed have sight of a prose life of Athelstan: 'Making of King Athelstan's Empire', 265–7; *idem*, 'Lost Life of King Athelstan'. Thompson, the most recent editor of William's work, agrees with Wood that William used a much older prose source, but adapted and paraphrased it for his own ends: William of Malmesbury, *Gesta Regum Anglorum*, ii, 117–18.

7. Bartlett, *Gerald of Wales*, 169.

8. Ibid., 178–81.

9. Ibid., 159.

10. Both Hoskins (*Westward Expansion*) and Finberg (*Lucerna*) examined the evidence for the Anglo-Saxon expansion into the south-west in the seventh century. Recently, Todd, *South-West to AD 1000*, 269–72, has provided a different perspective, while the more recent unpublished thesis of D. Probert examines the linguistic evidence for Devon and Cornwall in the early middle ages. For Cornish history, the most significant recent work is Olson's account of the early monasteries of Cornwall, Padel's discussion of the Cornish charter evidence and Orme's catalogue of Cornish saints' cults (see n. 4).

11. Olson and Padel, 'Tenth-Century List of Cornish Parochial Saints'.

12. Aldhelm, *Poetic Works*, 77, 173.

13. *ASC*, D, s.a. 825.

14. Ibid., s.a. 830.

15. Berresford Ellis, *Celt and Saxon*, 204.

16. *ASC*, D, s.a. 835, *recte* 838.

17. Canterbury, Cathedral Library, Register A, fo. 292; *Canterbury Professions*, 27 (no. 27).

18. Olson, *Early Monasteries*, 52–6.

19. S 1296.

20. *Anglo-Saxon Charters III: The Charters of Sherborne*, liv–lvi.

21. Keynes and Lapidge, *Alfred the Great*, 173–8.

22. *ASC*, C, s.a. 891.

23. *ASC*, B, s.a. 914; C, D, s.a. 915.

24. Ibid.

25. *Annales Cambriae*, 15.

26. Thanet (*Ruim*), Nottingham (*Tig Ghuocbauc*), River Wylye (*Guilou*), Dorset (*Durnguerir*), Exe (*Uisc*), River Frome (*Frauu*), Exeter (*Caeruuisc*), River Avon (*Abon*), Countisbury (*Cynuit*), Selwood (*Coitmaur*), Cirencester (*Cairceri*) and St Guerirr.

27. Keynes and Lapidge, *Alfred the Great*, 56, 250, n. 115; Smyth, *Alfred the Great*, 350.

28. I am very grateful to Paul Kershaw for allowing me to use unpublished material on Asser's audience.

29. S 1207.
30. Padel, 'Two Pre-Conquest Charters', 22–3.
31. Ibid., 22.
32. *Two Cartularies of the Benedictine Abbeys of Muchelney and Athelney*, 156.
33. Davies, 'Latin Charter-Tradition'; see also Broun, *Charters of Gaelic Scotland and Ireland*, for a partial revision of Davies's model; Padel, 'Two Pre-Conquest Charters', 20, also notes that the use of the term *coretis* for fish-pools is a Latinization of a Brittonic word.
34. O'Donovan, 'Interim Revision of Episcopal Dates', 109–10; Brooks, *Early History of the Church of Canterbury*, 210–13; *Anglo-Saxon Charters XI: The Charters of Exeter and Crediton*, iii–v.
35. Padel, 'Two Pre-Conquest Charters', 26.
36. Olson, *Early Monasteries*, 62–5.
37. A number of Old Testament names, for instance, occur among the priests of St Petroc's, who witnessed many of the manumissions discussed below.
38. William of Malmesbury, *De Antiquitate Glastonie Ecclesie*, 138.
39. Lapidge, 'Cult of St. Indract at Glastonbury', 182–4.
40. S 1296 and 1451a.
41. O'Donovan, 'Interim Revision of Episcopal Dates', 109–10; Brooks, *Church of Canterbury*, 210–13.
42. Canterbury, Cathedral Library, Register A, fo. 3v; BL, MS Add. 15350, fo. 112 (Codex Wintoniensis); William of Malmesbury, *De Gestis Regum Anglorum*, i, 140–1.
43. Olson, *Early Monasteries*, 75–8.
44. S 832 (977).
45. In this respect, these charters do fit some of the features discussed by Davies; Welsh charters of the twelfth and thirteenth centuries were also expressed as grants to the saint, not to an individual cleric.
46. Olson, *Early Monasteries*, 108–9.
47. Robertson, *Anglo-Saxon Charters*, 226.
48. Förster, 'Die Freilassungsurkunden des Bodmin-Evangeliars'. The manumissions have also been calendared by Finberg, *Early Charters of Devon and Cornwall*, and Hooke, *Pre-Conquest Charter-Bounds*, 70–82. The following references are to Förster's edition and Finberg's Calendar.
49. Förster, 36, Finberg, 81 (for the soul of King Eadred); Förster, 14, Finberg, 87 (for the soul of King Edgar).
50. Förster, 22; Finberg, 92.
51. Förster, 33; Finberg, 93; Förster, 50; Finberg, 88.
52. Förster, 22; Finberg, 92.
53. The most recent consideration of these texts has been by Pelteret, *Slavery in Early Medieval England*, 131–63.
54. Picken, 'Bishop Wulfsige', 34–8.
55. Hooke, *Charter-Bounds*, 82.
56. Förster, 22; Finberg, 92.
57. Olson, *Early Monasteries*, 73–5.
58. Rollason, 'Relic-cults', 92–6.
59. Lapidge, 'Cult of St Indract', 182–4; Rollason, 'Relic-cults', 101–2.
60. Olson, *Early Monasteries*, 92–3.
61. Ibid., 92.

62. Conner, *Anglo-Saxon Exeter*; Rollason, 'Relic-cults', 93–4.
63. Keynes and Lapidge, *Alfred the Great*, 102, ch. 107; William of Malmesbury, *De Gestis Pontificum Anglorum*, 399–400; William of Malmesbury, *Deeds of the Bishops of England*, 273.
64. Brett, 'A Breton Pilgrim in England in the Reign of King Athelstan', 43–70.
65. Rollason, 'Relic-cults', 94–5.

3
Address and Delivery in Anglo-Norman Royal Charters

Richard Sharpe

The writ is now widely recognized as an innovative diplomatic instrument, created in Anglo-Saxon England, developed by Anglo-Norman rulers, and by the end of the twelfth-century influential elsewhere. Its essence is that it was delivered to a particular person or body responsible for the appropriate aspect of the administration of the realm or the doing of royal justice. In diplomatic terms, this is expressed in the address clause which is generally the vital clue to the way a document would be used and therefore to what it was meant to accomplish. There was an inherent linkage between the nature of the transaction, the person or body to whom it would be delivered, and the address clause. Who actually delivered the document would vary according to the nature of the business too, but the documents themselves do not spell out this step in the process: that must be inferred from understanding the relationship between address and function.

The eleventh century appears to us now to be the key period in the evolution of the writ, though such a conclusion is bedevilled by issues of survival. All surviving pre-Conquest 'writs' are in fact what I should define more narrowly as 'writ-charters': that is, they are deliverable writs whose role was (or had developed into) that of charters. Anglo-Saxon writ-charters were addressed and delivered to the shire court, where they were publicly read before being returned to the beneficiary to keep for future use. Only after the Conquest do we see surviving examples of writs addressed to analogous bodies such as the officials responsible for the administration of areas (royal forests, for example) outside the juris-diction of the ordinary local courts. As early as the 990s, however, there is indirect evidence that the king addressed writs to shire courts that were not in their function charters: there survives the record of a plea referring to the king's order to the shire court of Berkshire to meet and decide the case (Robertson, *Anglo-Saxon Charters*, 136–9, no. 66; S 1454). The apparent post-Conquest development in the competence of the writ may be an accident of preservation: writs were short-life instruments, not intended for permanent retention, and it was only their progressive acquisition of charter-like functions that led some 'beneficiaries' (at least in circumstances where the writ ended up in the their hands) to preserve them. From the reign of Henry I, there was an increasing reason to keep certain categories of writ, and the great increase in the number of documents preserved from his reign is not simply an index of the increasing use of documentary procedures.

There is a good case to be made that the writ existed long before the emergence of the writ-charter addressed to the shire court (which I conjecture to have happened during the reign of King Edgar). We are here more concerned with its end. The reign of Henry I signalled the beginning of the end for the writ-charter through the establishment of a standard so-called 'general' address, which appears to have been undeliverable. The charter addressed generally and the charter addressed in writ form to a shire court continued side by side for about 60 years until the writ-charter was abandoned in Henry II's time.

We can classify transactions into two groups: notifications ('sciatis') and mandates ('mando', 'precipio', but also 'sciatis quod uolo et precipio', and sometimes 'mando' held back until after a notifying preamble). I shall spend little time on mandates, which are addressed and delivered to those ordered to do something, and in principle there is no restriction on who may be addressed. Mandates addressed to shire courts pose a problem: the court, in such cases, is not usually ordered to act but is instructed in certain facts rather than merely notified, and we have yet to understand the distinction implicit in the form. Notifications, communicating royal decision or consent or confirmation, were addressed and delivered to the appropriate body, most commonly the shire court. In that case, the address reflects the composition of the court, though variation in the formula used must be taken into account. Equivalent bodies are addressed in a similar way. The general address, which I shall deal with at the end, represents a distinct and interesting development.

For more detailed consideration, we turn now to the writ-charter. This is addressed, as I have said, to the shire court. This normally means that in the early eleventh century the address specifies the presiding bishop in the shire (Anglo-Saxon terminology refers to *scirepscop*), the ealdorman of the shire, and 'ealle mine Þegenas on Hamtunescire'. Most examples surviving have replaced the ealdorman with the earl, a reflection of change introduced in the reign of Cnut, and pre-Conquest examples refer to the specified individuals by name and role, 'Ælfheah biscop', 'Ælfric ealdorman', though the less important persons occasionally included in the address are simply named: they knew who they were, though we may not. Whether the late Saxon earls of Wessex or Mercia had been able to attend all the shire courts in their jurisdictions is questionable, but after 1066 most shires had no earl. In post-Conquest usage, therefore, the earl's place was taken in most shires by the sheriff, Latinized as *uicecomes*, 'earl's deputy'. The linkage between earl and *comes*, sheriff and *uicecomes*, and shire and *comitatus* may point towards a design for Anglo-Norman shiring that never came about: William I's earls still took their titles from shires, though their landed interests designedly overrode such territorial units, and (as with Norman *comtes*) earls only existed in parts of the country; Anglo-Norman earls were not destined to be the leaders of local government, a role left to sheriffs, very different figures from Norman *vicomtes*. In post-Conquest usage, it became common to refer to the specified individual more briefly than previously, often initial and role, sometimes name without role, and later (in specialized contexts) it would become role without name. When one tries to draw up lists of Anglo-Norman sheriffs, for example, it is sometimes unclear whether initials refer to the same person or not and sometimes even whether someone named without role was indeed one of the officers normally specified. Other changes introduced in the normal address clause are simple. The thegns of Old English are Latinized as *barones*, a word which we translate as 'barons' though that word did not mean in 1070 anything like what it meant in 1170; in the language of the shire court, the *barones* are the men who make decisions, and even in the setting of the king's court the word can have the same significance. From an early date, William I adds to the address his *fideles* 'sworn men' (deriving from Latin *fides* 'oath'), the ordinary suitors of the shire court, who were invisible in pre-Conquest writ-charters. What distinction is implicit in this addition in its contemporary context is not yet clear to me; nor was it necessary, since writ-charters will sometimes omit either barons or sworn men from the address.

The shire remains at the centre of eleventh-century diplomatic even in contexts that go beyond its internal business. As we see from the coronation charter of Henry I, this national communication was published by being read at the shire courts, to which copies were separately addressed and delivered (see p. 63). The St Albans historians have preserved one local text, addressed to Hugh of Buckland, sheriff, and all the king's *fideles* of Hertfordshire (omitting the bishop of Lincoln, for reasons unexplained); the Red Book of the Exchequer happened to preserve a copy of another local text, addressed to Bishop Samson of Worcester, Urse d'Abetot as sheriff, and the king's *barones* and *fideles* of Worcestershire, one of several acts copied in the Red Book from Worcestershire documents. By contrast, early legal collections from Winchester (MS Cotton Domitian VIII and *Quadripartitus*), as well as other early twelfth-century sources such as Richard of Hexham and the *Textus Roffensis* have preserved an archival version addressed to the king's *barones* and *fideles* without further specification. It would have been preferable for historians to find a formulary style, 'to N. bishop and M. sheriff and all my *barones* and *fideles* of Anyshire', but on any reading the style in the archival copy does not represent a general address. The mechanisms for drafting and publishing such an act were readily available to the new king, and one might suspect that the main constraint on how quickly the coronation charter could be got out into the shires was the time it would take for the king's goldsmith to carve the matrices of the great seal.

Much of this is very basic, but we have no handbook to the diplomatic, and I find that students of the period have not always grasped the norms. I am afraid that, where the situation is not the usual one of a writ-charter addressed to the court of the beneficiary's home shire, even specialists are not always clear about who is who.

To take an example, there is a series of three writs, issued by William Rufus and Henry I, continuing the exemption of the monks of Durham and their men from being impleaded in the king's courts concerning any possessions they held in the time of Bishop William of Durham. There is a complication here, inasmuch as the writ was first requested in a period of vacancy after his death but it was renewed in the same terms after the appointment of a bishop of Durham, so that it appears to involve the division of the interests of the bishop and the cathedral, but that is not what we are concerned with.

W. rex Angl(orum) Th. archiepiscopo et R. episcopo et omnibus uice-comitibus suis et fidelibus francigenis et anglicis regni Anglie salutem. Precipio et defendo ne monachi uel homines sancti Cuthberti ullo modo placitent uel respondeant de terris uel hominibus uel consuetudinibus uel aliis rebus de quibus saisiti erant die qua Will(el)m(us) episcopus Dunelmensis uiuus et mortuus fuit, sed ita bene et quiete et in pace omnia sua cum saca et soca et tol et team et infange<ne>theof et omnibus aliis consuetudinibus infra burgum et extra teneant sicut melius tenuerunt in predicto tempore. Et si quid inde postea ablatum est reddatur eis. Testibus W(illelmo) cancellario et W(illelmo) Peuerello. (*RRAN*, i, no. 481; *Facsimiles of English Royal Writs*, no. 12)

> William king of the English to Archbishop Th. and Bishop R. and all his sheriffs and sworn men French and English of the realm of England greeting. I command and forbid that the monks or the men of St Cuthbert shall in any way plead or respond concerning their lands or men or customs or other property in which they were seised on the day when William bishop of Durham was alive and dead, but they shall hold everything with sake and soke and tol and team and infangthief and all other customs in borough and out as well and quietly and in peace as they well held at the foresaid time. And if anything has been taken from them, it shall be restored to them. Witness William the chancellor and William Peverell.

There is no difficulty in interpreting Th. as Archbishop Thomas of York, but R. appears more problematic. The first volume of *RRAN* (often an unreliable witness in these matters) expanded it as referring to Robert Bloet, bishop of Lincoln; T. A. M. Bishop and Pierre Chaplais, who published the facsimile, expanded it as referring to Ranulf Flambard, bishop of Durham from May 1099, citing the confirmation of this grant by Henry I:

> Henr(icus) rex Angl(orum) G. archiepiscopo et R. episcopo et omnibus uicecomitibus et baronibus et fidelibus francis et anglis regni Anglie salutem. Precipio et defendo ne monachi sancti Cuthb(er)ti uel homines sui placitent ullo modo aut respondeant de terris uel hominibus uel consuetudinibus aut de ulla re unde saisiti <erant> die qua Will(el)m(us) Dunelmensis episcopus uiuus et mortuus fuit...(*RRAN*, ii, no. 767)

> Henry king of the English to Archbishop G. and Bishop R. and all sheriffs and barons and sworn men French and English of the realm of England greeting. I command and forbid that the monks of St Cuthbert or their men shall in any way plead or respond concerning the lands or men or customs or any other property in which they were seised on the date when William bishop of Durham was alive and dead...

In this case the second volume of *RRAN* (often less reliable than the first) expanded R. as Ranulf without hesitation. He was already bishop at the beginning of the reign, Durham is the beneficiary, and they neither looked nor thought one step further. At one level this is an exercise in solving cross-word puzzles, and there is a third document that must be brought into the picture, William II again:

> Willelmus [dei gratia] rex Anglie Thome archiepiscopo et R. episcopo et omnibus uicecomitibus et baronibus et fidelibus suis francigenis et

anglicis regni Anglie salutem. Precipio et defendo ne monachi sancti Cuthberti uel homines sui ullo modo placitent aut respondeant de terris uel hominibus uel consuetudinibus aut de ulla re unde saisiti erant die qua Willelmus episcopus Dunelmensis uiuus et mortuus fuit... Testibus Walkelino episcopo et Willelmo cancellario. Apud Salesburiam. (*RRAN*, i, no. 396)

William [by the grace of God] king of the English to Archbishop T. and to Bishop R. and to all his sheriffs and barons and sworn men French and English of the realm of England greeting. I command and forbid that the monks of St Cuthbert or their men shall in any way plead or respond concerning the lands or men or customs or any other property in which they were seised on the date when William bishop of Durham was alive and dead... Witness Bishop Walkekin and William the chancellor. At Salisbury.

In this case the date must lie between the death of Bishop William of Durham in January 1096 and that of Bishop Walkelin of Winchester, here attesting, in January 1098. Ranulf was not bishop of Durham until nearly 18 months later. Johnson and Cronne (*RRAN*), and Bishop and Chaplais (*Facsimiles of English Royal Writs*) must explain therefore why there is a different bishop, and from a different diocese, in the address clause of documents effecting the same outcome, if they are to defend the expansion Ranulf in the other two documents. In 1096 and 1097, there were four bishops in England with the initial R.: Robert Bloet of Lincoln, Ralph Luffa of Chichester, Robert of Chester, and Robert of Hereford. Now, I suspect that the editors of Volume i of *RRAN* simply picked Robert Bloet because he is frequently named in William II's charters and the other three are not. But this is not merely a puzzle: the address clause bears a rational relationship to the document.

The two bishops specified indicate where this document is expected to be delivered; it is primarily addressed to shire courts presided over by them. This is not formally a general address, though its compass is widened to include 'omnibus uicecomitibus', as well as all barons and sworn men, 'regni Anglie'. There was no shire court and no royal sheriff in Durham at this date, but the church of Durham had extensive interests in several shires, notably in Yorkshire and Nottinghamshire, where the archbishop of York presided, and in Lincolnshire, where the bishop of Lincoln presided. Other interests further south in Northamptonshire are also within the diocese of Lincoln. The point of this document was that the monks of Durham should deliver it to be read in any of the several shire courts south of the Tees where their interests were affected, but primarily in the shires where Archbishop Thomas of York or Bishop Robert of Lincoln presided.

It is easier to arrive at the correct interpretation by trying to understand how the document was used than by searching for parallels. A group of documents preserved from Bishop Ranulf's archive, however, provides a decisive parallel. *RRAN*, ii, no. 545 notified the shire courts of Yorkshire, Lincolnshire, and Northumberland that Ranulf has been restored to his bishopric in 1101; it is addressed 'Girardo archiepiscopo et R(oberto) episcopo Lincolniensi et O(sberto) uicecomiti et omnibus fidelibus suis de Euerwicschira et de Lincolnschira et de Northumberlanda'. Robert's see is specified, though Gerard's is not; similarly *RRAN*, ii, no. 575 gives Robert his name and title in full.

The interpretation of initials in the address *may* be informed by an understanding of the tenor of the act, the act *may* be interpreted through its address clause, but the two *must* fit together. In this case it would have been easier if the three texts had all specified the shires, but before 1100 it is rare to find even two shires specified (more examples to come, however). What would usually be done in such cases is to use a plural, 'of the shires where the church of Durham holds lands', though the specification of two or even three shires increased in Henry I's reign.

With sufficient space one might present an elaborate taxonomy of address clauses from the period; there are many variations, and it is worth attempting to understand them. There are several categories of variation.

First, within the category of writ-charters addressed to a shire, one has the broad distinction already seen between the address to a single shire and the address to those shires where the beneficiary has lands, a formula in use throughout the eleventh century. This is straightforward, though its use was declining in Henry I's time. Instead one finds documents that specify more than one shire; as for example in *RRAN*, ii, no. 613 for Abingdon, 'Rogero episcopo Salesb' et Roberto episcopo Linc' et Hugoni de Bochelanda et Willelmo de Oxeneford et baronibus suis omnibus et fidelibus Francis et Anglis de Berchescira et Oxenefordscira'; I shall mention one later that specifies three shires.

Second, there are variations in the formula used for the shire address. The basic form comprised four elements, bishop, sheriff, and the *barones* and *fideles* of the named shire. Occasionally the name of the shire is omitted, but the specification of bishop and sheriff leaves no room for doubting the status of the shire address. In some circumstances any one element may be deliberately omitted. So, for example, in notifications of the appointment of a bishop, or in grants to the bishop, he is omitted (*RRAN*, ii, no. 1243, original, appointing Richard de Capella as bishop of Hereford in 1121, unusually naming the three shires within his diocese, 'Henricus rex Anglorum Adam de Port et omnibus baronibus suis et fidelibus francis et anglis de Herefort scira et de Gloecestra scira et Salope scira salutem'). Similarly, in notifications of the appointment of a sheriff, the sheriff is omitted (*RRAN*, ii, no. 1034, Walter de Beauchamp as sheriff of Worcester). Other variations appear less deliberate than accidental, careless, or even captious, though I may simply not (yet) have understood the reasons behind them. For example, the inclusion of both *barones* and *fideles* was apparently not strictly necessary, and the omission of one or other seems unimportant. Very occasionally one finds two elements omitted: so, for example, when William II granted the church in the royal manor of Sutton (Berks) to Abingdon abbey, 1091 × 1094, the writ-charter is addressed to the sheriff and *fideles* of the shire, but the chronicle context in which it is preserved represents it as addressed (as one would expect with a transaction of this kind) to the shire court:

> Ecclesia uille regalis Suttune per hos dies regis dominio constabat soli subdita. Hanc ipse rex Willelmus iunior a Rainaldo petitus abbate eccelsie Abbendonie concessit, istas ad comitatum Berchescire inde litteras dirigens: 'Willelmus rex Anglorum Gilleberto de Brittewilla et omnibus fidelibus suis francigenis et angligenis de Berkascira salutem. Sciatis me dedisse...' (*RRAN*, i, no. 359; context from the Abingdon Chronicle, *Historia Ecclesie Abbendonensis*, ii. 36)

> At that time the church of the royal village of Sutton was accepted to be subject only to the king's lordship. At Abbot Rainald's request, King William the younger granted it to the church of Abingdon, sending these letters concerning it to the shire court: 'William king of the English to Gilbert de Bretteville and all his sworn men French and English of Berkshire greeting. Know that I have given...'

There is no apparent reason for the omission of the bishop in this instance; Salisbury diocese was not *sede uacante*; one might conjecture that the bishop had been separately notified of this transfer of advowson—this would be compatible with later procedure—but I have no evidence to explain the variation at this date.

Third, further elements may be included for a particular reason. So, the provost and burgesses of a borough may be included alongside the address to the shire court:

> Henricus rex Anglorum Will(elm)o Exon(iensi) episcopo et Ric(ardo) filio Bald(wini) uicecomiti et preposito Exon(ie) et omnibus baronibus et fidelibus suis Deuenescirê et omnibus burgensibus et ministris suis Exon(ie) salutem. Sciatis me concessisse ... (*RRAN*, ii, no. 1493)

> Henry king of the English to William bishop of Exeter and Richard fitz Baldwin sheriff and the reeves of Exeter and all his barons and sworn men of Devon shire and all his burgesses and officials of Exeter greeting. Know that I have granted ...

In some parts of the country, there appears to have been a local custom of including other individuals in the address clause, for reasons hardly understood. In Somerset the abbot of Glastonbury sometimes appears in address clauses (*RRAN*, i, no. 326, addressed to the shires of Somerset and Wiltshire), perhaps because he was too important to treat simply as one of the *barones* of the shire court, perhaps because of the interaction of his liberty and the shire's jurisdiction—but by contrast the no less important abbot of Bury St Edmunds does not appear in writ-charters addressed to the shire court of Suffolk. The joint shire court of Nottinghamshire and Derbyshire was always complicated, involving two bishops, one sheriff, but often other prominent laymen:

> Willelmus rex Anglorum Thome archiepiscopo et R(oberto) episcopo de Cestra et Rogero comiti et E. uicecomiti et H(enrico) de Ferrariis et W(illelmo) Peuerel et omnibus fidelibus suis francigenis et anglicis de Esnotingehamscire et de Derbiscire salutem. (*RRAN*, i, no. 337)

> William king of the English to Archbishop Thomas and Bishop Robert of Chester and Count Roger and E sheriff and Henry de Ferrers and William Peverell and all his sworn men French and English of Nottinghamshire and Derbyshire greeting.

Count Roger is not a local earl but Roger of Poitou, who held the title *comes* in respect of his French wife, but he was a major landholder in these shires, and we find him addressed in some other documents in the area; only rank puts him in front of the sheriff, while other major landholders follow the sheriff. But it is merely local custom that brings such names into the address. In parts of Lincolnshire, local custom included particular great men in the address; so for example we find the three successive husbands of Lucy, daughter of Thorold of Lincoln—Ivo Taillebois (*RRAN*, i, no. 406), Roger fitz Gerold (*RRAN*, i, no. 408), and Ranulf Meschin (*RRAN*, ii, nos 534, 535, 537, 727, 968)—each addressed and sometimes with precedence over the sheriff. In other parts of the county other local great men are named, but not in all parts of the county. We have perhaps some still-not-yet-understood reflection of the role of the 'parts' in the organization of the shire, rather as in Sussex the separate sheriffs of the several rapes are included as appropriate (*RRAN*, ii, nos 614, 810, etc.). In some cases we can see why there is variation from the normal formula in specific cases. So, for example, Robert de Lacy forfeited his English estates very soon after he had given land for the founding of an Austin priory at Nostell. His honour of Pontefract was put into the keeping of a subordinate, William Foliot, whose name appears after the sheriff's in the address of the earliest writ-charter confirming the founding of the priory (*RRAN*, ii, no. 1628), datable c.1115. Very soon afterwards the honour was assigned to Hugh de Laval, and in a renewal of the confirmation he is addressed before the sheriff (*RRAN*, ii, no. 1286). Other writ-charters for Nostell did not include the lord of the honour in their address clauses: this was done in specific circumstances, and in a form that nicely differentiates in precedence the lord of the honour and the official who had stood in during the vacancy. This detail reflects the intense degree of personalization built into the system of communication by writ-charter.

Fourth, in particular circumstances, the officers of shire court may be accompanied in the address clause by officers of higher rank, such as one or more of the king's regents during his absence in Normandy:

Willelmus rex Anglorum W(alchelino) episcopo et S(amsoni) episcopo et R(anulfo) capell(ano) et iustificatoribus suis et Waltero uicecomiti Glocestrie et omnibus fidelibus suis francis et anglis salutem. Sciatis me concessisse Herueo episcopo...T(estibus) W(illelmo) canc(ellario) et Vr(sone) de Abetot. Apud insulam de Wyct. (*RRAN*, i, no. 389)

William king of the English to Bishop Walkelin and Bishop Samson and Ranulf the chaplain and his *iustificatores* and Walter sheriff of Gloucester and all his sworn men French and English greeting. Know that I have granted to Bishop Hervey...Witness William the chancellor and Urse d'Abetot. At the Isle of Wight.

Here Bishop Walkelin and Ranulf Flambard, as usual at this date styled chaplain, were appointed regents for the king's absence in 1097–98 (and this was issued as he was about to sail from the Isle of Wight), while Bishop Samson and Walter the sheriff were the presiding officers of the shire court of Gloucester. The order of individual names reflects a complex precedence: bishops precede other clergy who precede laymen; in a second order of precedence the king's regents precede local officers; so Walkelin precedes Samson, but Bishop Samson precedes Ranulf the chaplain, while the unnamed *iustificatores* precede the sheriff. While there were occasions when men close to the king were sent to sit as justices in shire courts, it is not necessarily implicit in the address that this writ-charter was intended for such an afforced meeting. It is possible that it was intended for delivery, in separate contexts, to the king's regents and to the shire court of Gloucester.

A fifth cause of variation in address clauses of the same class of document is evolution in the course of time. I have mentioned the disappearance of the earl from the writ-charters of most counties. The conspicuous addition in Henry I's time is the inclusion of the king's justice, usually between the bishop and the sheriff and usually by name only without title, in the address to writ-charters and, in due course, the inclusion of justices ('iusticiis') in the same position in the general address. It would provide a useful dating criterion if we knew when Henry added royal justices to the regular personnel of shire courts, but it is more likely that we shall have to infer that from approximating the appearance of the change in address clauses. A little snag with this variation is its form, always abbreviated as *iustic'* in the Anglo-Norman period and often anachronistically expanded in cartularies (and editions) as *iusticiariis*, though one can demonstrate that the word is *iusticia* from the many documents that add an adjective, 'iusticia mea' (common in the clause *nisi feceris*); for example, 'Et nisi feceris, iusticia mea et uicecomes faciant' (*RRAN*, ii, no. 1566); in writ-charters the word should generally be treated as singular, though at times there might be two justices holding joint office in a particular region (for example, *RRAN*, ii, no. 754).

Now, there is a fundamental distinction between notifications such as writ-charters and writs that issue a command; it is a distinction usually reflected in the address clause. Where the king issues a grant or a decision by means of a writ-charter addressed to the shire court, there would *often* be a writ issued at the same time to instruct the sheriff alone, or to the sheriff and *ministri*, to put the king's will into execution. The survival of paired writs is unusual; one must suppose the sheriff had given back to the beneficiary the writ of execution. The editors of the *RRAN* sometimes print one member of such a pair and refer to the other as a 'duplicate', a fundamental misunderstanding. What particularly tends to mislead in such cases is if, after the address, the opening sentence rehearses the notification before issuing the command, the address is the most conspicuous clue to the correct categorization of the transaction. There are also rare cases where one document is issued with an apparently fused address clause and even with a switch from notification to command within the text of the document. Such hybrids can be confusing.

Here is a relatively clear example from the Abingdon archive that takes the form of a mandate but appears to address the shire courts of Berkshire and Oxford:

> Henricus rex Anglorum Rogero episcopo Salesbirie et Roberto Lincolie episcopo et Hugoni de Bochelanda et Willelmo uicecomiti de Oxeneford et omnibus baronibus et ministris suis de utraque scira salutem. Volo et precipio ut ecclesia de Abbendona et monachi habeant suas consuetudines in nauibus transeuntibus, scilicet in accipiendis allecibus et in mercatis faciendis, sicuti unquam melius et plenius habuit, tempore regis Eadwardi et patris et fratris mei, et meo tempore. Teste Willelmo episcopo Exonie. Apud Merlebergam. Et testibus Eustachio de Britoil et Patricio de Cadurcis. (*RRAN*, ii, no. 937)

> Henry king of the English to Roger bishop of Salisbury and Robert bishop of Lincoln and Hugh of Buckland and William sheriff of Oxford and all his barons and officials of either shire greeting. I will and command that the church of Abingdon and the monks shall have their customs in passing boats, namely in receiving herring and in making markets, just as ever it well and fully held in King Edward's time and my father's and mine. Witness William bishop of Exeter. At Marlborough. And witness Eustace de Breteuil and Patrick de Cadurcis.

The two bishops and the two sheriffs, the *barones* of the two shires, point clearly to the shire courts, but where one might expect mention of *fideles*, instead the phrase 'ministris suis' is meant for the officials who have been interfering in the monks' right to levy customs. This document was perhaps intended to be read at the two shires but then given back to the monks of Abingdon to show, as a writ would be shown, to any *minister* who sought to interfere with their collecting tolls from boats carrying fish or other merchandise along the Thames. The river formed the boundary between the jurisdiction of the two shires, and the authority of different *ministri* met in midstream. Hence the need to include two shires.

In a form analogous to the shire address, notifications would be addressed in special circumstances to the appropriate local officers, for example, in peculiar jurisdictions. In the case of *RRAN*, ii, 696, for example, Abingdon, it is addressed to the officials in Windsor forest:

> Henricus rex Anglorum W. filio Walteri et Croco uenatori et Ricardo seruienti et omnibus ministris de foresta Windresores salutem. Sciatis me concessisse Deo et sancte Marie de Abbendona totam decimam de uenatione que capta fuerit in foresta de Windesores. Testibus Roberto episcopo Linc' et Eudone dapifero. Apud Bruhellam.

> Henry king of the English to W. fitz Walter and Croc the huntsman and Richard the serjeant and all his officials of the forest of Windsor greeting. Know that I have granted to God and St Mary of Abingdon all the tithe of the venison that is caught in the forest of Windsor. Witness Robert bishop of Lincoln and Eudo Dapifer. At Brill.

There is every reason to think that the draftsmen had a very precise and up-to-date knowledge of what was needed in the different circumstances and localities. Of course, the king's clerks should always know who was bishop and who was sheriff in any given shire court—they would have prepared the writs of appointment and they may well have kept lists to remind themselves of the details—but the beneficiary, or the impetrant obtaining a writ, must have taken care to make sure that they knew which shire or shires (or other courts) were concerned with any particular transaction, and the beneficiary may have supplied other particulars. Occasionally one wonders whether one glimpses details in the clerks' knowledge. So, for example, in a writ-charter of William II for Bermondsey, the surviving copies (three antiquarian transcripts) all have a gap where one would expect the initial of the archbishop of Canterbury: 'Willelmus rex Anglorum [*blank*] archiepiscopo et G(undulfo) episcopo Rouesc' et H(amoni) dapifero et omnibus fidelibus suis francigenis et anglicis salutem' (*RRAN*, i, no. 340). The text refers to 'Robert my chancellor, that is, the bishop of Lincoln', providing a date between March 1093 when he was nominated bishop and September 1093 when he was replaced as chancellor. During this period he was usually referred to simply as bishop of Lincoln, and I infer that this act was probably drafted soon after his nomination. Anselm was nominated at almost the same time, but it was September before he accepted the temporalities: the draftsman appears to have known that there was about to be an archbishop but did not commit himself to writing the initial A; he still included Gundulf, who had been deputizing since Lanfranc's death.

At later dates, the level of current knowledge appears to diminish: in Stephen's reign, for example, we find the first example of a writ-charter that includes the words 'episcopo Lund(oniensi)' even though at the time this was issued the see of London was vacant: S(tephanus) rex Angl(orum) episcopo Lund(oniensi) et omnibus baronibus suis de Lund(onia) et de Essexa et de Heortfordsc(ira) et ministris et fidelibus suis omnibus tam clericis quam laicis francis et anglis salutem' (*RRAN*, iii, no. 521, datable to 1135 × 1137, during the long vacancy 1134–41).

I indicated that I should say little here about mandates. I want to mention just one category, and that is the general writ, adapted for various specific purposes. The usual pattern with a general writ is that it was addressed to all the king's sheriffs and officials of all England, so that the impetrant could carry it and show it to any official who needed to be instructed. The special form granting exemption from tolls was usually addressed to sheriffs, officials, and the reeves of boroughs and ports. Justices were added in due course, perhaps simply by analogy with the shire court, perhaps because they could help the impetrant secure his exemption, but not, I think, on account of any involvement in levying tolls. For those who were so involved, the word *balliuus* 'bailiff' emerges as a frequent term in the evolving address, either alongside *minister* 'official' (literally 'servant'), or in its place. There are examples from when Henry I was in Normandy, which begin by addressing Roger of Salisbury, the highest official in England (*RRAN*, ii, nos 1573, 1682), though I can hardly imagine the holder of the writ felt the need to go and show it to Roger.

The overwhelming impression conveyed by the address clauses of royal acts from before the Conquest right through to the early years of Henry I's reign is that of a well-organized system of communication. The beneficiary probably knew what parts of the system needed to be told something, the king's draftsmen knew who the officers of the courts were and the officials in peculiar jurisdictions, and they knew pretty much exactly who should be addressed in what circumstances. In the drafting of addresses, there was some licence, but not so much as seriously to confuse the picture.

What then of the general address? What purpose did it serve, and why did it come eventually to supplant the shire address and the local variations on it? Some form of general address can be seen in acts of William I and William II, but it is always very rare, usually confined to

Anglo-Norman diplomas. These early examples are also variable in form and, more conspicuously, different in their language from the address clauses of writ-charters. In particular, lay magnates are not distinguished but addressed under the imprecise designations of *proceres* or *optimates*. From these we may learn that there were circumstances in which the other available addresses were felt not to meet the need. In Henry I's time, the formulaic general address emerges, to the archbishops, bishops, earls, sheriffs, *barones* and *fideles* of all England. It first certainly occurs between 1106 and 1110, and it becomes more frequent in the 1120s and 1130s. (There is one example which, if authentic, would date from February 1102 (*RRAN*, ii, no. 564 for Eudo Dapifer), but other features of the act rouse suspicions.) Through Henry I's reign, I can say that there are 22 currently known examples of a general address surviving as originals and a further 73 authentic examples surviving only in copies. (I cannot provide precise figures for shire addresses yet, but the total is in excess of 700.)

There are a very few examples of acts with a general address and the specification of a shire. An original for the abbey of Tiron concerns a gift of property in Wales; it is addressed 'archiepiscopis et episcopis et omnibus baronibus et fidelibus suis totius Anglie et nominatim illis qui in Walis conuersantur' (*RRAN*, ii, no. 1187, datable 1107×1120). This remains in its character a general address: there were no local courts in Wales analogous to the English shires. Documents surviving as copies, however, from St Frideswide's priory, Oxford, and from Kirkham priory in Yorkshire, attach a shire to the general address: 'archiepiscopis episcopis abbatibus comitibus iustic(iis) baronibus uicecomitibus et omnibus ministris et fidelibus suis francis et anglis tocius Anglie et nominatim Oxon' (*RRAN*, ii, no. 1957 for St Frideswide's, datable 1129×1135); 'archiepiscopis episcopis abbatibus comitibus uicecomitibus et omnibus baronibus et fidelibus suis francis et anglicis totius Anglie et de Eboraciscira et de Northumberlanda' (*RRAN*, ii, no. 1459 for Kirkham, datable 1123×1129). Such rarities adhere to some intention of deliverability, but it is impossible to comprehend why they exist. They could at this date have perfectly well been drafted to address the shire courts; their rarity argues against any strong interpretation of their significance; but they attest to some sense that the general address was, on rare occasions, somehow inadequate in the eyes of at least one draftsman.

The questions of whether a charter generally addressed was still taken to the shire court for publication, whether indeed it was published at all, are impossible to answer. The Abingdon chronicle provides an insight into delivery of writ-charters, over and over again introducing those it quotes by saying that the king sent his letters to the shire. In the three instances where a charter generally addressed is quoted, the narrative introduces it thus: 'tales litteras totius regni Anglie primoribus misit' (*RRAN*, ii, 1259, datable to 1121×December 1122; *Historia Ecclesie Abbendonensis*, ii, 228), 'rex primoribus Anglie tales litteras suo sigillo munitas direxit' (*RRAN*, ii, 1641, datable to March×September 1130; *Historia Ecclesie Abbendonensis*, ii, 254). Whatever the writer, in the early 1160s, thought this meant—and he may have been merely interpreting the words of the general address—it suggests that he did not expect a document so addressed to be published at the shire court.

Why the king should choose to increase the use of seemingly undeliverable documents is also a hard question to answer. If his coronation charter could achieve nationwide publication through shire courts, and if there were adequate systems for addressing the courts relevant to holders of a multi-shire complex of rights, why the general address at all? And whence this form of it? I suspect that form provides the best clue to the origin of the general address. I have entertained several possible explanations for its genesis. One might, perhaps, guess that a Norman draftsman devised a general address, someone who was familiar with the general addresses used in the diplomas of French kings with their roots going back to Carolingian diplomatic practice. Big assumptions underlie such a guess: Who was in a position to devise such a formula, would that person have experienced Capetian forms, and why should he want to import this one to England, and this one alone, apparently without any substantive reason in the documentary mechanism? Since the words used are not the same, one must add the further supposition that in the devising of a formula for England the king's clerks chose to use the terms already in use in writ-charters in England rather than those used in the non-formulaic general addresses of William II's time.

Or one might, perhaps, see it as the logical extension of the writ-charter address to multiple shires. Before the Conquest that had been 'to the bishops, earls, and thegns of the shires where...', adding sheriffs and replacing thegns with *barones* and *fideles* would bring it into line with Anglo-Norman usage in writ-charters, and adding the archbishops would allow for a landholder who owned in Kent and Yorkshire or Nottinghamshire. The addition of justices between earls and sheriffs was a consequence of a change in the practice of writ-charters. Once the formula was framed, however, it acquired a different logic of its own, and came to incorporate other categories of great men who had no place in writ-charters. Abbots were the first, entering the general address before the end of Henry I's time and becoming usual in Stephen's; while abbots had been among the *barones* of the shire court, the shire address had not singled them out as a category and only rarely included a particular abbot. Over the centuries, the new general address would be augmented to include further dignities, but that need not concern us. One interesting point to reflect on, however, is this: sheriffs always precede *barones* until around the death of Henry I and the accession of Stephen, but thereafter *barones* are sometimes accorded precedence over sheriffs, though the precedence is inconsistent, even in the drafting of particular clerks, throughout Stephen's reign. This is the first signal that *barones* were beginning to be perceived as magnates, with higher precedence than royal officers such as justices and sheriffs; this precedence is consolidated in Henry II's time.

Or a third possible explanation for the general address is to suppose that it was in origin no such thing but simply an address to another grander court, the king's own, at which the archbishops, bishops, earls, and so on were gathered 'in concilio' (to use the expression of Henry I's place-dates). One way to test this possibility might be to look for any correlation in early examples of the general address and place-dates at the major courts held at Christmas, Easter, and Whitsun. There are some that lend support to this hypothesis: such as *RRAN*, ii, no. 1280, 10 April 1121, granting the heiress Sybil of Neufmarché to Milo of Gloucester, 'Apud Wintoniam eodem anno inter pascha et pentecost' quo rex duxit in uxorem filiam ducis de Luuain'; or *RRAN*, ii, no. 1485, a resolution in the king's court at Winchester in 1127, between Gloucester abbey and Gilbert de Miners. But there are others that argue against it, such as *RRAN*, ii, no. 1048, issued in 1114 at Holdgate Castle, 'Apud Castrum Helgoti in Scalopescyra', during the king's Welsh campaign. These three all survive as originals. I am not convinced that a wider search would clinch this line of reasoning.

There is a small group of documents concerning England whose address is in some way intermediate. A charter that grants tolls during certain fairs to the bishop of Lincoln, for example, is addressed, 'A(nselmo) archiepiscopo Cantuar(iensi) et Ger(ardo) archiepiscopo Eboracensi et episcopis suis et abbatibus et omnibus baronibus suis et fidelibus francis et anglis tocius Anglie' (*RRAN*, ii, no. 864). If this one merely substitutes names for the two archbishops while remaining a general address in category, that is not true of the act appointing Geoffrey as abbot of St Albans, which is addressed, 'Radulfo archiepiscopo Cantuarie et

Roberto episcopo Lincolnie et omnibus episcopis et comitibus et baronibus et uicecomitibus et ministris et omnibus fidelibus suis francis et anglis totius Anglie' (*RRAN*, ii, no. 1203). The bishop of Lincoln is here singled out as the presiding bishop in the shire court of Hertfordshire, but the nature of the abbey's relationship to the bishop and to the archbishop of Canterbury was perhaps already an active issue. Delivery appears to be notionally intended though it is not clear in what context it could be perceived as possible. These two acts come from a rather small group (others in it are *RRAN*, ii, nos 637, 885, 1687 for Fontevraud which names several bishops, and 1765 which addressed the archbishop of Canterbury by title but not by name).

If the general address does not represent a notional address to all members of the king's court 'in concilio', it is perhaps ironic that its use should have been increasing during exactly the period when the lords of honours with seigneurial jurisdiction began to imitate royal writ-charters, addressing them to the officers of the honour court. Extreme examples of this honour style come from the charters of Ranulf, earl of Chester, in the 1140s and 1150s: 'Ranulphus comes Cestrie episcopo Cestrie, archidiacono, omnibusque sancte ecclesie filiis necnon et constabulario, dapifero, iusticiario, baronibus, uicecomiti, ministris et baliuis, et omnibus hominibus et amicis suis salutem', 'Rannulfus comes Cestrie episcopo Cestriensi, abbati Cestrie, totique clero, constabulario Cestrie, dapifero, baronibus, iusticie, uicecomitibus, ministris et omnibus fidelibus suis Francis et Anglis'; secular examples are more common, such as, 'Ranulfus comes Cestrie constabulario, dapifero, iusticiario, baronibus, uicecomiti, ministris et balliuis et omnibus hominibus suis francis et anglis, clericis et laicis' (*Charters of the Anglo-Norman Earls of Chester*, nos 34, 63, 27, with silent and inconsistent expansion of abbreviations *iustic'* and *uic'*, where I should prefer 'iusticie', 'uicecomiti'). This is a relatively short-lived form, emerging in the late 1120s and 1130s and lasting into the early years of Henry II. Its apparent perception of the officers of the court is undermined by the inclusion in some examples of the perpetuity formula so common in private deeds but not used in authentic royal acts, 'Ranulphus comes Cestrie constabulario, dapifero, baronibus, iusticiario, uicecomiti Cestrie, tam presentibus quam futuris, et omnibus hominibus suis francis et anglis, clericis et laicis' (ibid., no. 26). These honorial acts demonstrate a trend towards including all *categories* of person without real regard to the *persons* themselves. The habit of mind that had already added abbots to the general address was clearly becoming settled. Whatever prompted the new form and whatever shaped its wording, it came to be treated as a general address and developed accordingly.

Now, the real question must be whether such a change is initiated as a change of diplomatic form or in response to a new institutional demand. With the exception of the small number of acts for which publication through being read before the king's court might have been judged appropriate, it is impossible to discern any practical rationale dictating why a particular transaction is drafted with the shire address or the general address in much of Henry I's time, throughout Stephen's reign, and in the early years of Henry II.

My own instinct is to see the general address, in the formula adopted early in Henry I's time, as an almost accidental emergence from the writ-charter for multiple shires. It addressed, in general terms, like the general writ, any court or individual to whom the document might need to be shown. It could therefore provide an all-purpose solution in cases where the circumstances were varied or complicated, though it was decades before it was widely adopted. Once devised, the formula was quickly treated as a truly general address rather than an all-purpose amalgam of other addresses; this must have happened by the time the abbots were added to the formula. Such an evolution for the general address over the first 20 or 25 years of Henry I's reign requires no supposition that it would be used in a wide range of circumstances, because for most purposes the standard shire address or the locally appropriate address met the need. The extension of its use was gradual.

The factors governing a choice between shire address and general address over the years from the later 1120s to the late 1160s were perhaps various. The charter as a form of document was emerging from the background of the writ-charter and it would be developed quickly by Henry II's chancery in the first years of his reign. The preference for personal addresses was giving ground in several contexts to generic addresses, even where a general formula was not used. The circumstances in which a writ-charter was appropriate may have been becoming less frequent, so that the locally specific form began to appear old-fashioned before it was obsolete. Writ-charters were always in the large majority over the general address in Henry I's time, they remained in a clear majority in the authentic charters of Stephen (which include about 150 examples of the general address and more than twice that number of shire addresses), but in the years between 1154 and 1170 the shire address was used in only a small proportion of Henry II's acts.

When the shire addresses cease, perhaps in the late 1160s, perhaps c.1170, some explanation is called for. It seems unlikely that it was simply that, after 60 years of what might have been choice, no one any longer wanted a writ-charter. It was more probably a central decision to stop addressing royal acts to shire courts. This may have been because such business as was transacted through royal charters was no longer published by being read in the shire courts. No specific act indicates exactly when or why the shire address ceased to be used, but the fact of its disappearance may signal change at the centre of the legal system as well as in the shires. Justices ceased to serve continuously in the shire courts; instead, men of the same rank and competence as might have been appointed justices in the shires joined justices from the common bench at Westminster in travelling on eyre from time to time to hear pleas in one or more shires. This change is reflected in the charters: where the clause *nisi feceris* would previously have mentioned 'iusticia mea' as the person who could enforce action over the sheriff, after this change the *nisi feceris* clause would impose the responsibility on the king's justices in eyre. As Nicholas Vincent has shown, this change appears to coincide with the introduction of *Dei gratia* in the regnal style in 1172–73; by then, 'iusticia mea' was obsolete, but there are few examples referring to justices in eyre before that point. From around the same time the settled availability of a central court at Westminster and of procedures dependent on the king's writ now tended to draw away from the shire courts those categories of business—disputes over land for which royal charters were cited in evidence, perhaps particularly where the private exercise of judicial privileges was in question—for which the publication of charters had been a precondition. And in the administrative sphere the question of monies to be collected by sheriffs was arranged between the sheriff and the court of the exchequer at Westminster. The shire court was no longer the forum in which such shrieval business was made public. The reasons, both legal and administrative, that had necessitated the writ-charter in King Edgar's time and sustained it through the eleventh century appear finally to have become obsolete. This does not equate with a reduction in the volume of business heard in shire courts, but it may well reflect the increasing centralization of the categories of business to which writ-charters had been relevant. The precise chronology of such changes remains elusive.

Meanwhile, however, while there were two forms in use, are we to suppose two procedures? Were charters generally addressed still taken to the shire court for publication? Indeed, were they published at all, or had diplomatic, perhaps—perish the thought—become less embedded in the mechanics of government? Might a beneficiary be willing to pay the king rather more for a document that he would not have to take to the shire court at all unless conflict arose but which should rather sit in his muniment chest? A change from an administratively well-structured procedure to one that was less tightly structured, less personalized, and less integrated into the local administration must be hard to explain, especially if we are to understand this change against a background of increased bureaucratization. It must surely reflect the increased emphasis on the central courts at the expense of the shires.

4

'A Lasting Memorial': The Charter of Liberties of Henry I

Judith A. Green

According to the chronicler Eadmer, Henry I made promises at his coronation, to maintain good laws and to abolish all oppressions and injustices, and had ordered 'all these promises confirmed by a solemn oath to be published throughout the kingdom with, by way of lasting memorial, a written document authenticated by his seal in witness of its validity'.[1] The Charter of Liberties of 1100 is, like *Laudabiliter*, one of the famous charters of the central Middle Ages. It is a crucial piece of evidence for our understanding of the situation in England in 1100, when Henry I seized the English throne on his brother's unexpected death, and because it was taken up by the opposition barons in 1214 as a basis for their demands for redress and reform. It provided a first draft of Magna Carta.[2] It has often been discussed, but usually in the context of political and constitutional history rather than as a charter, yet it has a good deal to tell us about the status and transmission of texts. The first section of this chapter is concerned with the genesis of the charter, and with the concessions made: why were these concessions recorded in charter form? The second section deals with the construction and transmission of the text. Finally, the seeming paradox of this charter is explored: if it achieved ultimate fame as a prototype for Magna Carta, it did not, however, establish a document template systematically followed by Henry's successors.

No original has survived, though there is a reference to one in the archives of Canterbury.[3] Many copies survive.[4] All but one from the twelfth and thirteenth centuries known at the time (more may obviously be discovered as the acts of Henry I are edited) were collated by Liebermann in his paper to the Royal Historical Society, and another was taken account of by the time the third volume of *Die Gesetze der Angelsachsen* was published.[5] Whilst the body of the text is transmitted with only minor textual variants, there are significant differences in the address clauses and the witness lists. The address clauses fall into two basic categories: first, those addressed to named individuals, and secondly those addressed generally 'to all bishops, abbots' etc.[6] In one important early sub-category of the first group the address was to the bishop of Worcester and the sheriff, Urse d'Abetot. The lists of witnesses are brief, and the names differ in different copies. One group of copies has both a general address clause and a general witness list 'all bishops, abbots' etc. It was this version which, it was suggested by Ludwig Riess, was a reissue of 1101 (see p. 64). According to Eadmer, the charter was sealed.

The Charter of 1100 is the first coronation charter to survive, but behind it lay the three-fold promises made at the time of their coronation by English kings since the late tenth century.[7] Pauline Stafford in an important paper demonstrated how these promises were linked with coronation rituals and with homilies by churchmen on good kingship.[8] She argued that Aethelred probably made a series of commitments in 1014 at a time when he was in acute difficulties, and that these were subsequently confirmed by Cnut in 1016 or 1017.[9] She suggested that clauses 69–83 of Cnut's lawcode may represent the text of a lost coronation charter.[10] Cnut certainly gave an undertaking to observe the laws of his predecessor, and doubtless pledged to do away with evil customs, but were his promises written down in the form of a charter? The same point is true of his successors: we hear of commitments but not of charters in the cases of Edward the Confessor and Harold Godwineson.[11] William the Conqueror certainly took the coronation oaths, as reported in Anglo-Saxon Chronicle D and the Worcester Chronicler,[12] but again there are no references to an amplified version, or to a coronation charter.

Ratification of custom or legislation could be recorded in different ways in eleventh-century England, as Patrick Wormald has demonstrated.[13] Cnut's two great lawcodes were in fact the last of their kind before the Conquest, but unofficial treatises or tracts, compilations, letters, writs, all survive. The 1100 text falls into the category of a writ-charter,[14] distinguished from the Conqueror's legislative writ-charters by its range. The Conqueror's confirmation of the customs of the Londoners in an original writ-charter in English still survives,[15] and, in copy form, the writ-charter ordering the removal of ecclesiastical pleas from the hundred courts.[16] The 'regulations concerning exculpation' also survives in copies.[17] Compilations of William's laws were made, which deal with a wider range of issues and survive in later manuscripts.[18] There is no clear evidence, however, that the Conqueror soon after his coronation or subsequently issued what might be described as a charter of liberties.

One might suppose that if his predecessors had issued such charters, then he would have followed precedent and have done so too.

On the other hand, two actions of William Rufus deserve more attention than they have had. The first occurred in 1088. According to the Anglo-Saxon Chronicle and William of Malmesbury, Rufus had sent out letters summoning the English to him, promising them 'the best law that there had ever been in this country', a prohibition of unjust tax, and a grant to 'people' of their woods and hunting rights.[19] The context here was that Rufus was faced with a major revolt against his occupancy of the English throne in favour of his elder brother Robert Curthose, duke of Normandy. Rufus had support, but he also faced powerful opposition chiefly from the survivors of the great men of the Conquest, especially Odo bishop of Bayeux, and the bishop of Durham, probably the most influential figure in royal government. Rufus therefore decided to make key concessions, and in considering these we find clear precedents for the charter of 1100.

First was 'the best law there ever had been', like the promises of Aethelred and Cnut and Henry's promise to restore the law of King Edward (clause 13). The second pledge, to prohibit unjust tax, may have had in mind the Conqueror's triple geld of 1084, the incidence of which, in conjunction with other military demands, led to the Domesday Inquest.[20] The 1084 levy may have been the first taken by the Conqueror on a country-wide scale.[21] At 72 pence per hide, it was certainly exceptionally heavy. The issue did not go away, because in 1096 Rufus had levelled a four-shilling geld to raise money for the first crusade, when customary exemptions may have been ignored.[22] The inclusion of tax and tax exemptions in 1100 may be seen as Henry's pledge on an issue which had clearly struck a nerve. In clause 13 in 1100, it was stated that the 'demesne ploughs of serving knights' were to be quit of geld so that they could be prepared to defend the kingdom.

The third concession Rufus offered, a concession of rights over woods and hunting, was probably a response to stricter control imposed by the Conqueror. It is not easy to establish quite what was on offer here, but the likelihood was that there was a lengthy and largely unrecorded three-cornered struggle for control over woodland and hunting rights between kings, lords, and peasants. Kings had woodlands on their demesne lands, and they also exacted services, some to do with the hunt, over outlying estates.[23] As great estates broke up into smaller manorial units, proprietorship of woodland and hunting rights may in some cases have passed to lords. II Cnut 80 had permitted freedom of hunting on private property, whilst strictly protecting the king's rights over his own land. William the Conqueror had extended a royal hunting reserve in Hampshire, the New Forest, attracting opprobrium in the process, but much more crucial for the future was the protection extended over deer and wild boar.[24] Rufus may simply have been promising a return to the traditional position. However, he seems not to have kept his promise, since Eadmer tells the story of a number of men from the English nobility who were sent to the ordeal for forest offences. From the fact that they got off, we may deduce that their trial was held to be unjust.[25] Evidently they had believed they had the right to hunt on their own lands, only to be brought before royal justices.

In 1100 Henry stated that he would retain his father's forests in his own hands by the counsel of his barons, but he made no other commitments. This suggests that he was not going to disafforest the New Forest and any other land taken into the royal forest by his father, whilst leaving open the status of any forests created since 1087 and the question of freedom for lords to hunt in their own lands. Orderic Vitalis was quite clear about Henry's desire to control hunting over much of the country, only allowing a few of the nobles freedom to hunt on their own lands.[26]

Rufus successfully surmounted the 1088 rising, but in 1093 he fell seriously ill and thought that he was dying. Those around his bedside advised him to make his peace with God by filling the many vacant churches, particularly the archbishopric of Canterbury which had been vacant since Lanfranc's death in 1089. In 1100 there was no reference to the prolongation of vacancies, possibly because Henry set about nominating to key vacant bishoprics and abbeys. He promised that the holy church of God should be 'free'; that he would neither 'sell it nor put it to farm', 'nor on the death of an archbishop, bishop, or abbot would he take anything from the demesne of the church or from its men until a successor had entered' (clause 1). The reference to 'selling' churches may be understood as a repudiation of simony, in accordance with reforming ideals, but the more specific phrases relate to the way vacant bishoprics and abbeys had been managed by royal officials.[27] Such practices can only be illustrated in England after 1066, and the scandalized comments of chroniclers indicate that Rufus, or rather his chief minister Ranulf Flambard, pushed these rights much further than was regarded as acceptable.[28]

A proclamation was written out and confirmed with the king's seal that prisoners, whoever they were, were to be released, all fines remitted, and all offences pardoned. Furthermore, Rufus promised to all his people good and righteous laws, unfailing observance of rights, and an examination of wrongs committed so thorough as to deter all others.[29] The liberation of prisoners, lifting of fines, and pardoning of offences, may be seen as part of the king's preparation for death. In 1087 the Conqueror had freed his prisoners, even—and against his better judgement—Odo bishop of Bayeux.[30] Orderic Vitalis's account of Henry's own deathbed, when he 'revoked all sentences of forfeiture pronounced on guilty men, and allowed exiles to return and the disinherited to recover their ancestral inheritances', covers much the same ground.[31] Clauses 8 (fines) and 9 (murder fines) should perhaps be fitted into this context.

Henry renounced the practice of taking all a man's property as security for fines as had occurred in his father's and brother's day, and said that in future forfeitures would be imposed as they had been before that time (clause 8). This is another promised amendment of the operation of justice. 'Forfeitures' were discretionary damages imposed for those who fell into the king's 'mercy' for offences which did not incur fixed fines. The transition from fixed fines to discretionary forfeitures is thought to have been under way by 1066 in England. The incoming Normans were used to the idea that men were 'in mercy' for their lives, lands, or chattels, depending on the nature of the offence.[32] Rufus had evidently imposed heavy fines and sureties, as the story of Rainbald, a knight of Abingdon abbey, made clear. The knight was facing royal lawsuits and was told to pay five hundred pounds to be reconciled with the king, and had to produce sureties, who had to find the money when Rainbald fled to the count of Flanders.[33]

In 1100 Henry remitted murder fines incurred earlier than the day of his coronation (clause 9), and he promised that in future murders would be dealt with according to the law of King Edward. The origins and development of the murder fine have attracted a certain amount of attention in recent years.[34] It seems most likely that it had originated before the Conquest, possibly as a means of protecting strangers travelling along the highways. After 1066 the Conqueror laid down that this protection was to apply to Normans, who were to be designated as 'permanent strangers', in Alan Cooper's phrase.[35] If, as seems likely, the Conqueror had made an important change in the murder fine, then this might explain Henry's promise to restore the situation as it had been under Edward the Confessor. It was levied on lords or, if the lords could not find the sum, from local communities. Its origins are thought to have dated back before the Conquest, and to have been reimposed by the Conqueror because of a need to make lords responsible for the actions of their men—whether this meant an intention of dropping the fine is not clear. In practice it continued, and the burden was shifted entirely onto the hundreds, whilst exempting certain lords.

To sum up: in 1088 we have a precedent for the confirmation of 'good laws' and abolition of evil customs, and in 1093 for pardoning debts and offences. On both occasions royal pledges were recorded in writing and disseminated. Here we have the precedents for the 1100 charter, together with an attempt to execute acts of contrition. When the other clauses of the charter are examined in more detail, we can see how they are a mix of concerns found earlier in Cnut's lawcode, reshaped to reflect the situation in 1100, and of grievances arising in the more recent past.

The opening of Henry's charter recalls his coronation: 'by the mercy of God and the counsel of the barons of the whole realm I have been crowned king; and because the realm was oppressed by unjust exactions, I, in respect for God and the love I have for you all, make free the holy church of God . . . and all evil customs with which the kingdom of England was unjustly oppressed I take away', and it ends 'the law of King Edward I restore to you with those emendations made by my father with the counsel of his barons'.[36] The report of Henry's coronation in the Anglo-Saxon Chronicle echoes this, 'before the altar at Westminster he vowed to God and all the people to put down all the injustices that there were in his brother's time, and to maintain the best laws that had stood in any king's day before him'.[37]

Other clauses of the 1100 Charter strongly recall II Cnut, as Stafford pointed out: the promises to alleviate evil customs, protection for widows and wards, reasonable reliefs, the right to devise money and to make a will, rights over royal forests, and the nature of landholding by military service.[38] When the relevant clauses of the two codes are compared more closely, however, it can be seen that although there may be continuity in the issues of concern, the solutions proposed reflected the changed circumstances of 1100.

Clause 2 on reliefs reflects II Cnut 70 and 71 on heriots, which laid down heriots or succession payments for earls, king's thegns, and lesser thegns. Lesser or median thegns were evidently regarded as falling within the ambit of the charter, and this helps to explain Henry's concern that concessions made in 1100 were to be granted by his men to *their* men. However, there were important differences between the form taken by the succession payments. Cnut's code spelled out precisely the kind and amount of military equipment that was to be handed over, whereas in 1100 reliefs were simply to be 'reasonable'. We may wonder whether equipment was routinely handed over before 1066; afterwards only cash sums were paid as reliefs in England, and the amounts were evidently regarded as negotiable. Moreover, in 1100 there is a direct reference to Rufus's reign: 'if any of my barons, earls, or any other who holds of me should die, his heir was not to buy back his land, as he had done in the time of my brother, but was to pay a just and legitimate relief'. The issue of reliefs from knights on ecclesiastical tenancies in chief, which Rufus is known to have exacted from the bishopric of Worcester during a vacancy, was also probably regarded as an unwarrantable novelty.[39]

Hard evidence that Rufus had been taking too much as reliefs in straightforward cases of lay succession is lacking. On two occasions very large sums are mentioned, but the circumstances in each case were exceptional. Robert de Bellême is said to have offered three thousand pounds for his brother's earldom of Shropshire, for instance, but this was for the title and powers of an earl.[40] He also offered a large sum for succession to the large honour of Roger de Bully. Robert was related to Roger, but he was possibly not his nearest male relative.[41]

Unlike land, chattels and money were devisable by will. Churchmen were concerned that men should not die intestate, and in clause 70 of II Cnut it was recognized that after the heriot had been paid the property was to be strictly divided amongst a dead man's wife and children. In 1100 Henry stated that if a baron or one of his men fell ill, he could dispose of his property and the king would confirm this. If, however, his man was prevented from making arrangements, his wife, children, kinsmen, or law-worthy men could make division 'for his soul' as seemed fit. One problem that might well arise was that an heir might obstruct such bequests, or might possibly seize goods in order to pay off the deceased's debts.[42] Such gifts were often made to churches, and churchmen had an obvious interest in seeing that they were implemented. For example, in about 1100 a man named Robert Latimer, a sheriff's officer in Kent, made a deathbed bequest for the sake of his soul to the church of St Andrew (Rochester) of marshland in the Isle of Grain which he held of Archbishop Anselm.[43] If the dying man was prevented from making bequests 'by arms or infirmity', his wife, children, kinsmen, or his men could do so on his behalf.[44] Payments for burial, mortuary dues, frequently proved to be contentious.[45]

Protection of widows and wards was conspicuous both in II Cnut 73 and clause 3 of the 1100 Charter. According to the former, widows were to remain unmarried for a year, and afterwards might choose their own husbands. If remarried within the year, they were to lose their morning gifts and all the property received from their first husbands (clause 73a), and second husbands were to forfeit their wergelds to the king (73a. 1). They were to pay heriots within 12 months if not before (73a. 4). Widows were not to be too hastily consecrated as nuns (73a. 3).

In clause 3 of the 1100 charter, childless widows were to have their dowers and marriage portions, and were not to be remarried against their will. If there were children, widows were to have their dowers and marriage portions 'whilst they remained chaste' (no intruders were to be provided for at the expense of the family's lands); the custody of children was to be given to widows or to kinsmen, whichever was deemed to be more appropriate and, as in the case of reliefs, the king ordered that his men should deal in the same way with their own men. Although the details differ, the evident concern to balance the interests of two families, and for an orderly transfer of lands and rights, is much the same. On the one hand, the widow's family was concerned to protect its investment in the marriage in the form of the marriage portion and dower. On the other hand, there were the interests of the deceased husband's family as represented by the heir to be taken into account.[46] Without raising the further issue of differences between Norman and English custom, we may see ongoing attempts to define how shares of a family's land were to be apportioned between husbands and wives, parents and children.

A striking point of difference between II Cnut and the Charter of Liberties is the concern shown in 1100 about control of women's marriages. If a baron or any other of the king's men wished to give a daughter, sister, niece, or any kinswoman in marriage, he had to speak with the king about it. The king promised that he would neither forbid such marriage nor charge for his permission, unless the marriage was to an enemy. It seems unlikely that earlier kings had not sought to regulate noble marriages. One possible inference from this clause is that the position of women as heirs had changed during the eleventh century, perhaps because noble families had adapted their inheritance strategies to preserve and transmit inheritances, or because of a greater emphasis by the church on the indissolubility of marriage. Another factor was the possibility that unlicensed marriages to women of royal, native, or Scandinavian descent might occur. Disputed successions after 1087 may have sharpened the issue, in that inheritances might pass to supporters of Duke Robert rather than supporters of Rufus or Henry, but they did not create the situation. In 1075 the Conqueror had allegedly tried (but failed) to forbid the marriage of the sister of Earl Roger of Hereford to Earl Ralph of East Anglia.[47] It seems reasonable to suppose that in a society where marriage was a way of building alliances, the king, or any lord, would want to ensure that marriages were not made with his enemies.

A second issue was payment for permission: here Henry rejected any idea of payment for licence to marry, of the kind that was extracted from unfree peasants in the form of merchet.

Even more striking is the second part of clause 3, the provision that if there were a daughter as *haeres* she was to be given in marriage with her land by the counsel of the barons. The sentence is as striking for what is not said as well as what is. In what circumstances were daughters heiresses? How were their marriage portions, which represented their share of their family's lands, to be distinguished from a much larger share, possibly the whole, to which they might succeed, especially if they had no brothers? And in what circumstances was one daughter to inherit the whole?[48]

Stafford has drawn attention to cases in late Anglo-Saxon England where great assemblages of land devolved through the female line.[49] She has suggested that in that respect the coming of the Normans may not have brought fundamental change. In Norman society, too, inheritances had descended through women. The case of Mabel de Bellême and Roger of Montgomery is one conspicuous example from the era of William the Conqueror.[50] We may suspect, however, that the issue was particularly sensitive in 1100 because of decisions in the recent past. The most obvious instance is perhaps that of Judith, widow of Earl Waltheof. She was a kinswoman of the Conqueror who, it was alleged, had refused to be married at the king's behest to Simon de Senlis. She took flight and, after taking counsel, she was advised to offer her daughter Matilda as the bride. The idea, it was later claimed, was that if the Normans retained the kingdom, the daughter would retain both Northampton and Huntingdon; if the English recovered the country, she would at least hold the latter, her father's county.[51] The bulk of Waltheof's lands passed via marriage to Simon, and this may well have been an unpopular decision with the Normans. His younger daughter, Adeliza, though well provided for, took a smaller share in marriage to the Norman, Ralph de Tosny.[52]

One of the few innovations of his father's day which Henry pledged to abolish was the money tax or *monetagium*, taken in the towns and counties, which had not been levied in the time of King Edward. This obscure impost has left few traces in the sources.[53] It was clearly to do with the king's financial rights over the coinage, and the way moneyers passed on a share of the profits they made. English coinage was of high quality, over 90 per cent silver; coining was effectively a royal monopoly, and kings threw the weight of their authority behind maintaining authenticity, and punished forgery severely. In III Aethelred clause 8 the death penalty was prescribed for moneyers found guilty of striking false coins, and in II Cnut clause 81 it was prescribed that anyone found with false money was to lose a hand and his property.[54]

Moneyers based in boroughs made the pennies according to a design which changed every few years, by reminting older issues.[55] By the later eleventh century the increasing need for coins and the inelasticity of the supply of silver increased the likelihood of debasement. In England no *organizational* change to the system of coining was made by William the Conqueror,[56] and it looks as though the *monetagium* may have been a new and possibly heavier tax on the money supply. One theory is that it was a payment in lieu of royal profits from changing the weight of coins,[57] but the reference in 1100 to a payment 'from the cities and the counties' not from the moneyers is intriguing, as there were other supplementary payments, such as those imposed on the sheriffs' farms, and by 1130 aids from counties and boroughs occur.[58] If clause 5 of the 1100 charter contains one of the few explicit references to the recent past, the underlying issue, that of maintaining the excellence of the silver coinage, is older, as is the reference to strict punishment for those caught with false money. Attempts to maintain the quality of the coinage and to punish forgery were of course to continue in Henry's reign, but these were only palliative measures until fresh sources of silver were discovered.

Henry's charter purported to have been 'given' on the day of his coronation, but what was given? By whom was it recorded, and in what form? Was it, like Magna Carta, ever reissued? The coronation took place in London only three days after Rufus's unexpected death in the New Forest. Henry had ridden from the Forest to Winchester and thence to London. He had little or no time, therefore, to ponder the details of a charter, though Richardson and Sayles speculated that he would have had at his fingertips an idea of the concessions he would need to make if he became king.[59] The pace of events must have been hectic. Henry's decision to press ahead with the coronation meant that neither archbishop was present, and, in all probability, very few magnates. As the great men arrived at court to offer their homage and allegiance, individual deals had to be negotiated to win their support, and to head off the possibility that individuals might look to Duke Robert for a better deal. These agreements sometimes left traces in the written records. What we may infer is that Henry took the customary oaths at his coronation and either on that day or subsequently decided to amplify his promises, to record them in writing, and to see that copies were distributed.

The overall consistency of the copies suggests that there was basically only one form of words agreed at the time. This is not to rule out the possibility that there were preliminary notes, if not drafts. The framing of the clauses on, say, reliefs and widows suggests that someone on hand had good knowledge of old English law, possibly Maurice, bishop of London, an experienced former chancellor,[60] and an ability to translate earlier custom into a form of words that addressed current problems (at the very simplest, the use of the term reliefs and not heriots, for example).

If the organization of the text is considered, we find that it begins with a report of the coronation rather like Henry's letter to the exiled Archbishop Anselm; promises freedom for the church (a variant of the first part of the triple coronation oath); and promises to remit evil customs. These are then listed (clauses 2–11). Then there are two clauses which seem to go back to the coronation oath, a declaration of the king's peace (clause 12) and a restoration of the laws of King Edward (clause 13), before the final amnesty clause (14). Perhaps what we have is a composite text, rather like the 'Hic intimatur' of William the Conqueror.[61] The first clause could be interpreted as an interpretation of the traditional protection of the church to take account of reforming ideas; then clauses 2–11 as redress of grievances; then the declaration of the king's peace, which was traditionally made at coronation, a promise of the laws of King Edward; and the amnesty clause tacked on the end.

When the discussions reached a certain stage, however, they were recorded, and copies were made sufficiently quickly that only one version of the body of the text was established as William of Malmesbury and Eadmer suggested, not draft versions.[62] One decision was obviously about the language or languages of the record: the surviving early copies are in Latin, and it may be that only Latin texts were distributed at the time, though the possibility that the original may have been distributed in French[63] and in English cannot be entirely ruled out.[64] It is evident that a copy was sent to each shire court, and that addressed to the bishop and sheriff of Worcester has survived, and this was the version later transcribed into the *Red Book of the Exchequer*. Were copies sent to other individuals, such as bishops, as occurred later in the case of Magna Carta? Roger of Wendover suggested that the abbeys received copies,[65] and Matthew Paris, no fan of Henry I, believed that the king subsequently sought to recover them all, so that only three copies survived, at St Albans, Canterbury, and York.[66]

If distribution to shire courts, and, possibly, to certain individuals accounts for those copies of the Charter with addresses to specific individuals, how are those with general address clauses to be explained, given their early date?[67] That included by Richard of Hexham in his chronicle as having been sent to the treasury is one of this type.[68] It may be that those responsible for copies might have used a general address clause simply because at the time they were writing they believed that this was the appropriate form. Nevertheless the form of words used, 'to all his barons and sworn men French and English', was not identical with later general address clauses where different social ranks were listed.[69]

Lists of witnesses could also be adjusted as deemed suitable: at Rochester Bishop Gundulf was included, and at Westminster Abbot Gilbert Crispin, for example. The Rochester copy comes from the *Textus Roffensis*, a collection of texts made within about twenty years of Henry's coronation.[70] If the general form of the text is that of a writ-charter, the closing *Valete* is redolent of a letter, and parallels Henry's letter to Archbishop Anselm announcing his coronation.[71] The shortness of the witness list might be explained on the score that the charter was intended to reflect the situation at Westminster on 5 August. However, the contrast between the 1100 charter and the long witness list of Stephen's Second 'Oxford' Charter is striking,[72] and with the careful list of witnesses and pledges to Henry's treaty with the count of Flanders of March 1101.[73]

At this point let us return to one particular sub-category, copies with a general address clause and witness list, which omit clause 12, the declaration of the king's peace. These include the version in the *Quadripartitus*, the *Red Book of the Exchequer*, and the version at Paris, the 'Unknown Charter', to which clauses about grievances under King John were appended. Ludwig Riess suggested that these represented a reissue of 1101.[74] His argument was that in 1100 Henry knew he could expect a challenge from his brother, Duke Robert. Henry had to take what steps he could to retain the loyalty of the aristocracy, many of whom were in secret negotiations with the duke. When it became clear that Robert was planning an invasion, Henry confirmed the pledges he had made at his coronation and called for oaths of allegiance, as is known from a single mandate surviving in the original. This was addressed to the bishop of Lincoln, the sheriff of Lincolnshire, and two named magnates, in which Henry confirmed the laws and rights granted at his coronation, bound them by oath to defend England against all men, especially his brother Duke Robert, and instructed them to take the oath from his tenants-in-chief and they in turn from their tenants.[75] Robert arrived in England, faced his brother near Winchester, and allowed himself to be bought off with a pension and a negotiated settlement, which also included an amnesty clause. Riess suggested the charter was reissued after this, when a statement about the king's peace, necessary in 1100, would have been otiose. However, there are other possible explanations for the omission of clause 12, the most obvious being a copyist's action. Another is that this 'king's peace' was that customarily granted at coronation, which was deemed to last eight days.[76] Perhaps clause 12 was intended to be linked to the amnesty clause. In 1101 Henry may well have renewed the pledges made at his coronation, but there is no evidence that written reminders, as it were, were distributed.

Rufus's promises in 1088 had been recorded and sent out in sealed letters, yet neither they nor the later version in 1093 have survived, possibly because, as Eadmer bleakly remarked, as soon as the king recovered, he swept them aside.[77] Henry's charter was widely distributed, and it was soon inserted into legal compilations. Within a few years it had been included in the *Quadripartitus* and the *Leges Henrici Primi*, and in the collection of laws made at Rochester, the *Textus Roffensis*.[78] At this point then, we turn to the seeming paradox that whilst the 1100 Charter did not create a template, it did achieve long-term immortality as the precedent for Magna Carta.

Henry himself is not known to have issued a charter for Normandy after his victory at the battle of Tinchebray in 1106, though his public commitments to the customs of his father, to the repression of robbery, and to instructing officials to uphold the laws are all redolent of familiar ideas.[79] In fact, as David Bates has shown, relatively few writs or writ-charters were issued for Normandy.[80] The idea of using writs or writ-charters for legislation thus may not have been as widely used in Normandy as in England. Possibly only the notification issued in 1135 amending the Truce of God legislation might be regarded as a parallel with the legislative writs for England.[81]

Stephen's first Charter was a short statement about his commitment to the liberties and good laws of his uncle, King Henry, and a grant of the good laws and customs of the time of King Edward. It was witnessed only by his steward, William Martel.[82] Henry II's Charter, witnessed solely by Richard de Lucy, was of the same type as Stephen's first.[83] By 1154, written copies of the coronation promises were evidently placed on the altar at Westminster Abbey.[84] It would appear that Stephen's first charter and Henry II's were both of this type.

Stephen was crowned very soon after the old king's death and, as in the preceding reign, there would have been a period following the coronation when the great men appeared at court to offer homage. He was also negotiating with churchmen. He needed their support and wished to demonstrate his credentials as a reformer. Hence the need for a second, more detailed, charter in which his promises concerning the church, the forest, and the activities of sheriffs and other officials were spelled out.

By 1154, Henry II did not feel the need to issue a second, more detailed list of concessions to follow up his coronation promises. If Richard and John did have their coronation promises recorded in writing, they have not survived in charter form. Hence when the barons in 1214 were casting around for precedents there were only two detailed coronation charters available, Henry I's and Stephen's second charter. Stephen's decisions had been set aside by Henry II, and the charter of 1100 alone dealt with a similar range of concrete issues which penetrated to the heart of baronial concerns such as lordship, land, service, taxation, forests, and law.

The charter of 1100 is important politically and constitutionally, but it is also revealing about the relationship between making and recording law and custom in early twelfth-century England. Henry was engaging in a traditional practice by promising good law and redress of grievances; he was not the first to record his concessions in the form of a charter; but the context in which he did so, the growing importance of the written word as a record of legislation and as title to grants of liberties, ensured that the Charter of Liberties was indeed a 'lasting memorial'.

Notes

1. Eadmer, *Historia Novorum*, 119.
2. Holt, *Magna Carta*, 222–6.
3. *Councils and Synods*, i, pt II, n. 653, citing London, Lambeth Palace, MS 1212 pp. 2 and 1330.
4. For a list see Liebermann, 'Text of Henry I's Coronation Charter', 21–48; *Die Gesetze der Angelsachsen*, i, 521–4; iii, 293–9. In the early twentieth century another copy was found at Manchester in the John Rylands Library, of which Liebermann then took account in *Die Gesetze der Angelsachsen*, iii, 296–9, see: *RRAN*, ii, no. 488.
5. These are discussed by Liebermann, 'Text of Henry I's Coronation Charter', 40–6 and *Die Gesetze der Angelsachsen*, i, 521–4.
6. On the terminology used for different kinds of royal documents (diploma, writ, charter, and writ-charter), and the different address clauses, see Sharpe 'Use of Writs', 248–53.
7. The *ordo* in the Dunstan Pontifical was described in the *Vita Oswaldi: Historians of the Church of York*, i, 436–8. For a discussion of coronation oaths see Foreville, 'Le Régime monocratique en Angleterre', 157–63.
8. 'Laws of Cnut and the History of Anglo-Saxon Royal Promises'.
9. Cnut was recognized as king in a ceremony in 1016 at Southampton, JW, ii, 484. Later chroniclers refer to a coronation in 1017, Ralph of Diceto, *Opera Historica*, i, 169; Gervase of Canterbury, *Historical Works*, ii, 55. An agreement between the English and Danes at Oxford in 1018 about the observance of King Edgar's laws is reported by JW, ii, 504.

10. For comment see: Lawson, 'Archbishop Wulfstan and the Homiletic Element', reprinted in *The Reign of Cnut King of England, Denmark and Norway*, 159.

11. *Life of King Edward*, 20–1, refers to this king as abrogating bad laws and with his witan establishing good ones, but no reference is made to a charter. For discussion of Edward's commitment to uphold good law see Maddicott, 'Edward the Confessor's Return to England in 1041'. The Worcester Chronicler gives the gist of Harold Godwinson's promises which evoke the spirit of a coronation charter: he is said to have revoked unjust laws, established good ones, became the protector of the church, cherished churchmen, showed himself humble and courteous to all men but rigorous to malefactors. He gave orders for the arrest of all thieves, robbers, and disturbers of the peace, and laboured himself for the defence of the country by land and sea: JW, ii, 600.

12. *ASC* D 1066.

13. Wormald, *Making of English Law: King Alfred to the Twelfth Century*, I *Legislation and Lawsuits*, pt 2.

14. *Die Gesetze der Angelsachsen*, iii, 293.

15. *RRAN*, ed. Bates, no. 180.

16. Ibid., no. 128.

17. This was described by Liebermann as W Lad: *Die Gesetze de Angelsachsen*, i, 483–4. William's order (*RRAN*, ed. Bates, no. 129) that sheriffs should refrain from taking demesne lands from bishoprics and abbeys should also perhaps be included, as it is comparable with the concern shown in Cnut's second lawcode (c. 69) that royal reeves were to provide for the king from his own property and that no-one should be compelled to give them anything as purveyance.

18. These are the collections referred to by Liebermann as Wl art, Leis Wl, and Wl art retr.

19. E 1088; William of Malmesbury, *Gesta Regum*, i, 546. William's slightly longer version says that the king sent letters to the English, and bound them to his service, promising good laws, a lightening of tribute and freer hunting.

20. Green, *Aristocracy of Norman England*, 228–34.

21. Ibid., 228.

22. Leges Edwardi Confessoris, c. 11, 2: *Die Gesetze der Angelsachsen*, i, 636.

23. For a brief survey, Faith, *English Peasantry*, 102–3.

24. For the creation of the New Forest see: Baring, 'Making of the New Forest'.

25. Eadmer, *Historia Novorum*, 102.

26. OV, vi, 100.

27. On regalian rights see: Howell, *Regalian Right*, xx.

28. Jared, 'English Ecclesiastical Vacancies'.

29. Eadmer, *Historia Novorum*, 32.

30. OV, iv, 96–100.

31. OV, vi, 448.

32. See the inquest into ducal rights in Normandy, Haskins, *Norman Institutions*, 277–84.

33. *Historia Ecclesia Abbendonensis*, ii, 54.

34. Garnett, '*Franci et Angli*', 116–20; O'Brien, 'From Morðor to Murdrum, 74–110. O'Brien's case for a pre-Conquest origin is convincing. However, the evidence that it was introduced by Cnut has been queried, Cooper, 'The Rise and Fall of the Anglo-Saxon Law of the Highway', 55–8. There is some doubt from

the syntax of Wl art ('Hic Intimatur') clause 3 whose lord was supposed to arrest the killer, the lord of the murdered man who might be thought to have responsibility for him as a man without his kindred, or the lord of the murderer, on the premise that the fine was intended to make lords responsible for reining in the killings of their men. The Latin reads 'Et si quis de illis occisus fuerit, dominus eius habeat . . .'.

35. Wl art ('Hic Intimatur'), c. 3; for comment see Cooper, 'Rise and Fall of the Anglo-Saxon Law of the Highway', 64.
36. 'Le sacre des rois Anglo-Normands et angevins', 204–5.
37. E 1100.
38. Stafford, 'Laws of Cnut and the History of Anglo-Saxon Royal Promises', 178.
39. For the relief which Rufus exacted from the knights enfeoffed on the bishopric of Worcester in 1095, Stubbs, *Select Charters*, 109; for comment Barlow, *William Rufus*, 235–6.
40. OV, v, 224–6.
41. OV, v, 226–7n.
42. *Treatise on the Laws and Customs of England*, VII, 5–8.
43. Tsurushima, 'Fraternity of Rochester Cathedral Priory about 1100', 329.
44. For a discussion of the precise significance of this clause, Sheehan, *The Will in Medieval England*, 389.
45. Brett, *English Church under Henry I*, 227.
46. The common law solution eventually devised was the writ of dower, Bianacalana, 'Widows at Common Law'.
47. JW, iii, 24.
48. Milsom, 'Inheritance by Women in the Twelfth and thirteenth Centuries'; Holt, 'Feudal Society and the Family', IV: 'Heiress and the Alien'; Green, 'Aristocratic Women'; Green, *Aristocracy of Norman England*, ch. 11.
49. 'Women and the Norman Conquest', 237–40.
50. OV, ii, 46–8; Thompson, 'Family and Influence to the South of Normandy'.
51. *Vita et Passio Waldevi*, in *Chroniques Anglo-Normandes*, ii, 123–6; for Countess Judith see: Keats-Rohan, 'Portrait of a People', 138–40.
52. *Complete Peerage*, vi, 639n; Holt, 'Feudal Society and the Family', IV: 'Heiress and the Alien', 8–9.
53. Bisson, *Conservation of Coinage*, ch. 2; Metcalf, 'Taxation of Moneyers'; Nightingale, 'Some London Moneyers'.
54. *Gesetze der Angelsachsen*, i, 230, 314.
55. Archibald, 'Coins'.
56. Dolley, *Norman Conquest and the English Coinage*.
57. Bisson, *Conservation of Coinage*, 20.
58. Green, *Government of England under Henry I*, 62–4 (surcharges), 75–6 (aids from counties and boroughs).
59. *Law and Legislation from Aethelberht to Magna Carta*, 32.
60. For Maurice see: Brooke with Keir, *London 800–1216*, 340–2. Foreville suggested that Maurice may have been responsible for the charter, 'La régime monocratique en Angleterre au Moyen Age', 162.
61. Clause 9 of 'Hic Intimatur' ends, 'this decree was enacted in the city of Gloucester'.
62. William of Malmesbury, *Gesta Regum*, i, 714.
63. For a thirteenth-century copy in French see Liebermann, 'Text of Henry I's Coronation Charter', 46–8.

64. Holt, 'Origins of the Constitutional Tradition', 15–16.
65. Roger of Wendover, *Flores Historiarum*, ii, 164. Dr N. Karn has suggested to me (pers. comm.) it was unlikely that the abbeys were sent copies, pointing out that the copy sent to the shire court of Hertfordshire contains no reference to the abbot of St Albans.
66. Matthew Paris, *Historia Anglorum*, ii, 111.
67. For the growing use of the general address clause, see discussion by Richard Sharpe, pp. 32–52.
68. 'De Gestis Regis Stephani et de Bello Standardii', in *Chronicles of the Reigns of Stephen, Henry II, and Richard I*, iii, 142. Wormald pointed out, however, that the copy which was later inserted in the *Red Book of the Exchequer* was not the form with the general address, but that for the bishop and sheriff of Worcestershire, *Making of English Law*, I, 400.
69. A point made to me by Dr Nicholas Karn.
70. Wormald, '*Laga Eadwardi*: The *Textus Roffensis* and its Context'.
71. Anselm, *Letters*, no. 212.
72. *RRAN*, iii, no. 271.
73. *Diplomatic Documents preserved in the Public Record Office*, I, *1101–1272*, 2; Van Houts, 'Anglo-Flemish Treaty of 1101', 169–74.
74. 'Reissue of Henry I's Coronation Charter'.
75. This mandate survives in the original, Lincoln Cathedral Treasury A. 1.1, no. 5, calendared *RRAN*, ii, no. 531.
76. O'Brien, *God's Peace and King's Peace*, 73–84.
77. Eadmer, *Historia Novorum*, 38–9.
78. Wormald, *Making of English Law*, I, 407–15; *idem*, 'Quadripartitus'.
79. OV, vi, 92–4, 98.
80. 'Earliest Norman Writs'.
81. *Coutumiers de Normandie*, i, pt II, c. lxxi.
82. *RRAN*, iii, no. 270.
83. Stubbs, *Select Charters*, 158.
84. *Correspondence of Thomas Becket*, i, no. 74.

5
Regional Variations in the Charters of King Henry II (1154–89)

Nicholas Vincent

In a well known, though perhaps apocryphal injunction to the future King Henry II, Henry's father, Geoffrey Plantagenet, is said to have urged the about-to-be-king to respect the diverse laws and customs of his dominions, and to preserve in equal measure the Angevin customs of Anjou, and the Norman and English customs of Normandy and England.[1] Over the past 300 years, much ink has been spilled in an attempt to determine the extent to which Geoffrey's injunction was obeyed.[2] Did the Plantagenet dominion under Henry II enjoy a centralized administration, sufficient to qualify it as a Plantagenet 'empire' in the modern sense of the term, or did it remain merely a diverse collection of lands, each governed according to local custom, ready at any moment to fracture, as after 1189 these lands were indeed to fracture, into a series of independent entities, Norman, Angevin, Poitevin or English as the case might be? The general consensus amongst twentieth-century historians, themselves merely echoing the opinion of David Hume set down as long ago as the 1760s, has been that Henry Plantagenet, whatever his imperialist aspirations, ruled no true empire but a haphazard collection of French and insular territories, at best a dominion or, as the French have grown accustomed to call it, an 'espace Plantagenêt', lacking a fixed capital or any unified body of laws, customs, coinage or administration.[3] Just as their lands were divided by geography, ethnic identity and language, historians have argued, so in their political organization these lands were never fully welded into a cohesive whole. In what follows, I do not wish this particular debate entirely to dominate discussion, not least because it is a debate in many ways founded upon a wholly anachronistic confusion between the medieval concept of *imperium* and the modern idea of 'empire', itself far from universally agreed. Nevertheless, if we were searching for one aspect of their rule in which the Plantagenets do indeed appear to have imposed a degree of uniformity upon their lands, then our search would very swiftly lead us to the letters and charters, and thence to the chancery of the king. Like Richard of Anstey, in the late 1150s compelled to travel from England to Toulouse in search of the king and his writs, so throughout Henry's reign, Poitevins converged upon London, Londoners upon Normandy, and Normans upon Anjou, to petition the king for the issue of written mandates and confirmations, letters and charters, by which the king's power could be enlisted in their support.[4]

In stating that these letters and charters issued from a centralized chancery we would already be stepping beyond certain fact, since the process by which the king's letters and charters were drafted, written, sealed and dispatched, itself remains to a large extent mysterious.[5] Of the 550 or so original charters of Henry II that still survive, a very large number—thanks to the work of T. A. M. Bishop, recently revised by T. Webber, a proportion as high as one in three—can be attributed to no identifiable 'chancery' scribe.[6] Some at least of these, we may assume a very large number, were written not by scribes attached directly to the king but either by the scribes of the beneficiary soliciting the document or by professional freelances drawing up documents as and when required. The degree to which the king's charters were written outside the chancery, and the extent to which the rate of beneficiary as opposed to central chancery production declined between the 1150s and the 1180s, are important questions to which answers will shortly be attempted, though not in this particular survey. But even were it to be admitted that the chancery remains an ill-defined and in many respects Protean institution, the sheer extent of its activities is hardly in doubt. Each letter and charter, however drafted and written, had to be validated by the application of one or other of the king's seals, for the most part by the application of the itinerant great seal. This in itself, combined with the fact that all the king's surviving letters were written in Latin according to a series of more or less strict linguistic formulae, suggests that of all the offices of Plantagenet government it was the chancery that was in many senses the closest to the king, the most susceptible to the king's personal will, and hence the most centralized expression of Henry II's rule. In what follows, I intend to examine various aspects of the evidence that the chancery has bequeathed to us, physical, formulaic and linguistic, in an attempt to establish whether particular diplomatic forms were reserved for particular regions of the Plantagenet dominion, and in the process to establish what the charters themselves may tell us of the king's approach to the various lands over which he ruled.

We must begin with a set of crude statistics, and with a very stern warning. The edition of Henry II's charters is now more or less complete, and in the process of being indexed. It comprises more than 3200 individual entries, mostly of surviving texts but also including several hundred notices of texts now lost. More than one-third of the entries that can be dated were issued during the early years of Henry's reign, for the most part before 1158, so that there is an imbalance between the surviving evidence for the first 4 as opposed to the last 30 years of the reign.[7] There is also a very considerable disparity within the collection between the number of texts surviving for England as opposed to all other parts of the Plantagenet dominion. As many as 2200 entries, or more than two-thirds of the collection, concern English beneficiaries, as opposed to a mere 600 for beneficiaries in Normandy, and a further 400 concerning beneficiaries in all other regions from Anjou to Ireland and from Aquitaine to Wales. Ireland, indeed, accounts for less than 30 texts, the whole of Aquitaine for less than 50.[8] There is also a marked disparity between charters surviving for lay as opposed to ecclesiastical beneficiaries on either side of the Channel, which results in an over-whelming bias in favour of letters and charters expedited for English and Norman churches and monasteries, with greater Anjou—Anjou, the Touraine and Maine—emerging in a respectable, but by no means lavishly documented third place. The reasons for this are to some extent archival, and result from the greater number of cartularies that survive for England and Normandy, and above all from the thirteenth-century and later practice of the English but not the French royal chancery of issuing and preserving inspeximuses of vast numbers of earlier English royal charters. Even within France itself, there are considerable archival anomalies between regions, so that the Dordogne, for example, or Gascony south of the Garonne can offer barely a handful of surviving medieval cartularies to set against the very considerable numbers that survive for Normandy or Anjou.[9] Lay cartularies are as rare in France as they are in England, and this, combined with the destruction of many of the great seigneurial archives and the feeble survival (and we may assume issue) of inspeximuses by the late medieval French royal chancery, contributes in no small part to the relatively small number of charters of Henry II recorded for lay beneficiaries in France.[10] Many of those that do survive are so peculiar as to give rise to the suspicion that in Normandy or Anjou after 1204 it was far easier for laymen to gain acceptance for forged charters of the Plantagenet kings than it was for the incoming Capetian administration to reject such charters as forgeries.[11]

Throughout, we must be on our guard against assuming that the greater survival rate of charters for England necessarily implies that it was English affairs that occupied the majority of the chancery's time. That said, the peculiar operation both of the English exchequer and of the English courts of law may well have involved the issue of far more writs and mandates than were ever expedited for Normandy or other parts of the king's dominion. We know from the *Dialogue of the Exchequer*, and from later exchequer practice, that each year the king was obliged to issue many hundreds of writs of *liberate*, *computate* or *perdono*, of which today only a handful still survive.[12] Likewise, when, from the 1190s, we first come across the enrolment or filing of English judicial writs, they survive in their hundreds for any particular law term or eyre.[13] Since many such writs either had no beneficiary or were intended to be returned by the beneficiary to the king's officers, it is not surprising that very few from the reign of Henry II have been copied into cartularies or survive as originals. For our knowledge of them we depend very largely upon the formulary-treatise known as *Glanvill*.[14] By contrast, the practices of the Norman exchequer and of the Norman law courts are much less well known, but may well have involved the issue of fewer writs. Although the surviving Norman pipe rolls of the 1180s clearly imply the presentation of writs and warrants, we have not a single surviving mandate from Henry II to the exchequer of Normandy, and not a single royal charter or writ, as opposed to final concords, specifically stated to have been issued at the Caen exchequer. Even final concords made in the ducal court survive only haphazardly for Normandy, apparently with nothing to compare to the feet of fines introduced to English judicial and archival practice from the 1190s onwards.[15] There is a caution here to the wary, both to guard against the chronologically imbalanced and Anglocentric nature of the surviving evidence, and to take into consideration the fact that even such important administrative institutions as the exchequer of Normandy would have vanished virtually without a trace were it not for the physical survival of their accounts.[16] Powicke long ago suggested that the exchequer of Normandy may well have been, indeed almost certainly had to be, matched by some sort of financial accounting system for the Plantagenet lands further south, in Anjou and Aquitaine.[17] The fact that no such Angevin or Poitevin exchequer is revealed to us from the surviving charters is no proof that such institutions never existed. In much the same way, whereas in England in the immediate aftermath of Henry II's succession, the king issued surviving charters to several of the earls of English counties re-awarding them the third penny of pleas, the absence of any equivalent to the third penny in France has ensured that no such awards or confirmations survive for the greater Norman or Angevin magnates.[18] Charters of Henry II awarding laymen either lands or offices in France are extremely rare. That they were originally issued in large numbers is not, however, seriously in doubt.

Our surviving evidence is further distorted by its archival history since the twelfth century, so that whereas beneficiaries were keen to preserve charters and confirmations, they were less keen to preserve much of the routine business transacted via royal writs. We have remarkably few exchequer or judicial writs, even for England. The judicial writs that survive tend to survive in clusters for particular monasteries, most notably for such houses as Abingdon, Crowland, St Benet Holme and Thorney which possess especially comprehensive cartularies or cartulary-chronicles in which the monks preserved copies of letters that elsewhere appear to have been considered beneath the cartulary makers' contempt. Cartulary makers in Normandy and Plantagenet France appear to have been even more selective than their counterparts in England. For Normandy we can depend upon only a handful of cartularies—the so-called 'Livre Noir' of Bayeux cathedral, and the cartularies of Montebourg and St-Sauveur, for example—to supply any real insight into the circulation of judicial writs within the duchy. Most Norman cartularies were compiled after the Capetian invasion of 1204, at a time when there was even less incentive than in England for cartulary makers to copy out archaic and, for the most part, entirely redundant Plantagenet writs. Writs of military summons, which must originally have been issued by Henry's chancery in their thousands, are rarer still. We now have only one remarkable and somewhat troublesome survival, copied into a formulary in the north of England which was itself then discarded, the writ surviving only because the piece of parchment onto which it had been copied was cannibalized to make a parchment seal tag.[19]

On a similar note, we must be on our guard against a further element of distortion introduced to those letters and charters that have survived. Less than a sixth of the survivals are preserved to us in their original form as sealed single sheets.[20] The vast majority have been passed down to us in the form of later chancery, cartulary or antiquarian copies. In the process, the original word order and even the words themselves have frequently been changed. The most obvious example of this lies in the use of the *Dei gratia* formula which, as Léopold Delisle so cleverly revealed, was introduced to Henry II's charters in the early 1170s, probably on the king's return from Ireland in the spring of 1172. I know of no example of a genuine charter of Henry II before 1172 in which *Dei gratia* was used. However, as J. H. Round pointed out, later copyists frequently introduced the formula to their versions of charters composed before 1172, assuming perhaps that it had been omitted by mistake.[21] In the same way, after 1199 and the introduction of *dominus Hibernie* to the royal style, those copying out charters of Henry II would occasionally introduce Ireland to the king's titles, in an attempt to make such documents conform with later practice.[22] What might be taken as a sign that any particular charter is forged can in reality result merely from later scribal conformism. To add even further chaos to the equation, Bishop unearthed examples of sealed single-sheet originals, apparently issued by the chancery after 1172 in renewal of earlier royal texts, introducing the *Dei gratia* formula but leaving their original, pre-1172 witness lists unaltered.[23] In this way, a writ of Henry II witnessed by Thomas Becket as chancellor, before 1162 but employing the *Dei gratia* formula introduced after 1172, is not to be dismissed out of hand as a forgery but could well be a post-1172 chancery renovation of an earlier, genuine exemplum.

Many of the instances that will occupy us in this chapter are taken from only one clause, the address clause to royal letters. Here, it is not only the *Dei gratia* formula that can lead to confusion. Genuine royal writs could be issued under any one of dozens of minor linguistic permutations. The class of writs and charters addressed to the sea ports, for example, would demonstrate the rich variety of forms that could be introduced in setting down the order and the identity of the addressees: justices, ministers and sheriffs; justices, sheriffs and all ministers; all justices and bailiffs and reeves and ministers, and so forth virtually *ad infinitum*. Copyists, especially French copyists, unfamiliar with chancery practice, had a tendency to misread or to misinterpret certain specifically Anglo-Norman words. In this way, it is notoriously difficult to determine whether the abbreviation *iustic'* should be expanded as *iusticie, iusticiario, iusticiis* or *iusticiariis*. French copyists often opted for the later, perhaps anachronistic form. In the same way, in a land with *vicomtes* but without sheriffs, the Latin abbreviation *vic'* for *vicecomes* could be misinterpreted as *vic'* for *vicarius* or even as *via'* for the distinctively French *viarius*.[24] As Richard Mortimer is right to remind us, linguistic or formulaic anomalies in originals, let alone in copies, cannot in themselves be read as proof of forgery, however loud they may set alarm bells ringing.[25] Above all, we should not expect perfect uniformity amongst documents produced not by a xerox machine but by scribes who were fallible and frequently exhausted individuals, capable on a wet Monday morning of turning out writs from which even so significant an element as the king's title as count of Anjou was omitted, let alone of introducing any number of minor variations in language and word order.[26]

With these reservations in mind, let us now pass to the charters themselves. Here, I shall begin with the evidence that the charters provide for the way that the king viewed his lands, territories and subjects, attempting to extract from the formulaic Latin of the charters some idea of the banal reality of Henry II's 'empire'. I shall then move on to consider whether particular regions retained particular diplomatic forms, and whether the language appropriate to a charter for Ireland, say, or Aquitaine changed when the chancery came to address affairs in other parts of Britain or France. In the *intitulatio* to every one of his surviving charters, Henry's name, *H(enricus)*, is followed by a standard list of titles and honours. The list itself is not without its ambiguities, since it is not easy to establish whether the standard abbreviations employed, *rex Angl'*, *dux Norm'* et *Aquit'* et *comes And'*, are to be read as applying to places or to people. Was Henry king of the English or king of England, count of the Angevins or count of Anjou? The conclusion drawn by Delisle, since accepted by all recent commentators, is that it is peoples, *rex Anglorum, dux Normannorum et Aquitanorum et comes Andegauorum*, that are in question, rather than places.[27] Although there are several twelfth-century beneficiary-produced originals in which *dux Normannie et Aquitanie* and even *rex Anglie or comes Andegauie* are expanded in full, Delisle's thesis remains in essence unchallenged.[28] On the one occasion where a recognized chancery scribe expanded the king's title, it was in the form predicted by Delisle, as *rex Anglorum*.[29]

As a king, Henry possessed a realm, a *regnum*, that seems to have been conceived of as an exclusively English affair. That this was so is not immediately apparent. When in 1154, for example, in his so-called 'coronation charter', Henry claimed to act 'for the honour of God and holy church' (*et pro communi emendatione totius regni mei*), are we to suppose a charter directed specifically to the realm of England, or to all of Henry's scattered lands?[30] When the king writes of 'the whole of my realm' (*totum regnum meum*, or some such phrase) is it England alone that is being referred to, or an entity that is much more broadly conceived?[31] An answer here is suggested by those charters in which Henry's realm is specifically distinguished from his other lands, and in particular from his lands 'across the sea' (*transmarinas*).[32] Likewise, a relatively large number of charters employ a formula, apparently inherited from the Anglo-Saxon kings, in which Henry claimed to be acting for his own soul and the souls of various other members of his family, as well as 'for the realm's stability and peace' (*pro stabilitate et pace regni*), 'for the realm's condition and preservation' (*pro statu et incolumitate regni*) or just 'for the realm's condition' (*pro statu regni*).[33] Although some such phrase occurs in at least four charters issued to beneficiaries in Normandy or Anjou, there are enough examples, including one for the Norman abbey of Mortemer, in which it is the stability and peace of the realm of England (*regni Anglie*) that is specified, to suggest that in these and all other cases it was the realm of England, rather than the totality of Henry's lands in England and France, that was being invoked.[34] Other stock formulae, in which the king awarded all such privileges 'as are held by any other church in my realm',[35] or in which he referred to the privileges that he himself enjoyed in his *regnum*,[36] are to be found exclusively in charters addressed to English beneficiaries, and on occasion are qualified so as to relate specifically to the *regnum Anglie*.[37] Likewise, whenever *regnum* is used in the sense of reign rather than realm, it is Henry's reign as king of England that is referred to, rather than his accession to rulership in any more general sense. We have, for example, a handful of charters in which the chancery, or more likely the beneficiaries themselves, sought to supply a dating clause according to Henry's regnal years, calculated from the time of his coronation as king of England in December 1154.[38] On occasion, Henry's reign in England, or his realm of England, is specifically contrasted with his rule as duke or his dukedom of Normandy.[39]

Just as Henry's realm was specifically English, so one of the chief external symbols of kingship, the crown, appears to have enjoyed specifically English connotations. The word *corona* itself occurs only in charters to English beneficiaries, save when Henry refers to the actual rather than the symbolic crown of King William I which, according to charters of St-Etienne Caen, Henry I had repurchased after William's death from the monks with whom the late king had deposited it.[40] Elsewhere, whenever the king refers to the 'pleas of the crown' (*placita ad coronam pertinentes*), 'the customs of my crown' (*consuetudines corone mee*), or to land and rights held 'from my crown' (*de corona mea*), the context is invariably an English one.[41] Combining both ideas, of realm and crown, in 1188 we find Henry, in a letter to the pope, describing the church of Canterbury as 'the head and crown of our realm' (*capud est et corona regni nostri*).[42] Such a reservation of the ideas of *regnum* and *corona* to England might on the surface appear a mere banality. However, we should remember here Warren Hollister's investigation of the nature of Anglo-Norman kingship, and particularly his demonstration that Henry I thought of himself not as king of some joint Anglo-Norman enterprise, but as a ruler who was a king in England but a duke in Normandy.[43] Clearly, the chancery clerks of Henry II continued to think in similar terms. Furthermore, we might also care to consider Paul Hyams's suggestion that the author of the legal treatise *Glanvill*, regarded by Hyams as an English equivalent to the Norman and northern French *coutumiers*, deliberately employs the term *regnum* in order to distinguish the laws of the realm of England, here treated as a unified body of laws above and beyond regional or honorial English custom, from the laws of the king's duchy of Normandy.[44] The concept of an English crown and a unified English realm may well have strengthened the centrifugal tendency towards a unified body of English law, privileging the king's law at the expense of the customary laws of the English regions.[45] At the same time, by establishing a distinct sense of identity between the English *regnum*, Plantagenet kingship and English law, the concepts of crown and *regnum* may have served to set English kingship and law apart from the authority and law exercised by the Plantagenets in their lands across the Channel. In short, we may have an indication here of one way in which England had already established a claim to its own distinctive kingship and laws, many years before the physical disintegration of the Plantagenet 'empire'.

This is not to suggest that Henry II's chancery lacked any terminology for the king's dominions as a whole. The word *dominium* occurs frequently in Henry's charters in the general sense of demesne lordship or lordly power, as for example when the king, in writs of naifty, deliberately excepts those fugitive serfs who may be found in his own demesne (*in dominio meo*).[46] For the rest, however, used in a more specific sense to imply territorial dominion, it occurs only in charters that are of dubious authenticity.[47] The even more exalted word, *imperium*, occurs in no genuine charter of Henry II, although it is to be found in one of the many forgeries attributed to Henry by the *bonshommes* of Grandmont.[48] 'Fatherland', or *patria*, is used only once in a context that implies the realm of England—when Thomas Becket is described as having been promoted 'father of the fatherland' (*patrem patrie*)—but elsewhere in a generic sense, applicable to regions both within and outside Plantagenet control.[49] By contrast, two other words are used frequently to signify Henry's wider territorial authority. The first is the word 'power' (*potestas*), as for example when the king exempts the monks of Mortemer from all toll, passage, and all customs 'in any place of our power, either on land or at sea' (*in omni loco potestatis nostre tam in terra quam in aqua*), or as when 'power' is set down as one of the wider concepts aspired to by individual kings.[50] Henry writes, for example, to the archbishop of Rouen that 'we know that whatever of honour, highness or power we have, our realm and other things committed to our rule, we receive each of them from our Lord and creator' (*quod quicquid honoris, celsitudinis, potestatis habemus, regnum etiam et cetera que nostro commissa sunt regimini, singula a domino et creatore nostro nobis collata scimus et profitemur*).[51] The other term, used very frequently to signify the extent of Henry's lordship, is 'land' (*terra*), both in the singular and the plural, so that the monks of Abingdon can be exempted from all toll and customs 'throughout all my lands and sea ports' (*per omnes terras meas et portus maris*),[52] and charters are frequently addressed to the bishops, justices and other faithful men 'of the whole of the king's land' (*totius terre sue*).[53] The fact that so vague a term as 'land' or 'lands' is used in this context reinforces the impression that Henry's 'dominion', perhaps to pedants better described henceforth as his 'territory', was never thought of as being united by anything save Henry's personal power and his claim to rule. Whatever the intellectuals at Henry's court may have written of his claims to rival Arthur or the imperial splendours of antiquity, the chancery employed terminology that was more prosaic and which ultimately suggests a far from imperial outlook.

The best that can be expected from the chancery in this respect is some recognition of the wide extent and, in particular, the cross-Channel nature of Henry's land or lands. This is acknowledged on occasion, as for example in addresses to the archbishops, bishops and so forth of the whole of the king's land 'this side and beyond the sea'. This particular expression, *citra et ultra mare*, which can be found fairly frequently in charters issued after 1172, occurs in only five charters from before that date, making its first certain appearance in 1166.[54] Given the great preponderance of charters surviving from the first ten years of Henry's reign, the non-appearance of *citra et ultra mare* before the 1160s is unlikely to be the result of accident, but suggests a subtle and deliberate innovation in the chancery's language. The phrase itself, perhaps quite deliberately, is used in an ambiguous way, failing to spell out whether it was England or France that was considered to lie 'on this side' or 'beyond' the sea. On two occasions in the 1160s, we find the term 'overseas' (*transmarina*) employed to distinguish the king's French lands from his realm of England,[55] and in another instance the term *cismarina* is used so as to imply that it is the French lands that lie beyond the sea.[56] In the same way, the language used for the king's Channel crossings can, on occasion, imply that it was England that was the homeland from which the king departed and to which he returned, for example as when Henry announced, in a letter to the monks of Canterbury, that through God's mercy he had 'returned' to England (*Deo miserante in redditu suo in Anglia*).[57] The phrase *citra et ultra mare*, however, is to be found in charters issued in Normandy to Norman or French beneficiaries, as well as in charters issued in England to English beneficiaries.[58] Herein lies our one very slight indication that the chancery was moving towards a more imperialist vision of Henry's authority. We might also note that for all of its dependence upon earlier Anglo-Norman forms, and despite its apparent awareness of the distinctions between Henry's English 'realm', and the dukedoms and counties that he ruled in France, Henry's chancery exhibited no very precise spatial loyalty towards England— hardly surprisingly, perhaps, given that at least some of the chancery officials, such as Stephen of Fougères, were themselves of French rather than English birth.

Charters frequently designate not only the geographical position but the specific names of the various lands under Henry's rule, and most frequently in addresses to the bishops, ministers or men of England and/or Normandy. Although we have at least three surviving originals, one for an English and two for Norman beneficiaries, in which Normandy is placed in this context before England, in the vast majority of cases it is England that takes priority over Normandy or any other region.[59] Charters in which the address is extended beyond Normandy or England are comparatively rare. In this way, although there are a dozen or so charters clearly intended for use in Ireland, on occasion specifically addressed to the king's Irish subjects (*Hibernienses*), in only four certain instances is Ireland itself (*Hibernia*) referred to in the address.[60] Elsewhere, we find occasional addresses to Anjou, Maine, the Touraine, Poitou, the Saintonge and the Auvergne, and within Britain to Wales and Scotland, or to various combinations of two or more of these territorial groupings.[61] In part, the relative rarity of such addresses, when compared to charters addressed to England or Normandy, merely reflects the archival imbalance between charters surviving for English and Norman beneficiaries and for those from all other regions under Plantagenet rule. Peculiar combinations, such as an address to the men of Scotland and Wales, or a privilege to the men of Pembroke addressed to England, Wales, Ireland, Normandy, Britanny, Anjou, Poitou and Gascony (*archiepiscopis, episcopis, abbatibus, comitibus et iusticiis, baronibus et vicecomitibus et omnibus fidelibus suis totius Anglie, Wallie, Hibernie, Normannie, Britannie, Andagauie, Pictauie, Gasconie*) tend merely to indicate forgery or later reworking.[62]

It is significant, nonetheless, that far more often than they specify geographical regions, charters are addressed to regional peoples. The most common instance of this comes in addresses to French and English men (*Francis et Anglis/Anglicis*), where for once it is possible to state that an invariable rule applies, ranking Frenchmen ahead of the English. The formula itself, of course, was introduced in the reign of William the Conqueror, and cannot by the 1150s be read as anything other than a formality, occurring even in charters granted to Norman monasteries involving exclusively Norman lands, in cases where an address to Englishmen might well seem redundant.[63] Besides the French and the English, there were other peoples living within Henry II's lands deemed worthy of address. The case of the Irish has already been mentioned. Elsewhere we find addresses to Welshmen, and even in one case to the French, English and 'Welshmen' of Cornwall and Devon (*Francis et Anglis et Wallensibus Cornubie et Deuonie*).[64] In one even more extraordinary instance the chancery appears to distinguish Cornwall from England, as in an address to the archbishops and men of all England and of Cornwall (*archiepiscopis, episcopis, abbatibus, comitibus, baronibus, iusticiis, vicecomitibus, ministris et omnibus fidelibus suis Francis et Anglis totius Anglie et Cornubie*),[65] but seems to have possessed no word other than *Wallenses* to distinguish Cornwall's inhabitants from their English neighbours, *Wallenses* in this context being perhaps better interpreted as a linguistic distinction, 'Welsh speakers', rather than an indication of ethnicity let alone of nationality.[66] Other peoples addressed or mentioned include the Norsemen *alias* the ostmen, the Scots and the men of the liberty of St Cuthbert designated under their ancient title as *haliwerfolk*.[67] We should note, however, that the inhabitants of the various regions of France are invariably addressed merely as Frenchmen, rather than as Normans, Angevins, Bretons, Gascons or whatever other regional, ethnic or linguistic sobriquets historians might assume them to have affected. We must bear in mind here, as throughout, that Henry's chancery was in most cases merely following practices and forms established many years before, by earlier English kings. Nonetheless, although slight, the evidence enables us to map something of the king's ethnographic perceptions, in which a distinctive realm or kingdom of England was set about with other northern peoples such as the Welsh and the Irish, and in which France, although divisible into territorial dukedoms, counties and regions, was inhabited by men who were first and foremost French. The chancery did adapt its forms to meet the needs of territories, such as Anjou, Poitou and Ireland, now joined to the Anglo-Norman domain. It did so, however, somewhat haphazardly and with no very clear perception that the king now ruled an estate that was very different, both in its extent and in its internal coherence, from the estate ruled by earlier Anglo-Norman kings.

Let us turn now from peoples and places to the distinctive documentary forms that such peoples and places inspired. I do not intend to dwell here upon mere regionalisms in vocabulary. It is hardly surprising, for example, to find land measured in different units in one part as opposed to another of Henry's territories. Cantreds are to be found in Ireland, perches only in England and Normandy.[68] Likewise rights, customs and taxes were on occasion described using regionally specific or archaic terminology which tells us merely what we already know—that laws and customs varied greatly from one region to another and especially between England and all other parts of Henry's dominion. *Bernagium* and *gravarium*, for example, are taxes which in Henry's charters are to be found exclusively in awards to Norman beneficiaries; *minagium* is a right found exclusively in charters for Anjou.[69] A charter renewing the privileges of the barons of Hastings to quittance from toll, lastage, *rivagium*, *sponsagium* and all wreck and *racatum*, like the apparently unique (and to a large extent mysterious) rights to *bellum et polam* found in a charter for the monks of Cerne, merely follows the terminology of what we must be suppose to be much earlier, Anglo-Saxon awards.[70] A confirmation for the Poitevin abbey of Charroux refers to the custom of *solaria* in such a way as to suggest that the word was sufficiently obscure, even in chancery, to require clarification in the king's charter: *solaria que auferebat in quadrigis, illud quod rotagium vocant*.[71] Such terms can on occasion be useful in weeding out forgery. In the example of the ancient right of wreck, for example, it is worth noting that all mentions of wreck occur in charters for English, and in single instances Irish or Norman beneficiaries applied to English lands, save in the case of three charters for the Norman abbey of St-Sauveur where the appearance of wreck merely adds to what are already grave suspicions over the charters' authenticity.[72]

In certain cases, terms and documentary forms known in England and Normandy are so rare elsewhere that we can indeed suppose that there were real differences in the king's approach to his various lands. The privilege of guild merchant, for example, widely known in England, appears in Normandy only at Rouen.[73] In Normandy, in general, and to an even greater extent further south, the king appears to have been sparing in his award of charters to the Norman, Angevin and southern towns.[74] The only two southern municipal charters of Henry II that survive, for the men of La Rochelle and the men of Angers, are clearly modelled upon one another, and seem, like the king's charter to the men of Rouen, to have been issued in the aftermath of the rebellion of 1173–74 as rewards for the loyalty of these towns in time of war.[75] Rather than confirm earlier or general municipal privileges, the charters for La Rochelle and Angers award very specific rights in respect to the estates of those who die intestate: rights that are very different from the sorts of communal municipal rights awarded in England. The mention of other privileges, now lost, said to have been issued by Henry II to such southern towns as Niort, Dax, Limoges and St-Junien should warn us to avoid any very certain hypotheses here, and above all not to assume that the king kept his French towns on a tighter leash than that allowed to the towns of England.[76] It was from the Norman customs of Breteuil, after all, that many of the English muncipal constitutions were later formed.[77] There is, however, some indication here that municipal charters, granted relatively frequently in England, were slow to emerge in the Plantagenet lands in France.

Just as the appearance of local customs should not surprise us, so it is only to be expected that royal charters issued in the north of England to northern beneficiaries, or in the south of France to southerners, are on occasion witnessed by individuals who attended the court only when the court was in their particular vicinity. Poitevins and Gascons, for example, such as the 13 southern bishops and barons who witness a charter issued at and on behalf of the abbey of La Grande-Sauve near Bordeaux, rarely if ever joined the court north of the Loire, or at least are virtually never to be found set down as witnesses to charters issued outside the duchy of Aquitaine.[78] Likewise, the 9 northerners who appear amongst the 14 witnesses to a royal charter in favour of Furness Abbey may have come to the king at Woodstock specifically for the issue of this award.[79] Even if they were more frequently at court, they are recorded as witnesses to virtually no other royal charters. These regional peculiarities in the witness lists may reflect the fact that large numbers of barons, both in England and in France, stood aloof from, or remained in sullen retirement from the court, a feature, as I have suggested elsewhere, that may apply not only to the Poitevins and the barons of Westmorland and Cumberland but to many of the greater men of Normandy.[80] Alternatively, as David Bates has demonstrated, the fact that the king's confirmation charters tended to be witnessed by men who had a particular interest in their award, may leave us with a misleading impression of the frequency with which Poitevins, northerners or Norman barons attended the court. Some, perhaps many such men, could have been in attendance at the court without their appearance being recorded in charter witness lists.[81]

Much more significant are the indications that specific documentary forms were reserved for specific regions. Some of these peculiarities are apparent merely from the outward, physical appearance of the charters. Thus we have at least three vast single-sheet *pancartes* for the abbey of St-Etienne at Caen, written in two—or in one instance four—columns, which appear to emerge from a local tradition of *pancarte* entirely distinct from the more ordinary run of English or Norman charters of confirmation.[82] Boundary clauses—a fundamental and surely extremely useful feature of Anglo-Saxon diplomatic, whose disappearance from chancery practice over the course of the twelfth century has never received the attention that it deserves—survive in charters of Henry II issued to northern beneficiaries, in Lancashire, Yorkshire and Dumfriesshire, but are virtually unknown elsewhere.[83] The greater royal charters of confirmation, known in England, Normandy and Ireland, and to some extent in Anjou, listing many dozens of individual estates, are virtually unknown south of the Loire, and this despite the fact that southern beneficiaries had access to papal confirmations that could be just as detailed and extensive as those available from the king. In Anjou and the south, it is noticeable that there are several charters for Angevin or Poitevin beneficiaries drawn up in the form of chirographs or general notifications of settlement, lacking the king's title at their head but nonetheless sealed with the king's seal.[84] In one instance, known to Delisle, we have both a notification of settlement, opening with the entirely atypical formula *Ego Henricus Dei gratia rex Anglorum... notum facio quod quedam controuersia*, and supplied with full dating clause *Actum in Ramis Palmarum, Andegauis, in aula mea, anno ab incarnatione domini MCLXVII, indictione xv* (24 March 1168), and a charter, addressed to the bishop of Angers without dating clause but rehearsing the same basic award under a much more conventional style: *Henricus rex Anglorum et dux Normannorum et Aquitanorum et comes Andegauorum episcopo Andeg'... Sciatis me concessisse et presenti carta confirmasse concordiam et finem qui factus fuit coram me*. The royal charter was apparently issued as an afterthought, to confirm, in more standard form, a settlement that had already been drawn up in non-standard terminology.[85] The survival of such forms, in the case of the abbeys of Ronceray and Montazay in forms that historians of eleventh-century France would classify as *notices* rather than *chartes*, has wide implications. It was partly upon the distinction between *charte* and *notice* that Georges Duby and others built their thesis that the tenth and eleventh centuries witnessed a fundamental breakdown in the instruments and hence the application of public authority. The fact that *notices* survive into an era in which there can be little doubt that Henry II was issuing publicly authenticated royal charters adds support to the counter-argument, advanced by Dominique Barthélemy, that the distinction between *chartes* and *notices* has been drastically overinterpreted.[86] Nonetheless, charters and *notices*, such as that issued by Henry II for the cathedral of Bourges in Berry or that recorded for the Breton monks of Locmaria, are issued in such peculiar diplomatic that we must assume either that they are forgeries or, more likely, that they were drawn up by scribes to a large extent unfamiliar with the practices of Henry II's chancery.[87] This very unfamiliarity may in itself be significant, since it suggests that royal charters and writs may have been solicited and awarded far less frequently to the men and monks of Berry or Brittany than to the men and monks of England and Normandy. The poor survival of charters from the south may well reflect twelfth-century reality, not just a later archival distortion of the evidence.

More difficult to detect, but no less significant, are the cases in which widely used and apparently standardized forms emerge, on investigation, to have very specific geographical limitations. We might begin here with the comparatively large number of charters—at least 78 of them—for the most part awarding or confirming quittance from toll and custom, in which the justices, ministers or reeves of sea ports are referred to in the address. Besides the vast proliferation of forms, varying in more or less minor detail from one such charter to another, we might note here the very strong Anglo-Norman bias to such awards. Some have a generic address, some are addressed specifically to England, some to Normandy and some to both England and Normandy, in a number of instances specifying particular ports—Southampton, Hastings, Dover, Barfleur, Caen, Ouistreham and Dieppe—which we must assume to have been the chief points of departure for cross-Channel trade.[88] A very few, issued for Welsh beneficiaries, are addressed to Wales as well as to England and/or Normandy, and in one instance, for the Lazarite order of Jerusalem, the address extends to a highly suspicious list of French lands, including not only Normandy but Anjou, Aquitaine, Poitou and Brittany, which hints at either forgery or reworking.[89] Charters of this sort were solicited by English, Norman and Welsh beneficiaries, and on occasion were awarded to northern French houses (Ourscamp, Vaux-de-Cernay, Tiron, Pontigny, Clairvaux and Gard) lying beyond the frontiers of Henry II's dominion, but no doubt in an attempt to make friends for the Plantagenets in regions that otherwise fell under the influence of Henry's rivals, most notably the kings of France. However, not one of these charters has survived either for greater Anjou or for Henry's lands further south. A quittance from toll for the abbey of Cercamp in the Pas-de-Calais is virtually unique in referring to the king's ministers of England, Normandy and Poitou, and might be explained by the fact that Cercamp possessed estates in Poitou which rendered such a clause peculiarly appropriate.[90] Whilst it might appear quite natural that sea ports should find no mention in charters for land-locked Anjou, no such explantion can apply to either Britanny or Aquitaine south of the Loire. Nor is it easy to explain why Breton, Angevin and Poitevin monasteries, some of which possessed extensive lands in England, appear to have shown no interest in soliciting quittances from toll on goods passing through the Channel ports. Even if the ports of Poitou or

Gascony were considered to be of lesser importance than Ouistreham or Hastings—an improbable suggestion, given the significance of Bordeaux and La Rochelle—toll itself was a major concern to the abbeys of the south, as demonstrated by the considerable number of charters solicited by the nuns of Fontevraud relating to tolls payable at La Rochelle, Saumur, Angers, Poitiers and on the Loire crossing at Les Ponts-de-Cé.[91] Either general quittances from toll for these southern houses were issued but have not survived or, as seems more likely, the general quittance from toll and its Anglo-Norman list of sea ports was a specifically Anglo-Norman instrument, solicited by northern beneficiaries in a tradition stretching back to the earlier Anglo-Norman kings, but deemed foreign to the traditions of Anjou and the south. My impression, for what it is worth, is that there was a difference between south and north in attitudes to toll itself. In England and Normandy, toll was something from which men and especially monks sought and obtained general exemption.[92] In the south, toll and other customs were more often treated as ducal perquisites from which part of the profit could be excused or diverted in alms to the religious, but from which general exemptions were virtually never awarded.[93] Toll indeed may have been so significant an element of the duke's income in Aquitaine, where the ducal demesne appears to have been far less extensive and far more depleted than in England or Normandy, that it was deemed to require very careful preservation.[94]

Just as toll may have been a tax whose nature, terminology and importance differed considerably between the various regions under Plantagenet rule, so other public obligations, although known under a uniform terminology, may have varied greatly between England and France. The most obvious example here is to be found in the king's forest jurisdiction. Forest rights are recorded from Aquitaine to Normandy, and according to the traditional interpretation of Norman lordship were introduced to England after 1066, whether or not the Anglo-Saxon kings already possessed a pre-existing concept of forest 'law'. However, although a terminology and an administrative machinery for the forests existed after 1066 in both England and Normandy, under Henry II it is by no means clear that the institutions and customs described under this terminology were necessarily the same on both sides of the Channel. In England we frequently encounter writs of the king addressed to the forest regarders of particular counties, designated as the *visores forestarum*,[95] or writs in which beneficiaries are freed from the forest regard (*regardum*).[96] By contrast, no such writs to *visores* or exemptions from *regardum* are recorded from Normandy. Instead, when the word *regardum* is encountered in Normandy it appears to define a seigneurial perquisite very different from the forest 'regard' that existed in England.[97] Likewise, although we possess two purported texts of Henry II in which Norman officials are assigned functions as forest 'regarder', both of these texts are highly suspicious and may well have been concocted after 1204 in the aftermath of the Capetian invasion of Normandy, perhaps in imitation of earlier English rather than earlier Norman practice.[98] Certainly, we should beware of assuming that a word used in Normandy necessarily has the same meaning when used in England, or that in this instance English forest administration was merely an imported copy of a pre-existing Norman model.[99]

In the same way that writs to the *visores forestarum* are to be found only in England, there appear to have been geographical limitations to another, even more familiar species of writ. From Henry II's reign we have at least 26 surviving writs of naifty (named after their description in *Glanvill* as *breues de natiuis*), commanding the restoration of runaway serfs.[100] All but one of these 26 writs were issued to English beneficiaries or to a Norman monastery clearly intending to apply the writ to its lands in England. The one exception, for St-Victor-en-Caux, is addressed to the archbishops and other ministers of both England and Normandy, suggesting that this too may have been intended for English use.[101] Even the place of issue of such writs, in all but three cases issued at English locations, indicates their peculiarly English nature, for the most part intended to speed the restoration to English landlords of serfs who had fled during the civil war of Stephen's reign.[102] Runaway serfs may have been just as great a concern to landlords in Normandy, Anjou or Poitou. The royal writ commanding their restoration, however, appears to have been reserved exclusively for use in England.

More subtle still are the variations that emerge from one of the most common of the surviving writ forms, in which a clause is inserted specifying the authority by which the writ may be enforced should its original addressee fail to act. Julia Boorman has recently made a study of such writs.[103] Her conclusions may require revision in the light of the 228 examples of the *nisi feceris* clause that can now be identified amongst the writs of Henry II. The basic intention of the clause remains the same in all 228 instances: to ensure enforcement by a higher authority. Thus in writs relating to churches and spiritualities, the bishop or archdeacon originally addressed may be warned that in the case of non-enforcement, the archbishop will be called upon to intervene.[104] Lay addressees are warned of future enforcement by their overlord, by the sheriff, or on occasion, as when it is the sheriff himself that is addressed, of future enforcement by an even higher authority.[105] It is these latter cases that are particularly intriguing, in which enforcement is deputed to a figure or figures known as the king's *iusticia, iusticie, iusticii* or *iusticiarius*, uncertainty here being heightened by the standard Latin abbreviation *iustic'*. Boorman has queried the meaning of this word, suggesting that it might refer to the county justiciars, the itinerant royal justices or even the abstract idea of royal justice with no particular individual in mind.[106] Another possibility, not considered by Boorman, is that it was the king's chief justiciar who was intended, Robert, earl of Leicester or Ranulf de Glanville, depending upon the date. In fact, a clear pattern emerges once the evidence is properly sifted. Let us begin here with England, where in a very few cases the enforcing authority is clearly intended to be the chief justiciar, either specified as *iusticiarius meus* or, as in six examples, named as Robert, earl of Leicester.[107] In only two cases before 1172, does the writ clearly specify that enforcement should be by the king's itinerant justice (*iusticia mea errans*).[108] Far more frequent are writs in which the justice is associated with a particular county, acting in association with the sheriff either as in a clause to be found in at least 25 writs specifying the justice and sheriff of a particular county, or as in a further five cases specifying the justice of Norfolk, Oxfordshire, Berkshire, Lincolnshire or Yorkshire.[109] Most common of all, accounting for at least 53 examples, are writs in which enforcement is left merely to *iusticia mea*, with no further details.[110] The use of the feminine *mea* for *iusticia*, rather than *meus* for *iusticiarius*, combined with the fact that when the king's chief justiciar is intended his name seems to have been given in full, as Robert, earl of Leicester, suggests that, unless otherwise specified, such writs were either intended for enforcement by the county justiciars or referred merely to the abstract idea of justice. This situation, however, changed dramatically over time. Of the 228 surviving writs with a *nisi feceris* clause, only 36 are to be dated after 1172, and of these 1 was directed to Ireland and 5 to Normandy, leaving only 30 such post-1172 writs for enforcement in England. Ten of the 30 specify the sheriff as enforcer, 3 the local bishop. Twelve, by contrast, introduce terminology not found before 1172 in which enforcement is deputed to the local sheriff and/or to *iusticie mee* or *iusticiarii mei de partibus illis*, now described almost as often in the masculine as in the feminine plural.[111] There can be little doubt here that we are witnessing a significant change, traced from other evidence by H. A. Cronne and by Lady Stenton, in which the county justiciarships were suppressed during the 1160s, to be replaced by the authority of the king's itinerant justices in eyre.[112] In only two cases, after 1172—one of them specifying enforcement by *iusticia mea de Oxenef'* and the other by the sheriff *vel iusticia mea*—do we find echoes of the earlier terminology, suggesting either that these writs have been misdated or that on rare occasions an archaic terminology might persist, despite what were otherwise very real changes both in terminology and in the practical enforcement of justice.[113]

The evidence considered so far is for chronological change. There are also very great regional variations. By no means all appearances of *nisi feceris* occur in English writs. At least 25 writs for enforcement in Normandy, and 1 each for Ireland, Maine, Anjou and the Saintonge, employ some such formula.[114] In Normandy, when justice is referred to in this context, it is invariably specified as that either of *iusticia mea* or of *iusticia mea Normannie*: a clause which does not change after 1172, and which Haskins assumed to refer to the body of Norman justices rather than to some chief Norman justiciar.[115] That this was indeed the case is suggested by at least one early writ in which the enforcing authority is named as Robert de Neubourg, seneschal of Normandy until his death in 1159, and in Normandy the figure closest in equivalence to the chief justiciar in England.[116] As with the English chief justiciar, the fact that writs intended for enforcement by the seneschal of Normandy can be so specific suggests that those that are not specific are unlikely to have been intended to refer to the seneschal. For the rest, the failure of Norman writs to adopt the new terminology used in England after 1172 suggests two possibilities: first is that the administration of justice within Normandy may have been less sophisticated than in England, or subject to lesser or to entirely different changes and reforms than those put in place in England from the 1160s onwards, and secondly that the royal chancery was aware that particular forms appropriate to England were not necessarily appropriate for Norman writs: a point that might well be overlooked given what has been assumed to be the bland uniformity of the chancery's language.

South of Normandy, yet further differences can be detected. Superficially, the very fact that writs employing a *nisi feceris* clause survive for Maine, Anjou and the Saintonge might be taken as evidence that a common administrative system functioned north and south of Normandy, as in all parts of Henry II's territory from Ireland to the Pyrenees. In reality, what is most striking about the 3 southern writs is the fact that there are only 3 of them out of a surviving total of more than 220. In two of the three surviving southern writs the *nisi feceris* clause refers to very specific individuals, in the case of the Saintonge to Hervey Pannetarius (one of Henry II's leading officials in Poitou), and in Maine to a man named as Pain, the seneschal—either Pain de Melna or Pain Mauchien, both of them recorded as seneschals of Maine under Henry II, although perhaps equivalent in rank to officials who elsewhere would be termed mere *prévôts*.[117] Only in Anjou does the clause employ the standard Anglo-Norman terminology, deputing enforcement to *iusticia mea*. Since this particular writ, for St-Florent, was issued at Brockenhurst in the New Forest, it is at least possible that the scribe who wrote it opted for the language of an English writ, perhaps precisely because such writs for the king's southern territories were so rare.[118] Despite the evidence amassed, most notably by Jacques Boussard, for the activity of Plantagenet officials in Anjou and the south, and despite the survival of occasional charters issued by, or in courts presided over by, such men, the great dearth of royal writs and mandates south of the Loire suggests either that there was no means by which such writs could be preserved—perhaps because they were returnable to the king's officials and were hence unavailable for copying into monastic cartularies—or else, more dramatically yet more plausibly, that Plantagenet administration even in Anjou, let alone in Aquitaine, was less sophisticated, less dependent upon written instruction from the king, and altogether less extensive or instrusive than Plantagenet administration further north.[119]

An even more striking example of both chronological and regional variation can be found if we bring together all the charters of Henry II in which a particular bishop is named in the address. All told, there are 384 such charters or writs, 220 concerning England and Wales (the Welsh diocese of St Davids accounting for only two of these), and 164 for the bishops of France. If we look first at the English examples, and divide them up both by diocese and by whether they concern ecclesiastical affairs or lay fee (not always an easy division to make), it is clear both that bishops are regularly named in the address to letters and charters concerning lay fee, which account for 165 of the 220 English examples, and that particular bishops, such as those of Canterbury (13 out of 18 of whose appearances in an address involve lay fee), Lincoln (34 out of 47), Norwich (only 6 out of 22), Winchester (15 out of 17) and York (30 out of 33), are addressed far more frequently than others. What is most remarkable here, however, is not merely the number of writs and charters addressed to these bishops, but the fact that every single one of the 165 examples involving lay fee can be dated before 1172, for the most part to the opening few years of the reign.[120] After 1172, there are only two undoubtedly authentic letters of Henry II that survive addressed to English bishops, all of them concerning spiritualities rather than temporalities.[121] An enormous number of such letters concerning spiritualities must have been lost, particularly if we assume that, like the later kings of England, Henry was accustomed to issue letters to the local diocesan or his official, in every case where he presented to an advowson under royal control. Not a single such letter of presentation survives for the whole of Henry's reign. Nonetheless, in respect to lay fee there is a remarkable change after 1170 or so, from a situation in which the local bishop was customarily addressed together with other officials in writ-charters, to one in which the bishop's name was entirely excluded from such writs.

Elsewhere in this volume Richard Sharpe has advanced an explanation for this change, based upon the administrative procedures of the chancery and the English county courts, rather than upon any very dramatic change in the relations between king and bishops. From the reign of Henry I onwards, Sharpe suggests, the previously standard address of writ-charters to bishop, earl and sheriff of a particular county or counties was replaced by an address to bishop, justice(s) and sheriff, and in course of time by an entirely general address to (all) archbishops, bishops, earls, sheriffs and so forth.[122] By the reign of King John, the writ-charter itself was to be entirely abandoned, replaced by more or less standardized letters patent, many of them now enrolled on the newly instituted patent rolls. This, according to Sharpe, supplies evidence that the county court, originally attended by bishops and earls, was now being abandoned as a forum for the publication and recital of royal charters. By locating the abandonment of the shire address—to bishop, justice(s) and sheriff—in the 1160s, the evidence assembled for the chancery of Henry II might well be thought to bear out Sharpe's contention that the writ-charter evolved to meet what were in essence procedural changes, and in particular to accommodate the declining significance of the county court. However, doubts remain. To begin with, it is by no means clear that by the 1160s the county court really had declined in significance or even that it had been abandoned as a forum for the publication of royal charters. Our knowledge of these courts is desperately inadequate.[123] Nonetheless, the functions assigned to them in Henry II's assizes, as places for the taking of inquests and oaths, and for the proclamation of royal commands, hardly suggest a diminution of their importance after 1160.[124] When evidence for the publication of royal legislation survives thereafter, most notably at times of political crisis in 1215 and again after 1258, it was the county courts that appear to have continued to serve as the chief forum for the publication of the king's laws.[125] For all we know, they may have continued to serve in the publication of more specific royal grants to monasteries and laymen. Certainly, it was the county court that was used for the public proclamation of royal letters of pardon, from the reign of King John, if not before, and, by the reign of Edward III, it was the county court that was being used as the venue in which impressions of the king's new seals were to be exhibited as proofs of their authenticity.[126] The only letter of pardon to have survived from Henry II's reign, issued before 1166, perhaps in 1158, in favour of Wido fitz Tece, previously disseised for the castration of Alan the Welshman, is issued under a general address (*iustic(iis), vicecomitibus et omnibus ministris suis Anglie et Wallie*).[127] The pardon must nonetheless have been intended for proclamation, most likely in the relevant county courts, supplying proof if proof were needed, that like many thirteenth-century letters patent without specific address, the absence of a specific address to a writ-charter does not preclude either public proclamation or the involvement of the county court.

From an early date, certainly from the time of Henry II, beneficiaries were accustomed to obtaining multiple engrossments of their charters from the king, clearly in order that one or other of the copies could be sent to courts meeting at some distance from the beneficiary archive without exposing the beneficiary's own copy to undue risk.[128] Whilst this does not prove that such charters were regularly recited before the courts, county or otherwise, the fact that from the thirteenth century onwards special judicial visitations, most notably the sessions of the forest eyre, were accustomed not only to the recital but to the copying into their written records of charters of franchise granted by earlier kings suggests that such charters had to be publically and regularly recited, not merely stored away, read only by their potential beneficiaries.[129]

The abandonment of what Sharpe has defined as the writ-charter's 'county' address—to bishop, justice(s) and sheriff—may well have other explanations than procedural changes at county court level. It could be, for example, that the traditional address came to be regarded as unnecessarily elaborate. In particular, as Sharpe himself has shown, the naming by initial or full Christian name of both bishop and sheriff could create problems of identification and, in cases where a particular named individual was no longer in office, could have led to the rejection of a writ as being no longer valid. It was for this reason that the papal chancery developed the use of the *gemipunctus*, in order to address the office of bishop in any particular diocese, rather than risk addressing a particular officeholder who might himself be dead or deposed by the time that papal letters arrived. In the same way, there is a marked tendency amongst the writ-charters that survive from Henry II's early years to avoid naming the bishop of any particular see, and above all to avoid specifying particular sheriffs save by the name of their county. Only a handful of writ-charters addressed to sheriffs by Christian name survives even during the first decade of Henry's reign, and the practice thereafter vanishes entirely.[130] In writ-charters addressed to bishops, although the name of the see is supplied, it is only rarely accompanied by the initial letter or Christian name of the particular bishop so addressed. Rather than risk such writs becoming invalid, the chancery, perhaps under pressure from beneficiaries, was moving towards a more general and hence much longer-lasting address that ensured the document's validity into the indefinite future. Such documents were probably still publicized, but under a form of words that had changed to meet a particular need. Furthermore, there is a coincidence between procedural and political developments in the 1160s, which surely requires explanation. The county address, naming a particular English bishop or bishops and hence proclaiming the bishops' involvement in the administration of royal government, vanishes at the precise moment that Henry II was most heavily engaged in his disputes with Archbishop Becket.

Earlier in the reign, the great frequency with which the archbishop of York and the bishop of Lincoln were addressed may well reflect a situation in which these two prelates, and perhaps others, were acting not merely as diocesans but as agents of royal government, perhaps as county justiciars, active in the re-establishment of justice following the late civil war.[131] The fact that the disappearance of the English bishops from such writs coincides so closely with the period of Becket's exile and murder suggests a deliberate innovation in chancery, either because the bishops were no longer attending the county courts or perhaps more likely because the king himself was forced to admit more stringent limitations upon the involvement of bishops in secular justice.

The situation in France, which could not have been controlled by any considerations of procedure in the county courts, so closely mirrors developments in England that we are surely correct to look to relations between church and king rather than to the county courts as the engine of change. The 164 surviving writs or charters addressed by Henry II to bishops in France may superficially appear almost as substantial a number as that which survives for England, suggesting that the French bishops were as closely involved in royal government as their English counterparts. However, 117 of the 164 French examples concern the one see of Rouen and can be explained without any need to assume that the archbishops of Rouen were heavily engaged in royal administration. Rouen was the only archbishopric in Normandy, so that in a general charter address that might otherwise be made to archbishops, bishops and ministers in Normandy it was only natural that the chancery should write not of archbishops in general but of the archbishop of Rouen, preferring the singular to the less appropriate plural. A glance at the letters and charters in question demonstrates that this was indeed so, and that Rouen is named for the most part only in charters involving lay fee with general address to the prelates and ministers of Normandy; this is a very different situation from that in England where before 1172 English bishops occur frequently and specifically in the address to writs as well as charters; hence the fact that after 1172 there is no great change in Normandy as there is in England, with at least 45 charters involving lay fee and a further 10 involving spiritualities continuing to be addressed to the archbishop of Rouen. For the rest, the other bishops of Normandy are only very rarely addressed, even before 1172, and not at all thereafter in cases that involved lay fee.[132] Further south, although there are occasional examples of mandates concerning lay fee before 1172 addressed to bishops, such as those of Le Mans or Poitiers, after 1172 these too tend to vanish.[133] The only exceptions appear to be single charters addressed after 1172 to the archbishop of Bordeaux and the bishop of Saintes, and four charters addressed to the archbishop of Tours.[134] Tours being the only archbishopric in Anjou, Maine and the Touraine, and Saintes being the only bishopric in the Saintonge, their incumbents, as at Rouen, may well have been included in such addresses as a mere linguistic formality.

Given that in Normandy and Anjou there was no local forum for the publication of charters equivalent to the English county court, and hence that the so-called 'county' address had never been used outside England, the disappearance of the French bishops from the address of writs and charters involving lay fee after 1170 cannot be explained either by reference to the county courts or by procedural changes to the 'county' address. The absence of the 'county' address in Normandy before 1170 certainly explains why so few writ-charters survive before that date addressed to Norman bishops. However, the total disappearance of named bishops from writs and charters issued after that date surely requires us to accept a change dictated by political rather than merely procedural factors.

What conclusions can we draw from all of this? First, it is clear that the chancery of Henry II was an institution that owed more to English than to continental practice. Its forms were for the most part developed from those used in England long before 1066, adapted and exported thereafter for use in Normandy, in Anjou and eventually even south of the Loire. Nevertheless, although the basic forms may have been English, they were consciously remodelled to comply with regional custom, regional variations in law and administration, and regional diplomatic traditions. Forms and practice were subject to evolution over time, so that the writs and charters of the 1150s, even in England, evolved to meet the administrative and political changes of the 1170s and 1180s.

Just as significantly, they evolved at a different pace according to regional as well as chronological imperatives. *Pancartes* survived in Normandy, boundary clauses in the far north of England. Toll was treated differently in England or Normandy than in Anjou or the south, and even when a particular vocabulary was applied in more than one region, the words themselves could disguise a far-from-standard set of meanings. Law itself evolved differently in Normandy than in England, so that documentary forms appropriate to Normandy by the 1170s were no longer deemed appropriate across the Channel. To accommodate this great variety, the king's clerks had to exercise a degree of expertise and sensitivity that may come as a surprise to those accustomed to view the Plantagenet chancery as a place of drab uniformity. The very fact that different localities required different documentary forms may itself provide one explanation of why so many letters and charters continued to be produced by beneficiary rather than by royal scribes, through to the very end of Henry II's reign. Far from suggesting that the chancery was itself inefficient or inade-quately staffed, such beneficiary productions may, in fact, suggest a very subtle awareness that certain forms were best left to beneficiaries to determine, according to particular local needs. To this extent, and reverting at last to the wider question of Henry II's pretensions to empire, the chancery was indeed the administrative hub upon which all manner of the king's subjects were obliged to converge. Its power, however, and with it the power of the king derived not from the imposition of unbending central authority, but from a willingness to follow the advice of Henry II's father, and hence to allow the English what was appropriate to England, and the Normans or the Angevins what was appropriate to Normandy or Anjou. Polities that remain adaptable to local circumstances are often the best and the most harmoniously governed. By contrast 'one size fits all' is the slogan of all shoddy operators, be they tailors, scribes or the builders of empires.

Notes

1. *Chroniques des comtes d'Anjou*, 224. The letters and charters of Henry II cited below will all be found in my forthcoming edition of *The Acta of King Henry II*. For economy of space, they are for the most part cited using the accession numbers that they have acquired in the office files, presently housed in the Cambridge University History Faculty. These numbers (1H and so forth, through to 5700H) do not correspond to the numbering system that will appear in the forthcoming edition. The edition, however, will be furnished with a concordance supplying both the accession and the final published numbers. Readers who meanwhile require details of particular charters cited

only by accession numbers are requested to write to the Angevin Acta project in Cambridge. For assistance and advice in the writing of this chapter I am indebted to all in attendance at the colloquium for which it was written. A particular burden of thanks is due to Judith Everard, Judith Green, Oliver Padel and Richard Sharpe.

2. For recent surveys here, see Hollister and Keefe, 'Making of the Angevin Empire'; Bachrach, 'Idea of the Angevin Empire'; Turner, 'Problem of Survival for the Angevin "Empire" '.

3. For recent historiographical overviews, see Vincent, 'King Henry II and the Poitevins', 104–6; Aurell, *L'Empire des Plantagenêt 1154–1224*, 9–18.

4. For Richard, see Barnes, 'The Anstey Case', 18, where Richard was forced to spend 14 weeks seeking out the king near Toulouse to obtain his writ.

5. For chancery practice, see the overview by Vincent, 'Why 1199?'.

6. Bishop, *Scriptores Regis*, with revisions and additions proposed by Tessa Webber incorporated into *The Acta of Henry II*. At the time of writing, there are known to be 542 original charters of Henry II surviving either as single-sheets or in photographic and other facsimiles of lost originals. Of these, 369 can be attributed to the work of some 29 scribes employed more than once 'in chancery', 84 being the work of Bishop's scribe XXXV (Germanus, the scribe) and 83 the work of Bishop's scribe XL (as yet anonymous), these two scribes accounting for 167 or 45 per cent of the charters attributed to the 'chancery'. Unknown or beneficiary scribes account for 173 charters, of which less than a dozen can be dismissed as blatant forgeries, with a suspicion of forgery hovering over a further 20 or so.

7. For an explanation here, see Holt, '1153: The Treaty of Winchester', 315.

8. For a list of charters issued to southern beneficiaries or concerning lands in the south, see Vincent, 'King Henry II and the Poitevins', 134–5, to which only a handful have since been added.

9. For the feeble survival-rate of cartularies from the Dordogne, see *Cartulaire de l'abbaye Notre-Dame de Chancelade*, 5, 9.

10. For further remarks here on differences between English and French archival practice, see *Acta of Henry II and Richard I, Part Two: A Supplementary Handlist of Documents*, 27–32.

11. See, for example, the remarkable list of offices conferred by charter upon Baldric fitz Gilbert, known to us only from copies preserved in the French royal registers: *RH*, i, no. 212.

12. For further details here, noting the survival of only two writs of *liberate*, and a single writ each of *computate* and *perdono* for the entire reign of Henry II, see Vincent, 'Why 1199?'.

13. For a file of 77 miscellaneous original judicial writs preserved from the Michaelmas term of 1199, and for a roll produced in 1190–91 by the Justiciar's chancery, listing 136 cases which must each have involved the issue of at least one routine writ of peace, see Richardson, 'Introduction' to the *Memoranda Roll for the Michaelmas Term of the First Year of the Reign of King John (1199–1200)*, lii–liv, discussing PRO KB26/12, printed in *Curia Regis Rolls of the Reigns of Richard I, John and Henry III*, i, 1–14.

14. *Treatise on the Laws and Customs of the Realm of England.*

15. For an incomplete but nonetheless useful list of concords made in the ducal courts of Normandy, see Haskins, *Norman Institutions*, 334–6. For a later example,

see Alençon, Archives départementales de l'Orne H3333, headed *Hec est finalis concordia facta in curia domini regis apud Cadom' ad scaccarium in termino sancti Michaelis anno tertio coronationis I(ohannis) regis Anglie, Garino de Glapion tunc sen(escallo) Norm', coram Sansone abbate Cad', Hugone de Chaneunba, Ricardo de Funteneto, Radulfo Labbe, Petro de Lions', Iohanne de Alenc' ceterisque iustitiis et fidelibus domini regis qui tunc ibi aderant.* Further examples are printed in *Rotuli Normanniae*, 6–17.

16. For an allusive reference in a charter of Henry II to new conventions made over Norman farms, apparently resulting from inquests of 1171 referred to elsewhere by Robert de Torigny, see *RH*, i, no. 418 (Fourcarmont 1741H).

17. Powicke, *Loss of Normandy*, 31, citing an order to the seneschal of Poitou in September 1200 (*Rotuli Normanniae*, 28) requiring a payment to be made *ad scaccarium nostrum*.

18. See *Foedera*, i, Part I, 41–2 (Arundel 1116H; Norfolk 1345H; Oxford 413H); Round, *Geoffrey de Mandeville*, 235–6 (Essex 4696H); *Rotuli Chartarum*, 53, 61b (Hereford 3938H), all to be dated to the opening two years of the reign. For what appears to have been a charter issued after 1168 confirming the earldom and the lands of his late father upon William son of earl Patrick of Salisbury, see *Bracton's Note Book*, iii, 248–9, no. 1235 (Wiltshire 5109H).

19. Vincent, 'William Marshal, King Henry II and the Honour of Châteauroux'.

20. For listings of the single-sheet originals, see *Acta of Henry II and Richard I*, to which a further dozen or so have since been added.

21. See here Vincent, 'Charters of King Henry II', 98–9.

22. For example, *Cartae Antiquae Rolls*, i, no. 253 (Jerusalem 2643H); *Early Charters of the Cathedral Church of St Paul's London*, 30–1, no. 42 (London 4372H); Brooks, 'Grant of Castleknock to Hugh Tyrel', 206–7 (Tyrel 4965H) and various of the copies of charters for Hilary, bishop of Chichester (689H), All Saints Dublin (833H), William fitz Audelin (2597H), the Jerusalem Lazarites (1049H), and Norwich Cathedral Priory (2406H). Forged charters of Henry II with Ireland in the title include *Calendar of Charter Rolls*, iv (1327–41), 217–18 (Wellesley 4269H); BL, MS Lansdowne 559, fo. 61r–v (Fitz Hucman 5227H).

23. For examples of such chancery renovation, see a lost charter to Mont-St-Michel (386H A3, known only from a facsimile), and BL, MS Additional Charter 6039 (Bordesley 21H); Bishop, *Scriptores Regis*, 35, 50, no. 288, 71, no. 724. Other possible examples are to be found in charters for Gervase of Cornhill (17H, cf. Bishop, *Scriptores Regis*, 35, 57, no. 427), the monks of Dover (430H) and Plessis-Grimoult (1756H).

24. For miscopied addresses to *vicariis* rather than *vicecomitibus*, see charters for the men of Angers (3857H); the lepers of Beaulieu (1938H) and the priory of Bohon (1651H), with an English example for St James' Canterbury (3303H). For addresses to *viariis*, invariably introduced in addition to *vicecomitibus*, see the examples of Domfront (1534H), Le Mans (1695H and 1693H), and St-Aubin (1545H). See *RH*, i, 220.

25. Mortimer, 'Charters of Henry II', 119–34, especially 133–4.

26. For the omission of the title 'count of the Angevins' (or 'of Anjou') from what appears otherwise to be a genuine writ, see PRO C148/168 (Malmesbury 4857H).

27. *RH*, Introduction, 196–207.

28. See, for example, Caen 379H (unidentified s. xii scribe, writing *dux Normannie et Aquitanie*); Cluny 1506H (unidentified s. xii scribe, writing *dux Normannie et Aquitanie*); Fitz Gamel 157H (unidentified s. xii scribe, writing *rex Anglie dux Normannie Aquitanie et comes Andegauie*, perhaps spurious); Fontevraud 1813H and Loire 1710H (unidentified s. xii scribes, writing *rex Anglie*); St-Evroul 561H (unidentified late s. xii scribe, writing *dux Normannie*); St-Valery 107H, 115H and 152H (unidentified, perhaps s. xiii scribe, writing *Anglie, Normannie, Aquitanie, Andegauie*, probably spurious); Wix 39H (spurious reworking, s. xii/xiii, writing *rex Anglie*). See also the peculiar forms *dux Antiquit(anorum)*, and *dux Acquitanie*, to be found in charters for Lire and Wix, 399H and 38H.

29. See, for example, Foucarmont 390H, written by Bishop's scribe XXXVI, with title expanded as *rex Anglorum*. *Anglorum* is also written out in full in Plessis-Grimoult 1517H, and St-Sauveur 1512H, both the work of unidentified s. xii scribes. A highly suspicious privilege for Westminster Abbey (240H, probably forged before 1200), surviving in duplicate originals, spells out all the titles in the form *Anglorum, Normannorum, Aquitanorum* and *Andegauorum*.

30. Stubbs, *Select Charters*, 158 (England 2665H).

31. For *totum regnum meum*, see Battle 102H; Durham 518H, and for phrases such as *omnes tenuras suas . . . in regno meo*, and *ubicumque fuerit in regno meo*, see Bassingham 350H; Hereford 4192H.

32. See here the phrase *iuxta clericorum et laicorum consilium tam regni nostri quam transmarinorum*, inserted into a letter of Henry II to the archbishop of Rouen: *Materials for the History of Thomas Becket*, vi, 78–81, no. 255 (Rouen 3081H).

33. See, for example, Cirencester 4037H; Coggeshall 2244H; Lincoln 2067H.

34. For examples addressed to Norman and French beneficiaries, some of them probably forged, see *RH*, i, nos 35 (Falaise 751H), 135 (Cherbourg 1560H), ii, no. 545 (Bois-Rahier 1831H). For a clear statement that such gifts are made for the *stabilitate et pace regni Anglie*, see Bordesley 69H; Flaxley 1328H; Mortemer 1536H. In another instance, an explicit distinction is drawn between the realm of England and the duchy of Normandy: *RH*, i, no. 1917 (Beaulieu 1752H, *pro statu et incolumitate regni mei et ducatus Normannie*).

35. See, for example, Alcester 3018H; Clerkenwell 92H; Faversham 1291H.

36. For example, Holme 828H; Ramsey 90H.

37. For example, Barking 1193H (*infra regnum nostrum Anglie*); Ely 281H (*in regno Anglie*); Faversham 1291H (*aliqua ecclesia regni Anglie*); Flanders 504H (*ad defendendum regnum Anglie*); Lincoln 1072H (*in regno meo Anglie*); Norton 1074H (*per regnum meum Anglie*); Stanley 16H (*cum Deo largiente adeptus fuerim regnum Anglie*).

38. See, for example, Angers 1627H; Bourgueil 3234H; Cirencester 4037H; Mont-St-Michel 1625 and 1626H; Winchester 3051H.

39. *RH*, i, nos 423 (Conches 1746H, confirming the *beneficia que ei dederunt et concesserunt in regno et ducatu meo Rogerus senior de Toenio*), 434 (Beaulieu 1752H, *pro statu et incolumitate regni mei et ducatus Normannie*), and see *RH*, ii, no. 643 (Fulk 1904H, spurious, but purporting to be sealed *sigillo regni mei necnon comitatus mei*).

40. *RH*, i, nos 152–4 (Caen 379H, 739H, and 1571H).

41. For pleas, see Campdavaine 1640H; Canterbury 854H; Cluny 1506H; London 191H; Ramsey 90H. For customs, see Biddlesden 61H; Bordesley 69H; Combe 658H and 2661H; Robertsbridge 1348H and 1356H. For lands and rights,

see Durham 518H; Fitz Harding 4318H; Godstow 2841H; Holme 828H; Lewes 1240H; London 4626H; Merton 1152H and 4026H; Winchester 949H.

42. *Epistolae Cantuarienses*, 160–2, no. 182 (Clement 4910H).
43. Hollister, 'Normandy, France and the Anglo-Norman Realm', 17–57, especially 53, n. 193, where Hollister, correctly, dismisses the appearance of the phrase *regia auctoritate* used in the confirmation clause to charters of Henry II in favour of the Norman abbeys of Blanchelande and Notre-Dame-du-Pré at Rouen (*RH*, i, no. 34, ii, no. 53 (1497H and 2525H)) as evidence of forgery. The same phrase also appears in an equally suspicious charter in favour of the hospital of Falaise (*RH*, i, no. 35 (751H).
44. Hyams, 'Common Law and the French Connection', especially 197, n. 23.
45. For the decline of regional customary law in England, see Brand, 'Local Custom in the Early Common Law', 150–9.
46. See, for example, Abingdon 2310H; *RH*, i, no.117 (Bordesley 69H, authentic: *totum dominium de Budifordia*).
47. See, for example, *RH*, ii, no. 626 (Bellière 1891H, probably forged: *de omnibus consuetudinibus in terra et in mari ad dominium nostrum pertinentibus*); ibid., no. 545 (Bois-Rahier 1831H, perhaps authentic: *ita quod in predictis scilicet terra et nemore nullam iusticiam nec aliquid dominium nec aliquid iuris nobis vel heredibus nostris vel etiam nostris successoribus retinemus*).
48. *RH*, ii, no. 728 (Grandmont 5249H: *omne ius et dominium utile et merum et mixtum imperium et superioritatem ad nos et heredes et successores nostros pertinentes*).
49. *Materials for the History of Thomas Becket*, v, 135, no. 72 (Louis VII 4898H), and for other uses, referring either to the Norman *patria* or to the *patria* of other parts of France, beyond Henry's dominion, see Louis VII 3077H; St-Evroul 1819H; St-Saens 5243H.
50. *RH*, i, no. 101 (Mortemer 1536H).
51. *RH*, i, no. 246 (Rouen 3081H).
52. Abingdon 497H, and cf. *RH*, i, no. 298; ii, no. 734 (Lonlay 1654H and 1965H).
53. For example, *RH*, i, no. 379, ii, nos 539, 721 (Amesbury 797H; Louroux 66H; Montjoux 112H).
54. Its first certain occurrence is in a charter issued during the siege of Fougères in 1166 (*Calendar of Patent Rolls*, iv (1247–58), 382–3, Fougères 2193H), and cf. *Sir Christopher Hatton's Book of Seals*, 192–3, no. 280; *RH*, i, nos 379, 403, 405 (Verneuil 1730H and Blanchelande 955H, both to be dated 1165 × 1173; Marshal 361H, to be dated 1166 × 1173, and Montjoux 112H, to be dated 1156 × 1173). Thereafter, for its appearance in 18 charters after 1172, see Amesbury 797H; Boscherville 32H; Fontevraud 592H; Henry II 1879H and 4856H; Mala Palude 1942H; Mont-St-Michel 1804H; Newcastle 4464H; Ourscamp 1968H; Philip 4960H; Rouen 1816H; St-Sauveur 391H, 1812H, 1934H and 1956H; Stixwould 2250H; Winchcombe 3013H; Witham 2472H.
55. *RH*, i, no. 240 (Louis VII 3079H, *quando a transmarinis partibus discessi et in Angliam veni*), no. 246 (Rouen 3081H, *iuxta clericorum et laicorum consilium tam regni nostri quam transmarinorum*).
56. *Materials for the History of Thomas Becket*, vii, 518–19, no. 773 (Exeter 1761H, *Sciatis quod per gratiam Dei prospera nauigatione applicui in Normanniam et inueni terram meam totam cismarinam in summa pace et tranquilitate*), although for a

reference to the lands of the king of England as *terra regis Anglorum cismarino*, clearly referring to the king's English lands, see Henry II 5305H.

57. *Epistolae Cantuarienses*, 297, no. 312.

58. For example to the monks of Blanchelande (955H) issued at Bur-le-Roi (*RH*, i, no. 405), or to the monks of Stixwould (2250H) issued at Nottingham: *Calendar of Patent Rolls, 1405–08*, 218.

59. See Biddlesden 61H and Caen 379H (both originals written by unidentified scribes); Foucarmont 390H (an original written by Bishop's scribe XXXVI), and see also Combe 658H, a cartulary copy of a text of doubtful authenticity.

60. For addresses including the king's *Hibernenses*, see Bristol 2596H, 3244H and 5283H; Dublin 833H, 844H, 2055H, 3258H (this last perhaps spurious); Fitz Stephen 3945H; Glendalough 3238H; Jerusalem 4671H; Labench 4969H; Lacy 3253H; Mellifont 4585H; Tyrel 4965H; Walter 147H. For addresses to the archbishops and so on of Ireland (*Hibernia*), see Fitz Audelin 2597H; Mellifont 2211H and 4585H; Pembroke 4124H (spurious); Walter 147H.

61. For the Saintonge, see Lewis, 'Six Charters of Henry II', 659, no. 1, 661–2, no. 3 (Dalon 3766H and 3767H). For the Auvergne, see *RH*, i, no. 389 (Ennezat 1718H). For an address to the archbishops and others including the French, English and Scotsmen of England and Scotland, see Barrow, 'Writ of Henry II for Dunfermline Abbey', 143 (Dunfermline 4022H).

62. For an address to the English, Norman, Welsh and Scotsmen and all other nations subject to the king's command (*Anglis, Normannis, Gualensibus et Scottis cunctisque nationibus sue ditioni subditis*) known only from a letter apparently concocted by Gerald of Wales, see *Expugnatio Hibernica*, 26–7 (Leinster 4673H). For the Pembroke address, see Walker, 'Henry II's Charter to Pembroke', 136–7 (Pembroke 4124H).

63. For a recent and extremely informative discussion of the formula, see Thomas, *English and the Normans*, 32–4, 68, 174, suggesting that after 1066 'French' was preferred to 'Normans' because to the English chancery *Normanni* implied not the Normans but the Scandinavian Vikings, and noting how the inclusion of Englishmen in the address can actually be read as an indication of the importance afforded to William I's English subjects. See also Short, 'Tam Angli quam Franci'. For charters of Henry II in which Englishmen are included in the address to what are otherwise entirely 'Norman' charters, see, for example, *RH*, i, no. 95 (Bernay 1532H), ii, no. 451 (Bohon 1760H).

64. Bowles, *Short Account of the Hundred of Penwith*, 21–2, no. 2a (Richard 4354H), and cf. *Cartulary of Launceston Priory*, 9, no. 10 (Launceston 4375H), for a charter to a Cornish beneficiary addressed to the king's French, English and Welshmen.

65. *Calendar of Charter Rolls*, ii (1257–1300), 305 (Truro 813H). As pointed out to me by Richard Sharpe, if the recipients of the charter (the men of Truro) had asked for Cornwall to be mentioned in the address, the formula adopted might have been the simplest way of working this into a standard general address.

66. For discussion here, I am indebted to Oliver Padel.

67. For the Scots, see above nn. 61, 62. For the Norwegians, addressed as the *Norenses*, see *Calendar of Charter Rolls*, iii (1300–26), 7, no. 1 (Lincoln 855H). For references to the 'ostmen' of Ireland, see Fitz Stephen 3945H; Waterford 4402H. For the 'haliwerfolc', see Conyers 3322H (perhaps spurious); Fitz

Gamel 157H, and for the word's significance, see Aird, *St Cuthbert and the Normans*, 5–8.

68. For cantreds, see Fitz Stephen 3945H. For perches, see Caen 739H; Coventry 835H; Croxden 1332H; Fairwell 2213H and 2438H; Kirkstead 282H, 3099H and 3100H; Mortemer 3877H; Nottingham 306H; Nun Appleton 2890H; St Albans 2417H; Ste-Barbe 1984H; St Osyths 829H; Stixwould 2862H; Vascoeuil 4724H.

69. For *bernagium*, see Caen 739H; Préaux 1921H; St-Sauveur 1812H and 1660H. For *gravarium*, see Bernai 1532H; Chartres 247H (covering land in Normandy); St-Sauveur 1597H and 1812H. For *minagium*, see Bois-Rahier 1831H (probably spurious); Fontevraud 1737H, 1776H, 1813H, 1881H and 1909H; Grandmont 5249H (spurious). For the Norman taxes, which appear to represent either the legacy or more likely the eleventh-century revival of Carolingian antecedents, see Musset, 'Que peut-on savoir de la fiscalité publique en Normandie?'; Bates, *Normandy before 1066*, 153–4. For various others of the localized taxes and public revenues collected further south, see Boussard, *Gouvernement d'Henri II Plantagenêt*, 249–51.

70. *Calendar of Charter Rolls*, iii (1300–26), 221 (Hastings 896H); *Calendar of Charter Rolls*, ii (1257–1300), 143 (Cerne 796H).

71. *RH*, ii, no. 733 (Charroux 1964H), also referring to *operaria etiam circa monasterium que vulgo dicuntur estaus*.

72. Wreck is referred to in Abbotsbury 4687H; Caen 379H (for the abbey's English lands); Cerne 796H; Dublin 2055H; Ely 279H; Hastings 896H; Holme 828H; Hythe 892H; Lesnes 945H; Ramsey 2559H and 3093H; Romney 4024H; Rye 5399H; St Albans 1843H; St Osyths 829H (probably spurious); Tynemouth 802H; Winchester 3044H and Wymondham 3151H (probably spurious). For its appearance in the three suspicious charters for St-Sauveur (1598H, 1660H and 1812H), see *RH*, i, nos 197, 307, ii, no. 515.

73. *RH*, ii, no. 504 (Rouen 1806H), confirming to the tanners of Rouen *gildam suam et pillanum et tanum et unctum suum et omnes consuetudines et rectitudines gilde sue*.

74. See here the remarks of Musset, 'Le problème des chartes de franchises'.

75. For La Rochelle (1814H) and Rouen (1816H), see *RH*, ii, nos 519, 526. The previously unpublished charter to Angers (3857H), survives in Oxford, Bodleian Library, MS Carte 91 (SC 10537), fo. 90v.

76. Dax 4498H; Limoges 5160H; Niort 4492H; St-Junien 5161H, all known merely from mentions in later royal confirmations.

77. See here Bateson, 'Laws of Breteuil'.

78. *RH*, i, no. 25 (Grande-Sauve 1399H).

79. *English Lawsuits from William I to Richard I*, ii, 327–8, no. 364 (Furness 14H).

80. Vincent, 'Henry II and the Poitevins', 113–14; Vincent, 'Les Normands de l'entourage de Henri II Plantagenêt', 82–8.

81. See here Bates, 'Prosopographical Study of Anglo-Norman Royal Charters', an article of fundamental significance to those attempting to bridge the gap between the study of diplomatic and the writing of medieval history.

82. *RH*, i, no. 154 (Caen 739H), the two originals examined by Delisle being written in book hand across two columns, with a third exemplum, written in book hand across four columns, surviving at Caen, Bibliothèque municipale ms. 355 (in fo. 148), no. 1. From the same abbey, see also *RH*, i, no. 152 (Caen

379H, written in double columns), and on a similar scale, see also the charters for Ste-Barbe-en-Auge (407H and 1984H) and La Trinité at Caen (1870H), all surviving as originals: *RH*, i, no. 169, ii, nos 601, 756. For the tradition to which they belong, see Bates, 'Chartes de confirmation et les pancartes Normandes du règne de Guillaume le Conquérant', 96–8.

83. See, for example, Byland 299H (perhaps spurious); Fitz Donald 4497H; Furness 14H. For an isolated southern example, see the bounds of Witham abbey's estate set out in Witham 2472H.

84. See, for example, *RH*, nos 129 (Tours 3685H), 136 (Ronceray 3744H), 140 (Bourgueil 3234H), 283 (Fontevraud 3848H, with the counterpart original, not noticed by Delisle, surviving at Poitiers, Archives départementales de la Vienne, Carton 12, dossier 1, no. 1); Thomas, *Les Comtes de la Marche de la maison de Charroux*, 127, no. 110 (Montazay 3486H).

85. *RH*, i, nos 267–8 (Angers 1631H and 1632H), and cf. *RH*, Introduction, 283–6.

86. Barthélemy, 'De la charte à la notice', and note that it is from the same archive of St-Aubin that we derive the examples cited above n. 85.

87. *RH*, ii, nos 449 (Locmaria 3850H), 538 (Bourges 1825H).

88. Although quittances from toll are common amongst the charters of both Henry I and Stephen, I can find only one example before 1154 of a quittance that spells out the names of individual ports in this way.

89. For the specification of particular Channel ports, see for example Furness 5288H; Louth 911H; Meaux 1996H; Newbattle 4389H; Newminster 800H; Revesby 1H; Rievaulx 2031H; Rufford 343H; Savigny 1520H; Stoneleigh 2656H; Thame 2986H; Tintern 873H; Woburn 923H.

90. *RH*, i, no. 437 (Cercamp 382H).

91. *RH*, i, nos 224, 260, 413, ii, nos 457–8, 503, 516–17, 614, 655 (Fontevraud 378H, 387H, 1613H, 1737H, 1776H, 1813H, 1881H, 1909H, 3718H, 4948H). A general exemption from *tailles*, known only from a notice in Evreux, Archives départementales de l'Eure H1438, p. 13, no. 32 (Fontevraud 5125H), may well be misattributed to Henry II or represent a confusion between general and specific exemption from toll.

92. For toll in Normandy, see Musset, 'Recherches sur le tonlieu en Normandie à l'époque ducale'. For related public taxes further south, see Bienvenu, 'Recherches sur les péages angevins'.

93. Amongst Henry II's southern charters, or notices of charters now lost, see a notice of a lost charter to the monks of Belleperche (4322H) exempting them from customs on two measures of salt each year to be transported up the Garonne; an apparent exemption from customs for the demesne goods of the monks of Les Châtelliers (4926H); quittance from péage on salt and all other customs granted to the monks of Dalon within the Saintonge (3766H); an exemption from custom throughout Poitou, Aquitaine and Gascony supposedly granted to the men of Dax (4498H); a grant of péage on the bridge of St-Pandelon (dép. Landes) to the ancestors of Raymond Jean de Domo Nova (*Calendar of Liberate Rolls*, i (1226–40), 125, 5100H); what may have been a customs' exemption for the canons of Dorat (3844H); an exemption from péage for the nuns of Jarsay (3661H); various specific customs' exemptions for the monks of Luçon (*RH*, i, no. 32, 1496H); rights to market granted to the men of Niort (4492H) but significantly reserving the duke's right to péage; exemption to the monks of Sablonceaux from péage and custom payable at

Poitiers, Chizé, Benon and La Rochelle (*RH*, i, no. 23, 1397H); an exemption from customs to the monks of St-Jean-d'Angély apparently limited to their lands in England (*RH*, i, no. 41, 2712H), and a grant of péage from the fair at Thouars to the monks of St-Laon at Thouars (*RH*, i, no. 436, 1754H).

94. As suggested by Gillingham, *Angevin Empire*, 64.

95. Eynsham 1286H; Fitz Osbert 2843H; Merton 1321H; Ralph 1293H, addressed to the regarders of Oxfordshire, Buckinghamshire, Hampshire or Yorkshire, and cf. Longueville 1992H which involves both England and Normandy.

96. For example, Beeleigh 1243H; Boscherville 1854H (covering lands in England); Bristol 1235H; Bromfield 4323H. Altogether there are at least 23 charters of Henry II which refer to or offer exemption from the regard.

97. See *RH*, ii, nos 745 (Aunay 769H, *et apud Mannunicel duos campos . . . quos campos dedit eis cum redditu frumenti inde proueniente exceptis reguardis*), 747 (Bondeville 1976H, *et decimas censuum et regardorum totius redditus sui*), 756 (Ste-Barbe 1984H, confirming a *decimam reguardorum in panibus*); Arnoux, 'Actes de l'abbaye Notre-Dame-du-Val', 29–31, no. 7 (Val-Notre-Dame 4154H, confirming a *donationem . . . de mesagio Susane iuxta virgultum suum quod valet ut dicitur annuatim iii. quarter(ia) frumenti et regard(um)*). For an earlier use of the term, specifying the obligation of four men of the vill to serve *pro regardo*, see *Recueil des actes des ducs de Normandie*, no. 224 at 430, and cf. 468 *sub regardum* where the term is defined merely as a 'taxe'.

98. *RH*, i, no. 212 (Fitz Gilbert 1606H, *et predictus Baldricus est regardator et pasnagator mearum forestarum, habens tantum in donis et liberationibus regardi et pasnagii quantum unus ex mag(ist)ris regardatoribus et pasnagatoribus meis per totam Normanniam*); ii, no. 705 (Mala Palude 1942H, *et debet esse unus ex regardatoribus forestarum mearum ad custum meum, et debet habere suum pasnagium liberum et quietum in omnibus forestis meis ad omnes porcos suos, et debet habere ad Natale viginti solidos vel quatuor porcos*). Haskins (*Norman Institutions*, 103, 117–18), whilst recognizing the oddities of the second of these charters, accepted it as irrefutable evidence of the existence both of regarders and of a forest regard in twelfth-century Normandy.

99. In both England and Normandy there is much that still remains obscure about the history of forest administration, despite the efforts of Young, *Royal Forests of Medieval England* and Roquelet, *La Vie de la forêt Normande*.

100. For terminology here, see *Treatise on the Laws and Customs of England*, 53–4.

101. For St-Victor (1046H), where the mandate comes as part of a more general confirmation of lands and liberties, see *RH*, ii, no. 596. All the other writs, including one for the English lands of Jumièges (*RH*, i, no. 92, 960H), are addressed generally to the justices etc of England, save for an isolated writ addressed to the sheriff of Suffolk (Malling 1161H). For prototypes of the writ of naifty, issued from at least the time of King Stephen, see *RRAN*, iii, no. 672, and cf. no. 552; Van Caenegem, *Royal Writs in England from the Conquest to Glanvill*, 336–43, 466–77, nos 103–24. Note that at least three of the writs issued by Henry II, requiring the return of serfs who had fled since the death of Henry I, were intended for the use of monasteries not themselves founded until after 1135: Bordesley 2856H; Coggeshall 4694H; Faversham 4397H.

102. The only such writs not issued in England are those for Coggeshall (4694H, issued at Rouen), Llanthony (4163H, issued at Lyons-la-Forêt) and St-Victor (1046H, issued at Lillebonne). Intriguingly, two of the 26 writs were issued at Westminster 'at the exchequer' (Cirencester 4042H; Mauduit 4001H) which is otherwise a comparatively rare place of issue. Only two such writs (Abingdon 2310H and St-Victor 1046H) can be dated after 1172, the majority being datable to the opening years of the reign.
103. Boorman, 'Nisi feceris under Henry II'.
104. For example, see *St Benet of Holme, 1020–1210*, i, 24, nos 41, 26–7, 48 (Holme 2927H and 2932H, warning the bishop of Norwich *et nisi feceris, archiepiscopus Cant' faciat*).
105. For example, see *Historia Ecclesia Abbendonensis*, ii, 348–9 (Abingdon 2300H), ordering the bailiffs of Droitwich to ensure the monks possession of their salt workings, *et nisi feceritis, vic(ecomes) meus de Wirec'sir' faciat*.
106. Boorman, 'Nisi feceris', 92–5.
107. For *iusticiarius meus*, see Gloucester 2347H; Spalding 3346H. For Robert earl of Leicester specified by name, see Athelney 3367H; Burton 3777H; Bury 2962H; Mandeville 4754H (Robert de Valognes or earl Robert); Rievaulx 1994H; Valognes 5067H. In other examples, it is likely that *iusticiarius* is being used to imply the county justiciars. For enforcement deputed to the sheriff and *iusticiarius*, or the *iusticiarius* and sheriff of a specified county (Yorkshire), see Hexham 3315H; Selby 2377H and 2380H. For enforcement deputed to the *iusticius vel vicecomes meus de Northf'*, see Holme 2921H.
108. Aubigné 710H; Thorney 207H.
109. For the last five examples cited here, see Colchester 2896H (Norfolk); Oxford 116H (Oxfordshire); Reading 3978H (Warwickshire); Spalding 3351H (Lincolnshire); York 3108H (Yorkshire).
110. For the first ten examples here, see Abingdon 493H, 2301H and 2305H; Athelney 4286H; Belvoir 1846H and 1847H; Binham 4320H; Burton 3798H; Canterbury 119H; Colchester 2897H.
111. For *iusticiarii mei de partibus illis*, see Cirencester 4047H and 4049H; Newnham 2044H. For *iusticie mee de partibus illis*, see Bardney 2542H; Crowland 4180H; Gloucester 5026H; Lire 3186H; Reading 3965H; St Albans 2637H; Shrewsbury 338H; Winchcombe 4058H; York 3110H, and see also Godstow 4078H (*iusticie mee*); Scriptor 2371H (*iusticiarii nostri*).
112. Cronne, 'Office of Local Justiciar in England'; Stenton, *English Justice Between the Norman Conquest and the Great Charter*, 65–70.
113. Both survive as originals: *Facsimiles of Early Charters in Oxford Muniment Rooms*, no. 81 (Oxford 116H, written by an unidentified scribe, deputing enforcement to *iusticia mea de Oxenef'* 1172×1175, as noted by Boorman, 'Nisi feceris', 94); *Rufford Charters*, iii, 440, no. 825 (Rufford 4014H, written by Bishop scribe XL, deputing enforcement to *vicecomes vel iusticia mea*, 1181×1188). Whilst the Oxford writ could conceivably be a post-1172 chancery renovation of a mandate issued as early as 1165, the Rufford writ is witnessed by Robert, archdeacon of Nottingham, not promoted to his archdeaconry until after 1179 at the very earliest. Furthermore, whereas in charters or writ-charters, renovation may have been a relatively common phenomenon; in writs of execution, intended to enforce particular circumstantial orders, the likelihood of renovation is greatly reduced.

114. For Ireland, see Cursun 4810H. For the others, nn. 115–118.
115. For Norman examples, after 1172, directed either to *iusticia mea* or to *iusticia mea Normannie*, see *RH*, ii, nos 500 (St-Valery 1803H), 688 (Cherbourg 1931H), 701 (Marmion 1940H), 712 (Mont-St-Michel 1948H), 732 (St-Wandrille 1963H), and see Haskins, *Norman Institutions*, 93–4.
116. *RH*, i, no. 21 (Bayeux 1395H).
117. Paris, Bibliothèque nationale, ms. Dupuy 499, fo. 26v (Ars-en-Ré 3833H); *RH*, i, no. 355 (Le Mans 1696H), and for Pain, see Boussard, *Gouvernement d'Henri II Plantagenêt*, 359.
118. *RH*, i, no. 91 (St-Florent 1529H).
119. For Plantagenet administration in Anjou and the south, see Boussard, *Comté d'Anjou sous Henri Plantagenêt et ses fils, 1151–1204*, and Boussard, *Gouvernement d'Henri II Plantagenêt*.
120. Economy of space forbids me from publishing full lists below. Such lists will be supplied in the introduction to the new edition of the *Acta of Henry II*.
121. *Reading Abbey Cartularies*, i, 234–5, no. 283 (a petition to the bishops of Chichester and Exeter, Reading 3976H, possibly reworked but from what was almost certainly a genuine model); BL, MS Additional 35170 (Newstead cartulary), fo. 147v (to the bishop of Worcester, Newstead 2606H). See also a notification concerning temporalities, supposedly addressed to the bishop of St Davids, but almost certainly forged or substantially reworked: *St Davids Episcopal Acta, 1085–1280*, 93, no. 69.
122. See pp. 32–52.
123. The best general guide remains that by Palmer, *County Courts of Medieval England*, which is nonetheless concerned chiefly with the legal rather than the general procedural functions of the courts.
124. See, for example, the Assize of Clarendon and the English Assize of Arms, in Stubbs, *Select Charters*, 170, c. 1, 171, cc. 7–8, 184, cc. 10, 12.
125. For the use of the county court in publishing the king's ordinances after 1258, see for example *Documents of the Baronial Movement*, 17, 312–15.
126. For letters of pardon, see Hurnard, *King's Pardon for Homicide*, 59–67, as drawn to my attention by Paul Brand. For the authentifcation of royal seals, see Tout, *Chapters in the Administrative History of Medieval England*, iii, 81, n. 1, v, 137–8.
127. BL, MS Harley 6072, fo. 17r (Fitz Tece 3316H), reading *Sciatis me rededisse Guidoni filio Tece totam terram suam unde diseisitus fuit per ementalationem Alani Wallensis, unde ipse Guido diffamabatur, et quantum ad me pertinet predictum delictum ei condonasse, et ipse Guido faciat pacem cum parentibus dicti Alani*, with three witnesses, issued at Durham.
128. This explanation is clearly set out by the author of *Chronicle of Battle Abbey*, 312–13, commenting on the production of multiple copies of a charter Henry II issued in the 1170s. For the charter referred to here, which once existed in triplicate and which still survives in duplicate originals, and for further remarks, calling in to question the reliability of the Battle Chronicle in matters of historical detail rather than in matters of diplomatic procedure, see Vincent, 'King Henry II and the Monks of Battle', 269–70.
129. From the mid-thirteenth century large numbers of early royal charters are assigned a prominent place in the records of the forest eyre, now for the most part to be found in the PRO class E32. As is well known, from the

1270s onwards they were also produced in large numbers across the country for the *Quo Warranto* pleas of the general eyre, many since published
from the eyre rolls (PRO JUST1) in *Placita de Quo Warranto*.

130. It might be objected here that a large number of such writs were issued, but
being returnable were not available to be copied into cartularies. This does not,
however, apply to writ-charters which were regularly preserved in cartularies.

131. For King Stephen's award of the justiciarship of Lincoln and Lincolnshire to
Bishop Robert Chesney (1154), see *RRAN*, iii, no. 490; Cronne, 'Office of
Local Justiciar', 23–4.

132. All told, we have four charters or writs of Henry II addressed to the bishops
of Coutances, four to the bishops of Evreux, two to the bishop of Sées, and
one each to the bishops of Avranches and Lisieux, all to be dated before
1172.

133. See, for example, letters concerning lay fee addressed to the bishops of Le
Mans: *RH*, i, nos 70, 107, 292, 352, 354, ii, supplement, no. 22 (Le Mans
1514H, 1540H, 1693H, 1695H; Perseigne 1648H; Sanson 2007H); Boussard,
'Trois actes d'Henri II Plantagenêt', 53–5 (St-Jean 3649H). For Poitiers, see
RH, i, nos 378, 436 (Fontevraud 1712H; Thouars 1754H).

134. For Bordeaux, see *RH*, ii, no. 519 (La Rochelle 1814H). For Saintes, see Boussard,
'Trois Actes', 55–6 (Dalon 3767H). For Tours, see *RH*, ii, nos 475, 520, 597
(Grais 1866H; Tours 550H, 1785H); Oxford, Bodleian Library, MS Carte 91,
fo. 90v (Angers 3857H).

6
Before Charters? Property Records in Pre-Anglo-Norman Ireland

Máire Herbert

The second half of the twelfth century saw the introduction into Ireland of charters which were similar in form and content to those in use elsewhere in Europe. The development was part of a process whereby Irish political and ecclesiastical structures had drawn closer to the European mainstream through intensification of external contacts. Irish rulers sought to exercise wider powers and to enhance institutions of government. Ecclesiastical reformers not only urged the adoption of diocesan structures, they also supported the foundation of religious houses affiliated to European reforming communities such as Augustinian canons and Cistercians.[1] From the second half of the twelfth century, grants by Irish kings to these new communities were recorded in internationally recognizable Latin charters.[2] Does this adoption of European documentary practice signal fundamental change? To set twelfth-century process in context, I propose to give a brief overview of Irish records of property transactions in the pre-Anglo-Norman era. My purpose is to trace developments rather than to focus closely on particular texts.

Early Irish evidence of pragmatic writing seems scarce and tenuous compared to that of other areas in Western Europe.[3] Indeed, in Ireland scholarship appears to be a particular focus of literate activity, though it would be rash to assert that scholarly production flourished at the expense of utilitarian documentation.[4] Questions of transmission loom large. Texts from early Christian Ireland are available to us because they escaped Viking devastation through being taken to continental Europe, or because they were chosen for recuperation and preservation in the eleventh century and beyond. Records of legal transactions, if they were not destroyed along with the ecclesiastical books with which they were probably associated, may also have been discarded in a changed post-Viking world.[5] Thus, the quest to outline the context in which the Latin charter was adopted in Ireland has to rely on fragmentary indications rather than on continuous documentation.

Record-keeping in early Ireland, moreover, must be assessed in the light of the fact that Christianity and literacy were not part of the legacy of incorporation into the Roman empire, but were assimilated into an Irish society with its own language, learned organization, and law. Vernacular Irish law-texts, compiled from about the seventh century onwards, provide for an Irish society within which the church is situated, while canon-law texts from the same era legislate for an ecclesiastical community which was a component of the wider social body.[6] In the matter of contract (as in other matters), we see interaction, mutual influence, and synthesis. Ecclesiastical legislators acknowledge established procedures involving sureties and witnesses, with writing as an additional stipulation, while vernacular law counts 'godly old writings' among seven things which facilitate legal decision.[7] In an early Irish context, ecclesiastical and secular institutions accommodated to each other, while each maintained its own priorities.

In assessing the evidence, moreover, we need to take account of multiple forms of the written word. For example, early Irish law's 'immoveable rock', witnessing to boundary or ownership, comes to be inscribed from perhaps the fifth century,[8] so that the 'ogam in the pillar-stone' is acknowledged (alongside sureties and witnesses) as one of the types of evidence which serve as proof of title to land.[9] Moreover, though names inscribed on stone, whether in Ogam script or in Roman letters, are far from constituting a formulaic statement of possession, we have at least one instance where a transaction is implied. An inscription in Roman script on a standing-stone at Kilnasaggart, Co. Armagh, dated to the early eighth century states *In loc so tanimmairni Ternohc mac Ceran bic ar cul Peter Apstel*: 'This place, under the protection of the Apostle Peter, Ternóc son of little Ciarán bequeathed it.'[10]

The vernacular statement on the inscription may be set alongside Latin hagiographical statements of a few decades earlier in Tírechán's late seventh-century account of St Patrick in the Book of Armagh.[11] Here, grants, formally signalled by Latin verbs such as *immolo*, are assigned to Patrick and to God.[12] The use of a formulaic vocabulary of offering suggests that Irish ecclesiastics had some acquaintance with charter terminology, while the Kilnasaggart inscription indicates that such terminology could be adapted for vernacular use. Indeed, examples of both Latin and Irish records are found in a collection of documents, datable around the year AD 700 and transcribed into the Book of Armagh a century later.[13] Some of these documents read like an extension of

Tírechán's narrative, situating property grants and church foundations in the context of Patrick's preaching in various parts of Ireland. Others are bare records of property transfer.[14] In texts that are otherwise in Latin, the vernacular may be introduced for specific property details like a boundary clause. Moreover, the Irish language is also the medium for entire records, such as a detailed transaction of buying and selling, and a testament delivered 'between the chancel and the altar' of the church of Druim Lias (in present-day Co. Leitrim) in the presence of local nobility and monastic *familia*.[15] We may suppose that major churches like Armagh were more likely to have capability in drafting Latin legalese than the outlying Patrician communities whose records were being copied into Armagh's Patrician archive. Indeed, their copyist in the Book of Armagh is openly condescending about materials which he terms *per Scotticam imperfecte scripta*, and he asserts that he could have penned them in Latin, if he chose.[16]

There is evident lack of uniformity, therefore, in the recording of early Irish property transfers. It is well established that the documents are narrative accounts of property settlements enacted in a public ceremony, their enforcement apparently guaranteed by sureties. Therefore, the texts are evidentiary rather than dispositive.[17] Certain formulae recur in both Latin and vernacular records, especially the use of specific verbs of offering or grant, the destination of offering to God and saint, and the specification that grants were to be 'for eternity', 'until Doomsday'. Such formulae are also used when grants to saints are recounted in early Hiberno-Latin hagiography.[18] Were other formal constituents absent from memoranda of transactions, or were they lost in transmission? The vernacular *Cáin Éimíne Báin*, literally 'The Law of Éimíne the Fair', in fact is a contract between ecclesiastical and secular powers in Leinster, preserved through having been reconstituted in a later hagiographical narrative.[19] The fundamentals seem to involve exchange of considerations, whereby the Leinstermen and their king granted various privileges to Éimíne's church and possessions in return for spiritual support. (The subsequent narrative explains the grant in terms of the saving of the king and his nobles from plague by the voluntary substitution of Éimíne and his monks.) Significantly, the formal content includes disposition and statements of sanction, as well as a list of 15 sureties or guarantors (*rátha*) of whom eight are identifiable in the genealogical records of the era around the late seventh or early eighth century.[20] Thus, in the midst of a hagiographical melodrama, we find embedded evidence of a vernacular contract from around the year AD 700, and therefore roughly contemporaneous with documents preserved in the Book of Armagh.

Eighth-century Irish ecclesiastical legislation indicates that written records should constitute the primary evidence in cases where two churches dispute ownership of a piece of land.[21] Within this context, the chirograph may have been utilized in some Irish ecclesiastical circles. Though no physical example survives, Hiberno-Latin glosses in manuscripts of the eighth and ninth centuries indicate that their Irish writers understood a chirograph to be a bisected document with either party to an agreement retaining one half.[22] This usage corresponds to insular practice rather than that of the contemporary continental milieu in which the glosses were probably written. Did Irish churchmen choose this mode of record as particularly suited to inter-church contracts? The earliest chirographs come from England, so the neighbouring island may well have been the immediate source of Irish exemplars. However, as the early Irish church absorbed influences from a variety of areas, we ought to be hesitant about concluding that all legal documentary models in the early Irish church derived from Britain.[23]

Whatever the provenance of its exemplars, written property documentation in pre-Viking Ireland seems to have been primarily a matter for churches, and, among churches, practice seems to have varied. There is no hesitation about adapting formal terminology for vernacular use, and the concern in both languages appears to be the transmission of key concepts rather than unchangeable formulae. There is no indication that the physical form of the document was considered particularly significant. We may infer that the Book of Armagh materials rely on single-sheet originals, but again we ought not posit uniformity.[24] Indeed, within early Irish society, standing stones on boundaries and crosses marking monastic perimeters evidently had stronger semiotic impact than vellum pages, however elaborated.[25]

The compilation of the Book of Armagh at the beginning of the ninth century was probably designed as a normal product of the Armagh *scriptorium*,[26] but in fact it constituted an act of conservation, accomplished in the shadow of threat. Already Vikings had begun to raid the Irish and British coasts, and the activity of Irish *scriptoria* was disrupted. Some scholars migrated with their books to the continent. Annals and hagiography invoked Irish saints as avengers of attacks on their churches rather than as recipients of offerings.[27] After some respite from the latter part of the ninth century, the renewal of Viking pressure thereafter seems to have greatly diminished written production for much of the tenth century. The content of codices produced in eleventh- and twelfth-century Ireland indicates that their compilers sought to reinstate both religious and secular texts of the pre-Viking era, using various means of textual mediation to bridge an evident gap in use and comprehension. It seems likely, therefore, that monastic writings which escaped devastation had been consigned to safe strongholds and withdrawn from use for a significant time.[28]

An annal report in the year 939 that *Canóin Pádraic* was enshrined thus seems to document the enclosure of the Book of Armagh as well as its veneration.[29] Indeed, as the Book is thereby emblematic of tenth-century hiatus, so too its reappearance reflects an Irish political and cultural revival beginning around the close of the same century. When the Munster ruler, Brian Bóruma, visited Armagh in the year 1005 as part of his campaign for the kingship of Ireland, he made a generous donation of gold, and acknowledged his support for Armagh's rights to revenue. This affirmation is written into the Book of Armagh, on a page which otherwise records an early eighth-century property record.[30] Such placement is probably not fortuitous. Moreover, the Latin hagiographical framing of the affirmation links it stylistically with the earlier claims on behalf of Patrick in the Book of Armagh.[31] Yet while the eleventh-century entry thereby connects with the past, is it also innovative? As Armagh's prized volume was inscribed by Brian's accompanying scholar, Máel Suthain, in the presence of the king, writing set a formal seal on the assertion that Brian, *Imperator Scottorum*, assented to Armagh's privileges on his own behalf and on behalf of his successors.[32] Transaction and the making of a written record are thereby being linked, and the new holder of Irish sovereignty is being associated with the textual proceedings of a formal agreement.

Certainly, ambitious Irish rulers followed Brian in seeking ecclesiastical support, and eleventh-century records show that churches capitalized on this by gaining concessions from rulers, especially in the wake of secular trespass on ecclesiastical property.[33] The written record of such eleventh-century transactions is clearly ecclesiastical, surviving in the form of brief annal statements, and in property records which had been entered contemporaneously into the Book of Kells.[34] The Irish language is the medium of all of these transactions. The annal statements may abbreviate documents like those of the gospel-book, since they share both verbal formulations and a focus on the reception of grants from kings as recompense for offences against the church.[35] The ceremonies of donation reflected in the documents may well have taken place in an ecclesiastical setting, so kings may have been present while a written record was made. Yet ecclesiastics clearly were in control of what was written, as the statements of grant usually recall the royal offences that occasioned them.

Did the entering of property transactions in the Book of Kells represent continuity or change? In the light of what we know of variant practice within the Irish church, we cannot rule out the possibility that legal transactions of the pre-Viking era had been contemporaneously recorded in gospels and other sacred volumes. Yet the materials written into the Book of Armagh at the beginning of the ninth century were already a century old, and were included to ensure the completeness of the Patrician archive.[36] After the ceremonial entry of the year 1005, no other documentary record survives in the Armagh volume. We may tentatively infer, therefore, that the recording of transactions in Irish gospel-books had not been routine, but rather was the product of special circumstances, when significant proceedings were transacted in an ecclesiastical setting.[37] Such was the case in Armagh in the year 1005. Similarly, the earliest identified entry in the Book of Kells, dated between 1073 and 1087, depicts the king of Tara acting in concert with the abbot and community of Kells to grant a property.[38] The sole record in our third gospel, the Book of Durrow, documents an exceptional property arrangement agreed between the community of Durrow and the neighbouring monastic community of Killeshin at the beginning of the twelfth century.[39]

There is only one attested case where a precedent was set. For over a half century following the first known entry, monastic officials used empty spaces in the Book of Kells to document their own personal property transactions as well as grants to the ecclesiastical settlement.[40] Since a grant of the first half of the eleventh century is entered retrospectively in the final decades of the same century, we may assume that written property-records were already being kept in Kells.[41] The change to gospel-book recording had evident elements of continuity, since monastic officials involved in the first transaction were also central to the following proceedings.[42] Did they take the view that property documentation gained security by closer association with 'the great gospel of Colum Cille', a book that was simultaneously a relic of the patron saint as well as a sacred text?[43] Whether considered as conservation or as innovation, the Kells decision allows us a direct view of vernacular recording of property transactions. As the constituents of the documents range through grant, sale, property dispute, and ecclesiastical immunity, comparable material from pre-Viking times is not extensive.[44] Nevertheless, the sum of evidence suggests that the Kells records follow existing Irish models. Purchase agreements, while linguistically modernized, are comparable to a vernacular text in the same genre in the Book of Armagh.[45] Phrases concerning suretyship are reminiscent of phrases in *Cáin Éimíne*,[46] and the use of sanctions in a majority of Kells statements of grant parallels their use in the *Cáin*.[47] That Irish pragmatic documentation follows pre-Viking usage is consistent with what we know of Irish cultural history in the eleventh century. The early phase of post-Viking revival had to draw on the surviving scholarly resources of Irish monastic libraries without any initial influx of external materials.[48]

Towards the end of the century, however, certain Irish churchmen and rulers were made aware of external developments in ecclesiastical and secular life.[49] Direct contact with reformist prelates like Anselm, archbishop of Canterbury, seems to have persuaded Ireland's most powerful king, Muirchertach Ua Briain, that he should take an active role in church reform. Presiding over the Synod of Cashel in the year 1101, he made the grand gesture of granting the royal site of Cashel itself 'to the Lord'.[50] It was, according to an annalist, 'a grant such as no king had ever made before'.[51] Political opportunism may have been at least as much a consideration as ecclesiastical support, since Cashel had been the hereditary site of the rival dynastic power in Munster.[52] Nevertheless, Muirchertach's act was clearly influential. Active patronage of the church became part of the role of power-seeking rulers. Hitherto, the records had depicted Irish kings granting property as reparation for offences against saints or as propitiatory offerings to obtain supernatural succour during crises.[53] Muirchertach, however, had seized the initiative and given positive value to the idea of ruler as benefactor. We may be sceptical about the extent to which promotion of reform ideals prompted all subsequent Irish rulers' ecclesiastical grants. Yet it is evident that twelfth-century rulers espoused the idea that power was both demonstrated and enhanced by generosity to churches.

How important was the written record of such generosity? We would expect a significant transaction like the donation of Cashel to be duly documented. The fact that some of the conventional vernacular grant formulae are discernible in surviving notices reinforces this view.[54] Yet no full statement of grant survives. Moreover, the event is conspicuously absent from the Annals of Inisfallen, which were being compiled within Muirchertach Ua Briain's own realm.[55] Could it be that an annal account was perceived as redundant because the formal record had been ceremonially written into a Munster holy book? We can only speculate. Certainly we have indications that Irish royal grants were documented in the twelfth century. Annals of the years 1127 and 1143 incorporate summary accounts of grants to Connacht churches by Toirdelbach Ua Conchubair, the most powerful king of the time.[56] Inclusion of detail such as boundary clauses suggests that the annals rely on documents similar to those associated with Kells.[57] Indeed, a sometime ally of Toirdelbach Ua Conchubair, the ambitious Tigernán Ua Ruairc, king of Bréifne, was making endowments to Kells around the same time, as he campaigned to establish his rule in the region. The original records of Ua Ruairc's grants are now missing from the Book of Kells, though they survive in later copies.[58] Some contemporaneous twelfth-century records do survive in the gospel-book, however, giving us sufficient grounds for concluding that twelfth-century vernacular documents are formally similar to those of the previous century.[59] Yet there are hints that account is now being taken of the sensibilities of royal benefactors. For instance, the record of a grant of Toirdelbach Ua Conchubair in an annal entry of 1127 states that the king gave the land *uadha féin*, 'of his own accord', while a grant by Ua Ruairc to Kells includes the king's titles and the extent of his dominion in fulsome (and perhaps exaggerated) terms.[60]

We may infer, therefore, that Irish rulers were becoming more aware that the written record afforded a means of enhancing the propaganda effect of donation. While practice clearly varied between kingdoms and churches, in the first half of the twelfth century leading Irish rulers evidently used ecclesiastical grants strategically and utilized public occasions to promote their role as benefactors. The Kells documents indicate that Tigernán Ua Ruairc was present as a witness in the year 1133 when the community of Kells made a grant to its dedicated religious. He himself granted a property on the occasion of the consecration of a church in Kells.[61] His presence at such ecclesiastical gatherings most likely meant that he was present at the inscription of the record in the gospel-book. The land which Ua Ruairc granted to Kells may well have been disputed border-land, wrested in the course of his campaign to dominate the Irish midlands. That such expediency could be documented as liberality 'to God and Colum Cille' in records in the Book of Kells was assuredly a bonus for the ruler.

What was the attitude of rulers to the new reformist communities? Insofar as we can tell, rulers of the mid-twelfth century offered patronage wherever advantage might be gained, without particularly distinguishing between traditional and reformist foundations. Kells's benefactor, Tigernán Ua Ruairc, seems to have granted lands also to the Augustinian canons of Navan. The record survives through its reiteration in a later Latin charter.[62] As with nearby Kells, the ruler's strategic interests in the territory may have been as significant a factor in the grant as religious motivation.[63] The memorialization of the Navan grant by Latin charter conferred ecclesiastical approbation, as did the Kells records, but did so in a format that was European rather than vernacular. Did Ua Ruairc and his secular counterparts share churchmen's awareness of the international character of the documentation? Or was it simply a further useful means of bolstering royal pretensions?

The sum of evidence suggests that there was no sharp divide between traditional ecclesiastics and new reforming communities as far as royal benefaction was concerned. In the matter of documentation, whatever the attitude of kings, Irish annalists took an inclusive view of the records produced by the various ecclesiastical beneficiaries. We have already inferred that vernacular property documentation of the eleventh and twelfth centuries served as annal source-material. It would appear that new Latin charters were similarly quarried. A record of the consecration of the church of the Cistercian foundation of Mellifont in the year 1157 incorporates a property grant to the monks by Ireland's leading king, Muirchertach Mac Lochlainn, king of Cenél nEógain.[64] While a charter recording this transaction has not survived, phrases reflective of Latin charter usage are rendered in the vernacular. For instance, the king is said to offer the townland *do raith a anma*, 'for the benefit of his soul', an evident echo of *pro salute animae meae* of contemporary Latin charters.[65] The same king, Muirchertach Mac Lochlainn, figures in the Book of Kells transaction of the year 1161, granting freedom from secular imposition to the neighbouring church of Ardbraccan. In this instance the vernacular record follows the mode of other transactions in the gospel-book, with a statement of the conditions agreed, and a list of sureties who guaranteed fulfilment.[66] The first name among the sureties is that of Gilla Meic Liag, successor of Patrick, that is head of the church of Armagh, and a leading figure among Irish ecclesiastical reformers.[67] Clearly there was no necessary connection between adherence to reform and dissociation from vernacular documentation procedures in pre-Anglo-Norman Ireland.

In fact, there appears to be pluralist toleration of a range of modes of property documentation at least up to the period of establishment of Anglo-Norman influence towards the end of the twelfth century. From the seventh century onwards, Irish ecclesiastical communities had incorporated property records in hagiographical texts, and emphasis on property and property rights is particularly notable in vernacular Lives throughout the twelfth century.[68] Yet hagiography could be used in conjunction with other modes of property documentation. An annal of the year 1176 records that Ruaidrí Ua Conchubair, 'king of Ireland', offered the church of Tuaim Achaid 'to the Lord and to St Berach' forever. The full immunity of the property was guaranteed by named ecclesiastical and secular magnates, headed by the archbishop of Tuam.[69] The annal, evidently based on a written record similar to those of the Book of Kells, uniquely includes the guarantor list.[70] A vernacular Life of St Berach conveys the information through another medium.[71] The narrative recounts how the saint's plough-team ran wild, and made a circuit of named places. Places ploughed along the way are claimed for Berach, including Tuaim Achaid.[72] By situating ownership of the site in the saint's lifetime, hagiography presented the grant as an affirmation of an existing right, and thereby, perhaps, made it more acceptable to the local community most directly concerned. It also unambiguously identified the saint as beneficiary and protector.

In the vernacular Life of St Mochua of Balla, prose narrative recounts the offering of a site to the saint, while the boundaries of the area granted and the dues owed by its inhabitants to the saint are rendered in Irish verse.[73] There must be a strong presumption that, in this instance also, the underlying information may have been available in the form of a written grant with boundary clause and specification of property dues. In the case of the Life of Mochua, reception of the written record is facilitated for a non-literate public not only by providing story context, but also by presenting factual details in Irish verse as an aid to memory. Saints' Lives formed the basis of preaching to laity, and thus could transmit property information widely. While clerics might refer to documents, and while rulers might at least acknowledge their existence, traditional Irish ecclesiastical establishments could not afford to overlook the social milieu in which they were situated and the population with which they were deeply enmeshed. Twelfth-century hagiography therefore does not represent a rejection of formal property documentation, but rather transposes it into a form communicable in particular situations.

We may conclude that the adoption of the European Latin charter to record grants by Irish kings to monastic houses of reform observances did not immediately transform the processes of property documentation. Instead the new Latin model was integrated into a complex tapestry of recording practices, reflective of the complexity of the Irish ecclesiastical world even as it sought to reform itself and to adapt more fully to the organizational structures of Roman Christendom. The transformation of the Irish church was accomplished more slowly in some areas than in others. The foregoing grant of property in the west of Ireland to St Berach comes almost a decade after the beginning of Anglo-Norman incursion into Ireland. Thus, though Anglo-Norman influence may have been the most decisive factor in securing Latin charter use in Ireland, we must not assume that change was always uniform and unidirectional. The interaction between the Irish ecclesiastical world and that of Latin charters continues to offer fruitful ground for exploration.

Notes

1. See, for instance, Gwynn, *Irish Church*; *idem, Twelfth Century Reform*.
2. See Flanagan, 'Content and Uses', 113–32.
3. Stevenson, 'Beginnings of Literacy', 127–65.
4. On scholarship in particular, see Charles-Edwards, 'Context and Uses of Literacy', 62–82.
5. On the association of documents with sacred books and relics, see Clanchy, *From Memory to Written Record*, 154–7.
6. See, for instance, Charles-Edwards, '*Corpus Iuris Hibernici*', 141–62; *idem, Early Medieval Gaelic Lawyer*; Ó Corráin, Breatnach, Breen, 'Laws of the Irish', 382–438; Breatnach, 'Canon Law and Secular Law', 439–59.
7. Full references to the primary sources and translations of the relevant secular law texts *Di Astud Cor, Berrad Airechta*, and *Gúbretha Caratniad* are given in Charles-Edwards, *Early Medieval Gaelic Lawyer*, 64–5; For canon-law texts, see Wasserschleben, *Irische Kanonensammlung*. See also McLeod, *Early Irish Contract Law*; Charles-Edwards, 'Construction of the *Hibernensis*', 209–37; Mac Niocaill, 'Admissible and Inadmissible Evidence', 332–7.
8. The old Irish term *ail anscuichthe* is also used to designate unshakeable evidence in early Irish law. On ogam inscriptions, see McManus, *Guide to Ogam*, passim; for specific reference to early Irish law, see 163–6.
9. McManus, *Guide to Ogam*, 164.
10. Text in *Corpus Inscriptionum Insularum Celticarum*, ii, 114–15. My translation differs somewhat from that offered by Stokes and Strachan in *Thesaurus Palaeohibernicus*, ii, 289. See Hamlin, 'Early Irish Stone Carving', 291.
11. The text is edited and translated by L. Bieler in *Patrician Texts*, 122–67.
12. For examples and discussion see Doherty, 'Some Aspects of Hagiography', 303–7; Stevenson, 'Literacy in Ireland', 19–28.
13. Styled *Additamenta* by J. Gwynn in *Liber Ardmachanus*, pp. lxiv–lxvi; texts edited and translated by L. Bieler in *Patrician Texts*, 166–79; commentary 46–9.
14. Stevenson, 'Literacy in Ireland', 28–9; Doherty, 'Some Aspects of Hagiography', 305–6.
15. *Patrician Texts*, 172, lines 14–22, 27–32.
16. Ibid., 178–9, item 17.1.
17. Davies, 'Latin Charter-Tradition', 262–3; *eadem*, 'Charter-writing and its Uses', 101–2.
18. *Vitae Sanctorum Hiberniae*, ed. Heist, 125.32, 129.46, 143.60, 161.5–6, 166.22. On the dating of these Lives see Sharpe, *Medieval Irish Saints' Lives*, 297–339.
19. Poppe, 'New Edition of *Cáin Éimíne Báin*', 35–52.
20. Poppe (op. cit., 36) points out that witness (*recte* guarantor) list and sanction form clear entities in the text. What counts as disposition is partly obscured and inverted by its remake in hagiographical form. On the guarantors, see Poppe, 'List of Sureties', 588–92. On suretyship, see Thurneysen, 'Aus dem irischen Recht V', 364–96; McLeod, *Early Irish Contract Law*, 16–21.
21. Wasserschleben, *Irische Kanonensammlung*, 117–18, ch. 24; translated by Sharpe, 'Dispute Settlement', 183.
22. Bischoff, 'Zur Frühgeschichte des mittelalterlichen Chirographum', 118–22; *Glossae Divinae Historiae*, 205, item 606. See also Mac Niocaill, 'Admissible and Inadmissible Evidence', 333–4.

23. Bischoff, *Latin Palaeography*, 36. On Brittonic adaptation of the term chirograph, see Davies, 'Charter-writing', 103–4.
24. The Book of Armagh account of the bringing of an *edoc[h]t* or testament from Sletty seems to imply an actual document. See *Patrician Texts*, 178–9.
25. See, for instance, Hamlin, 'Early Irish Stone Carving', passim.
26. Sharpe, 'Palaeographical Considerations', 3–28.
27. Note, for instance, entries in the years 881, 895 and 942 in *AU*[2].
28. I have discussed this evidence more fully in a forthcoming paper, 'Crossing Historical and Literary Boundaries'.
29. *CS* at the year 938 (*recte* 939).
30. *AU*[2] 1005.7; Liber Ardmachanus, fo. 16v; *Patrician Texts*, 47.
31. In this regard, see Sharpe, 'Palaeographical Considerations', and Broun, *Charters of Gaelic Scotland and Ireland*, 44–6. I accept that the wording was not directly imitative of a particular Book of Armagh text, but am inclined to the view that the content is shaped by hagiographical style rather than being reflective of lack of knowledge of basic charter elements.
32. For translation of the entry, see Broun, *Charters of Gaelic Scotland and Ireland*, 45, n. 158.
33. See, for instance, *AFM* in the years 1044 and 1072.
34. The Book of Kells records have been edited by Mac Niocaill, *Notitiae*, and subsequently, with translation, as 'The Irish "Charters"', 153–65. I will refer to the texts established in the latter edition, citing *Kells* and Mac Niocaill's numbering.
35. Compare the accounts of royal behaviour in *Kells* 4, *AFM* 1033, 1074. See also Herbert, 'Charter Material from Kells', 67, for the inference that *Kells* 2 may have been a response to the slaying of an aspirant to the kingship of Tara in the bell-tower of Kells in the year 1076.
36. Note the opening statement of the *Additamenta* in *Patrician Texts*, 166–7.
37. On other insular evidence, see Jenkins and Owen, 'Welsh Marginalia in the Lichfield Gospels, 37–66; Jenkins, 'From Wales to Weltenburg?', 75–88 (I am grateful to Dáibhí Ó Cróinín for kindly providing me with a copy of the latter).
38. *Kells* 2. On its primacy in the gospel-book, see Herbert, 'Charter Material', 67.
39. Text and translation by Best, 'Early Monastic Grant', 135–42. See Sharpe, 'Dispute Settlement', 170–3.
40. *Kells* 1, 2, 3, 5, 7 are all in the gospel-book itself. *Kells* 9, 10, 11, 12 survive in seventeenth-century transcripts. See Mac Niocaill, 'Irish "Charters"', 154.
41. *Kells* 4. See Herbert, 'Charter Materials', 62, 67–8.
42. Evidence from the Kells documents regarding the officials and community is set out in Herbert, *Iona, Kells and Derry*, 98–108.
43. The 'great gospel of Colum Cille' is so called in *AU*[2] 1007. While there is no certainty, it is highly probable that the Book of Kells is the volume in question.
44. For discussion of the content of the various documents see Herbert, 'Charter Material' passim.
45. *Patrician Texts*, 174–5, VII (2), (3), (4); *Kells* 3, 5, 7, 9, 10, 11.
46. Poppe, 'New Edition of *Cáin Éimíne Báin*', 44.10; *Kells* 5, 10, 11. It may be significant that the term *ráth* which had specifically designated a paying surety is used most consistently in *Kells* in the context of purchase. On the *ráth* in early Irish law, see Kelly, *Guide to Early Irish Law*, 168–71.

47. Poppe, 'New Edition of *Cáin Éimíne Báin*', 47.13; *Kells* 1, 2, 3, 4. See also Herbert, 'Charter Material', 63. In *Kells*, sanctions seem to be used more consistently in cases of grant than in the case of other kinds of property transaction.

48. Herbert, 'Crossing Boundaries' (forthcoming).

49. See n. 1.

50. Gwynn, 'First Synod of Cashel, 1101' in his *Irish Church*, 155–79.

51. *AFM* 1101.

52. Ó Corráin, 'Nationality and Kingship', 25.

53. *FM* 1044, 1072, 1095.

54. *ATig* 1101, *CS* 1097 (*recte* 1101), *AFM* 1101. A version of the proceedings of the synod is also incorporated into a late medieval genealogical account of the Ua Briain royal family, *Senchas síl Bhriain*, in *Caithréim Thoirdhealbhaigh*, i, 174–5.

55. *AI*. On its provenance, see p. xxviii.

56. *ATig* 1127, 1143. On the latter entry, see also Ó Corráin, 'Nationality and Kingship', 24.

57. Both annals detail the boundaries. Compare *Kells* 8.

58. A copy of *Kells* 8 (1) and (2) is also found in a late eighteenth-century copy. See Mac Niocaill, 'Irish "Charters" ', 154. On Ua Ruairc's activities and connection with Kells, see Herbert, *Iona, Kells and Derry*, 96–7, 106–7.

59. *Kells* 1, 5, 7.

60. *ATig* 1127, *Kells* 8 (2).

61. *Kells* 2, 8 (1).

62. Brooks, 'Charter of John de Courcy', 39.

63. Ó Corráin, 'Nationality and Kingship', 25.

64. *AFM* 1157.

65. For Muirchertach Mac Lochlainn's Latin charter to Newry Abbey see pp. 125–6.

66. *Kells* 6.

67. On his career, see Herbert, *Iona, Kells and Derry*, 111–12.

68. See Doherty, 'Some Aspects of Hagiography' passim; Herbert, 'Latin and Vernacular Hagiography', 327–60 (especially 346 and bibliography).

69. *AFM* 1176.

70. Its closeness in form to Kells material has already been noted by Mac Niocaill, *Notitiae*, 6.

71. *Bethada Náem nÉrenn*, ed. Plummer, i, 22–43, translation, ii, 22–43.

72. Ibid., i, 38–9 (xxiv (74)), ii, 38.

73. *Lives of Saints*, ed. Stokes, 137–46, translation, 281–9. The passage occurs at 142, 286, §§ 4759–84.

7
Irish Royal Charters and the Cistercian Order

Marie Therese Flanagan

This chapter focuses on the Latin charters issued by Irish kings in favour of Cistercian communities, or houses that were to become affiliated to the Cistercian order, in an effort to explore the role that Cistercian houses may have played in the promotion of document production in twelfth- and early thirteenth-century Ireland. The numbers of surviving Irish royal charters are pitifully small by comparison with English, Scottish, or Welsh charters, but nevertheless they shed valuable light both on documentary use and aspects of the political and religious history of the period and raise important questions, even though many of them are incapable of secure resolution owing to the partial nature of the evidence and paucity of the texts.

The most plausible context for the adoption of the European Latin charter by Irish kings in the twelfth century is the pan-European church reform movement that began to transform the western church and Christian culture from about 1050 onwards and to have a discernible impact on the Irish church certainly from no later than 1100 and probably some decades earlier.[1] Extant Irish royal charters are overwhelmingly in favour of what may be termed reformist religious communities that had adopted, or were in the process of adopting, continental monastic observances. Accepting the premise of the adoption of a new type of charter in Ireland as a concomitant of the church reform movement and also the key role of beneficiary diplomatic, the question may be asked which of the continental monastic orders was most influential in the dissemination of a new type of Latin charter in Ireland, and specifically royal charters? The Cistercians are conventionally regarded as the most advanced in institutional terms of the new monastic observances of the twelfth century and might *a priori* be considered likely to be an important agency in the dissemination of the European

Latin charter in Ireland. Certainly, their promotion of the Latin charter has been emphasized in other peripheral areas of Europe. In the case of Bohemia and Poland, the Cistercians have been assigned a major role in transmitting charter use; indeed in Poland their deployment of charters has been described as a Cistercian 'strategy'.[2] How far were the Cistercians 'missionaries of charters' in Ireland?[3]

Of 11 extant twelfth-century charters issued by Irish kings, 6 were in favour of Cistercian houses, or what became Cistercian houses. A striking feature of those charters is the diversity of their diplomatic and the ambiguity of the status of the religious communities in whose favour the charters were issued. One ready explanation might be that the six charters span 25 years from the earliest around 1157 to the latest around 1185, and that variation and change over such an extended period is only to be expected; another might be that they were issued by three different kings. The diversity of the twelfth-century texts is high-lighted by the marked contrast with four charters issued in the early decades of the thirteenth century by different benefactors in favour of the mother-house of Cîteaux which are identical in their internal formulae notwithstanding that they were written by local scribes attached to the households of the kings of Connacht and of Thomond, as detailed in the attestation clauses.

In terms of diplomatic, the distinctive features in the twelfth-century Irish royal charters is important testimony to their authenticity, but it remains to provide a satisfactory explanation for such peculiarities as discrepancies between the issue-dates of individual charters and the foundation-dates of the benefiting houses as recorded by the Cistercian order. One way forward is to explore the Irish royal charters in favour of Cistercian beneficiaries in the light of recent re-evaluations of the origins and growth of the Cistercian order. Traditionally, the Cistercians have been depicted as institutionally the most developed of the new religious observances of the twelfth century with an emphasis on uniformity of liturgical practice and of governmental structures that were elaborated by an annual chapter held at Cîteaux, which drew up statutes that were binding on all Cistercian houses. Their managerial and entrepreneurial drive is considered to have placed them also at the forefront of economic growth—twelfth-century predecessors of colonial frontiersmen. A further distinctive feature was the rapid expansion in the number of Cistercian houses. By 1215, the year of the Fourth Lateran council which endorsed the Cistercian institution of the annual chapter and enjoined its adoption by other non-affiliated religious communities who were urged to draw on the advice of local Cistercian abbots,[4] more than 500 Cistercian monasteries had come into existence, 34 of which were in Ireland.

The conventional portrayal of Cistercian growth has undergone radical re-evaluation, most recently and comprehensively in the work of Constance Berman.[5] Berman has sought to highlight that much of what historians have written about Cistercian origins has been derived from non-contemporary Cistercian in-house narrative accounts of their own history that have been too uncritically accepted. In the so-called primitive Cistercian narrative and legislative texts, it is necessary to distinguish between the rhetoric of foundation-myth and the reality. The *carta caritatis*, which may be described as the first constitution that laid down a legislative framework, conventionally dated to 1119, has been re-dated by Berman to after 1165. The implications of that re-dating are profound since in Berman's view the document emerges as a means of bringing under centralized administrative control, no earlier than the second half of the twelfth century, a large number of loosely affiliated houses that shared Cistercian customs. Only in the 1160s was a constitution first written, and only from the 1190s and later were devised the five filiations to which abbeys were tied as mother- and daughter-houses. In short, the 'invention' of a Cistercian order only appeared in the third quarter of the twelfth century. Once an institution, such as the annual chapter, became established, its component parts, notably affiliation and visitation, evolved quite quickly over the remainder of the twelfth century. There were, however, considerable differences between what it meant for an abbey to adopt Cistercian practices in the 1140s and what adopting those customs meant by the 1190s.

Another feature of the Cistercian foundation-myth is what Berman has termed its portrayal of apostolic gestation, whereby a mother-house sent out an abbot and a symbolic apostolic community of 12 monks to establish a new community in a site that was isolated and far from habitation. In Berman's view, the language of wilderness-sites in the Cistercian texts is more rhetorical than true and derived from motifs drawn from the Old Testament and sayings of the Desert Fathers. In the Burgundian region, the heartland of Cistercian origins—the area in which both Cîteaux and Clairvaux were situated—foundation by charismatic leaders of new communities *ab initio* may have been the norm. However, that idealized model of 'apostolic gestation' did not provide the invariable pattern for Cistercian expansion. A process of incorporation of independently formed reformist communities was just as important to Cistercian expansion, if not more so. Berman based her detailed case studies on houses in southern France in the first half of the twelfth century on a systematic analysis of charter evidence and there identified incorporation of pre-existing reformist houses and their properties as a key feature of Cistercian expansion. It is useful to try and test her conclusions against the admittedly very sparse evidence afforded by Irish royal charters in favour of Cistercian houses.

A feature that has supported descriptions of apostolic gestation has been the practice of tracing Cistercian expansion by five filiations, or families of monasteries. The manuscript evidence suggests that the Cistercians only began to create such filiation-trees from the 1180s onwards, once visitation had been prescribed by the general chapter. Organizational trees for visitation purposes were still in the process of revision in the early thirteenth century.[6] Moreover, filiation-trees required that multiple events in the foundation or incorporation of an individual house had to be condensed into a single date. For almost a century after the foundation of Cîteaux in 1098 there was no hierarchical control of those monastic communities that came to be formally affiliated to Cîteaux. Independently formed houses that in their early stages could be described as pre-Cistercian, or proto-Cistercian, only gradually began to coalesce into an order. It was only in the second half of the twelfth century that more genuinely Cistercian foundations were made by the sending out of colonies of monks to virgin sites. If Cistercian growth not only occurred by initiatives emanating from Burgundian houses, but also originated with local reformist groups that became attracted to Cîteaux and its practices, it is imperative to explain how such dispersed reformers came to learn of the Cistercians. In the case of Ireland, it is singularly fortunate to have Bernard's account of the reformer Malachy's two visits to Clairvaux in 1139 and 1148, and his desire to introduce continental monastic observances into Ireland; and the fact that Malachy died and was buried there in 1148 ensured a continuing Irish contact with Clairvaux in the immediate aftermath of his death. One question that naturally arises in an Irish context is whether there was a distinctively Burgundian, or more precisely Clarevallian flavour, to the Cistercian houses in Ireland. The first Irish Cistercian house, founded in 1142 at Mellifont with the help of monks from Clairvaux, as intimated by Bernard in his letters to Malachy and in his *Life of Malachy*, may give a misleading impression about the way in which other Irish Cistercian houses came to be founded.[7] Bernard's account conforms with the ideal of apostolic gestation, in that monks supplied by Malachy were trained at Clairvaux and their number augmented by others drawn from that house.[8] Bernard also uses familial language: he refers to Mellifont having five *filiae*, or daughter-houses, by the time that he was completing his *Life of Malachy*, probably around 1151 and certainly before his own death in 1153. Apart, however, from one house which he mentioned in passing in another context, he did not name the *filiae* nor offer any details about an institutional link between Clairvaux and the Irish houses.[9] On the evidence of the Irish royal charters, the pattern of new foundation, as exemplified at Mellifont, did not apply in all Irish cases. The Irish charters provide evidence for existing monastic communities adopting Cistercian customs, in other words for the phenomenon of pre-existing, or proto-Cistercian, communities and their subsequent incorporation. Of the six extant twelfth-century charters issued by Irish kings for communities that became affiliated to the Cistercian order, none provides unambiguous evidence for wilderness foundation, nor an active role taken by a mother-house.

Berman examined over 8000 charters relating to southern French houses dating from the 1130s to the 1250s and noted the near total absence of the term *ordo Cisterciensis* to describe religious houses in the first half of the twelfth century.[10] There were noticeably few usages before the 1140s. Furthermore, the earliest references to a Cistercian *ordo*, in Berman's view, signified a particular *ordo monasticus*, or form of the monastic life, rather than an institutional group. Only after about 1150 did *ordo* begin to acquire the new meaning of an institution characterized by administrative structures of visitation, legislation, and annual conventions of abbots.

Bernard's *Life of Malachy* makes an allusion to the *ordo Cisterciensis* when referring to a young man who according to everyone's report was leading a holy life among the brothers according to the *ordo Cisterciensis*:

> Apprehensumque manu sua tradidit abbati Congano nostro, et ille fratribus. Ipse vero iuvenis, adhuc, ni fallor, vivens primus conversus laicus Suriensis monasterii, testimonium habet ab omnibus quod sancte conversetur inter fratres *secundum ordinem Cisterciensis*.[11]

Bernard's usage here may be said to support Berman's interpretation that *ordo Cisterciensis* originally denoted a particular way of monastic life, or liturgical community, rather than an administrative structure. In a letter to Diarmait Mac Murchada, king of Leinster, that was probably occasioned by Diarmait's foundation of Baltinglass Abbey in 1148, Bernard wrote 'participem vos facimus in omnium bonorum quae in domo nostro et in omni ordine nostro fiunt et fient'.[12] This is more ambiguous in distinguishing between the *domus* of Clairvaux and 'all our order' which might plausibly be translated as 'our group', but the context of prayers for the welfare of Diarmait Mac Murchada again suggests an emphasis on *ordo* as a liturgical community.

It is in fact likely that it was the liturgical observances that Malachy had encountered at Clairvaux which he was most immediately concerned to introduce into Ireland. Such issues as the type of location in which abbeys should be founded, consistency about distances between agricultural units owned, and ownership of churches, tithes and mills would have been secondary. Analogy may be drawn with Malachy's known interest in the Augustinian abbey of Arrouaise in Flanders which he also visited. In 1179 Gualterus, abbot of Arrouaise, recorded that in the time of his predecessor, Abbot Gervasius (1121–47), Malachy had visited Arrouaise and had its *consuetudines* and *usus ecclesiae*, its *ordo* and its *divinum officium* copied and brought back to Ireland, where he persuaded a number of religious communities and clergy of *sedes episcopales* to adopt it.[13] That Malachy was interested primarily in liturgical practices is suggested by the fact that he viewed the customs of Arrouaise as particularly suited for cathedral-churches. In any case, it could be argued that at the time when Malachy met Bernard in the 1140s, the distinctively Cistercian contribution still related more to the internal reform of individual monastic communities and the creation of what Brian Stock has termed a 'textual community'.[14] The early Cistercian community was intent on reforming monastic practice by newly inspired reading of ancient texts from the Benedictine rule to the Song of Songs and a return to the spirituality of the Desert Fathers, and it was bound together by concepts of monastic love. Letters, treatises, sermons, and commentaries circulated ideas about monastic *caritas* and the behaviour of monks and abbots.[15]

Berman's emphasis on a more gradual growth of the Cistercian order and the incorporation of existing religious communities may help to explain certain features of the Irish charter evidence. The earliest extant charter-text in favour of an Irish Cistercian house was issued in 1157 by Muirchertach Mac Lochlainn, king of Cenél nEógain but styled king of Ireland, to the monastery of Newry. The Newry charter is precocious in an Irish context (and, if Berman is correct, also in a European context) in containing a reference to the Cistercian *ordo* ('condonavi et confirmavi in honore beatae Mariae et sancti Patricii et sancti Benedicti patris et fundatoris *ordinis Cisterciensis*, monachis Deo servientibus in Nyvorcyntracta').[16] The usage here, alongside the allusion to St Benedict as *pater et fundator* of the *ordo Cisterciensis*, suggests that the latter signified the particular way of life of the Newry monks. What was distinctive about the Cistercian *ordo* for the draftor of the Newry charter was the use of the Benedictine rule. The grantor, Muirchertach, believed in the efficacy of the liturgical observances of the monks of Newry. His charter expressed the aspiration that the monks would pray for the welfare of his soul and that he would be able to participate in all the good works, masses, [liturgical] hours, and prayers that would be offered in the monastery until the end of time ('ut particeps sim omnium bonorum, missarum et hororarum et orationum que in monasterio ipso fient et usque in consummationem seculi'), which may be interpreted as an articulation of the benefits of confraternity. *Ordo Cisterciensis* in this charter cannot therefore be unambiguously interpreted as signifying an institutional affiliation. It may be significant that the Newry charter identifies the monastery by its vernacular name Ibar Cinn Trácta, not *Viride lignum*, as it came to be recorded in the Cistercian filiation-tables.[17] Liturgical *ordines*, or order books, the *ecclesiastica officia* of the Cistercians, were developed earlier than the constitutional documents and they provided the most necessary supplements to the rule of Benedict for any twelfth-century reformist community wishing to adopt the practices associated with the monks of Cîteaux. The customs in the *ecclesiastica officia*, furthermore, could be adopted before any of the issues about formal relationships between houses need have arisen. In sum, a distinction between intra- and extra-mural arrangements needs to be kept in view.

A feature not only of the Newry charter but of all the extant Irish royal charters in favour of Cistercian houses is the dual dedication to the Virgin Mary and St Benedict. All Cistercian houses were dedicated to Mary, but a dedication that also included Benedict is more unusual. In England, in the period up to 1216, only four Cistercian houses had a patron saint additional to the Virgin, and in no case was it Benedict.[18] The dedication to St Benedict in the Irish charters suggests that what was initially perceived as distinctive about the Cistercian houses was their use of the Benedictine rule.

The earliest extant original charter of an Irish king is that of Diarmait Mac Murchada in favour of Abbot Felix and the *conventus* of Osraige, with a date-range 1162×1165.[19] This pre-dates by almost twenty years the filiation-date of 1184 recorded for the monastery in the Cistercian *tabulae* under its Latin designation, *Vallis Dei*.[20] That filiation-date conflicts not only with the evidence of Mac Murchada's charter but also with a privilege of Pope Lucius III issued on 15 February 1183 in favour of the 'monasterium sancte Marie Vallis Dei instituti Cisterciensium', although the chronological discrepancy in that instance is less marked.[21] From Mac Murchada's charter it may be inferred that a series of land-grants was offered to Abbot Felix and the *conventus* of Osraige for a prospective monastery ('ad monasterium...construendum'). *Conventus* may be presumed to refer to a religious community, whereas *monasterium* was intended to signify the actual church building, which, on the evidence of the charter, had yet to be constructed.[22] The identity of Abbot Felix and of the *conventus* of Osraige remain unknown. Osraige in the twelfth century could refer either to the kingdom of the Mac Gilla Pátraic kings, or to the newly constituted diocese of Osraige that was coterminous with Mac Gilla Pátraic's kingdom. The site of a specific monastery termed *Osraige*, however, is otherwise unattested. It serves to highlight what little can be recovered about the background to this foundation and the stages by which it may have become a Cistercian house. The charter illustrates, however, that it is necessary to bear in mind the distinction between dates when communities were formed, when such communities began to adopt Cistercian practices, when they affiliated with a Burgundian congregation, and when they were formally attached to filiation-trees. Each may have been a separate event in the evolution of Cistercian institutions. A further anomaly arises from the fact that in the Cistercian filiation-tables the mother-house of *Vallis Dei* is named as *Jeripons* and its foundation-date given as 1180, that is, 15 years later than the issue of Diarmait Mac Murchada's charter for Abbot Felix.[23] There is also evidence that, like Killenny, Jerpoint was in existence before its recorded filiation-date, since a charter issued by John, lord of Ireland and count of Mortain, c.1192 confirmed

> omnes donationes terrarum et tenementorum quas Hibernienses eis fecerunt rationabiliter ante primum adventum comitis Ricardi in Hiberniam et nominatim rationabilem donationem quam Dumvaldus rex Ossoriae eis fecit...sicut carta memorati Dunvaldi regis testatur et distinguit.[24]

This implies that Jerpoint was in existence 'before the first coming of Earl Richard into Ireland', that is before August 1170, and also that it was in receipt of a charter from Domnall Mac Gilla Pátraic, king of Osraige, who died in 1176,[25] that is, before its Cistercian filiation-date of 1180.

Diarmait Mac Murchada's charter to Abbot Felix may be said to afford evidence for incorporation as a feature of Cistercian expansion in Ireland. The name Cell Lainne suggests a pre-Cistercian phase. St Petrán of Cell Lainne is named in early genealogical collections.[26] The place-name list in the charter includes Ard Petráin 'the height of Petrán', two other *Cell* names, besides Cell Lainne, one *Dún* name, one *Ráith* name, one *Lis* name and five *baile* names, that is all place-name elements which indicate established settlements. These then were not *novalia*, lands that had to be reclaimed and brought into agricultural use.

The second extant twelfth-century original charter of an Irish king is that of Domnall Ua Briain, king of Thomond, in favour of the monastery of Holy Cross.[27] In its external characteristics, its shape and spacing, its elaborately elongated handwriting and its unusual scissors-type *et* abbreviation, it is very different from Diarmait Mac Murchada's charter to Abbot Felix of Osraige. The Holy Cross charter also suggests the incorporation of a pre-existing religious community, or at any rate of existing church-lands. Of the 11 place-names in the charter, one has a *cell* prefix and seven a *baile* prefix + personal name. The first place-name in the list, Celluactairlamudni, suggests an early church-site, although the name is unattested before its occurrence in the Holy Cross charter. A letter of protection from King Henry III in 1233 referred to the monastery *de sancta Cruce de Octerlan* indicating that Celluactairlamudni was the actual site of Holy Cross.[28] The dedication to the Holy Cross occurs alongside Mary and St Benedict, and *Sancta Crux* was the name by which the monastery was incorporated into the Cistercian filiation-tables under the year 1181.[29] That the place-names, which are listed without descriptors, reflect an earlier settlement pattern that had obtained prior to the assertion of Ua Briain dominance in the north Munster area by the twelfth century is most tellingly indicated by the paired place-names 'Baile Uí Chorcráin et Uí Conlígáin'. Conlígán son of Corcrán occurs in the genealogy of the Cenél Conaill, a segment of the Eóganacht Chaisil.[30] The names therefore suggest an association with the Eóganacht dynasty which had lost control of the area to the Uí Briain by the twelfth century. The place-name evidence, indicating long-established landed estates, conflicts with the Cistercian order's ideal of wilderness-sites and prescriptions against the acceptance of tenanted land. Although the Cistercians may have criticized the economic regimes of older monasticism and avowed their eschewal of tenanted lands, the Holy Cross charter reveals that they too were involved in the very practices that they denounced.

A charter of Domnall Ua Briain to Kilcooly Abbey survives in a fifteenth-century transcript and is more problematical in that it may have been rewritten or interpolated.[31] Since its witness list is missing, it cannot be dated more narrowly than by the regnal years of Domnall Ua Briain (1168–94). According to the Cistercian filiation-tables, Kilcooly was attached to the Cistercian order in 1184.[32] That Kilcooly had an earlier existence as a religious community is indicated by its *cell* name-form, by aerial photographs that reveal the existence of an earthwork to the east of the Cistercian remains,[33] and by the named beneficiary in the charter-text, Gregorius 'Olanan', who is variously styled *comarba* ('heir') of Colmán and *comarba* of Mag Airb. The title *comarba* of Colmán establishes a link with the early church of Daire Mór in the district of Mag Airb. The *Félire Oengusso*, a martyrology compiled c.800, commemorates Bishop Colmán of Daire Mór under 31 July.[34] A valuable piece of information about Daire Mór is contained in the (undated) life of Mo Chóemóc of Liath Mo Chóemóc (Liath Mór alias Leighmakevoge in tld Leigh, Co. Tipperary) which states that Colmán was in his monastery of Daire Mór, *nemus magnum*, 'the great wood', when he foretold the foundation of Liath Mo Chóemóc and its growth as a *civitas*. Abbot Mo Chóemóc visited Bishop Colmán at Daire Mór, who lamented to him that his own *locus*—situated as it was on the border with Munster and Leinster, and, in consequence, plagued by constant warfare—would often be deserted, so that sometimes there might not be even a single priest in residence. Mo Chóemóc thereupon promised that should such dereliction occur, he would ensure that Daire Mór would be served by a priest from his church.[35] The hagiographer further volunteered that not more than four miles separated these two churches. The sole reference in the annals to the church of Daire Mór occurs in 1014, when the death of Conaing mac Find, abbot of Daire Mór and of Liath Mo Chóemóc, is recorded,[36] confirming the hagiographical portrayal of a close link between the two churches. It might be expected from the allusion in the charter-text to the *comarba* of Colmán that the nucleus of the Cistercian house of Kilcooly comprised the church-site of Daire Mór, except that Daire Mór is not actually mentioned in the charter-text, while Gregorius is described locationally by the more unusual title of *comarba* of Mag Airb, that is as *comarba* of a district in north Munster rather than a named church. The reason is apparent from a charter of John, lord of Ireland and count of Mortain, c.1192–93, in favour of Matthaeus (Muirgius Ua hÉnna), archbishop of Cashel, confirming the possessions of the see of Cashel and in which are included the *villae* of Daire Mór and of Liath Mo Chóemóc.[37] It may be assumed that those two early church-sites had been allocated to the reform-constituted diocese of Cashel prior to the foundation of the Cistercian abbey of Kilcooly. Hence Gregory's distinctive geographical title of *comarba* of Mag Airb. The charter includes the Cistercian designation, *Arvus campus*, 'the ploughed plain', a play on the vernacular *Mag Airb*, 'the rough plain'.[38] Since the charter cannot be more narrowly dated than 1168×1194, it could post-date the recorded Cistercian filiation-date of 1184, but in any case it affords evidence for a pre-Cistercian religious community that was incorporated into the Cistercian order.

A charter of Diarmait Ua Dimmusaig, king of Uí Failge, offers another instance of incorporation.[39] The charter, dated 1177×1181 on the evidence of the witness list,[40] was issued in favour of the 'monks of Ros Glais'. According to the Cistercian *tabulae*, the monastery of *Rosea vallis* was affiliated to the Cistercian order on 22 October 1189, yet again indicating a discrepancy between the issue-date of the charter and the recorded filiation-date.[41] The charter-text also has the dual dedication to the Virgin Mary and St Benedict. It is likely that a monastic community at Ros Glais had opted for reformist monasticism under the Benedictine rule before it was formally affiliated to the Cistercian order. There was an early Irish church-site dedicated to St Éimíne at Ros Glais, 'the green copse'. From that vernacular place-name derived the Latin designation of the Cistercian house, *Rosea vallis*, 'the blooming valley', which is not used, however, in Diarmait Ua Dimmusaig's charter-text, suggesting that Cistercian filiation was not yet completed, while the founding saint, Éimíne, provided the later vernacular *Mainistir Éimin*, 'the monastery of Éimíne'. In 1199 the general chapter of the Cistercian order gave permission to *Rosea vallis* to celebrate the feast of St Éimíne, indicating a desire on the part of the Cistercian community to retain a link with its pre-Cistercian origins.[42] The continuance of the cult of Éimíne, within what by 1199 more legitimately can be termed a monastery of the Cistercian order, may have been important in retaining local patronage and protection from its Irish patrons.

Although there are no references to Ros Glais in the annals, evidence for the continuing cult of Éimíne in the twelfth century is furnished by the mention in 1177 of the *Bachall Éimíne*, 'staff of Éimíne', a relic listed among nine others as having been captured by John de Courcy at the siege of Downpatrick.[43] Liturgical and literary evidence is more extensive. The feast of Éimíne of Ros Glais is listed in Irish calendars under 22 December.[44] On the evidence of those with whom Éimíne is most frequently associated chronologically, he flourished in the seventh century. A series of texts depict Éimíne and his foundation at Ros Glais enjoying a close association with the kings of Leinster. A prose text in old Irish, *Cáin Éimíne Báin*, recounts how during a plague Bran Mut, king of Leinster (d. 693) and his retinue, sought counsel from Éimíne on whether they should enter the religious life. The saint proposed a death-pact, namely that he and 49 members of his community would offer their lives to God in place of the king and his associates, with Éimíne substituting for King Bran himself. In return, Éimíne's church was to be granted special privileges in perpetuity by the kings of Leinster including ecclesiastical immunity and royal protection.[45] The list of sureties to *Cáin Éimine* includes Dímmusach mac Congaile of the Uí Failge whom Diarmait Ua Dímmusaig, the grantor of the twelfth-century charter, would have claimed as a progenitor.[46] Éimíne further offered the king his bell as hereditary property, warning him that if he should ever give cause to have it struck against the saint, on that day his life would be cut short, he would not attain heaven, and none of his heirs would succeed as king. A versified elaboration of the prose narrative of *Cáin Éimíne Báin* is contained in a late middle Irish poem on the distribution of Éimíne's relics after his death. In the poem Éimíne's *mias* or paten is specifically associated with the Uí Failge.[47] The Cistercian monastery of Monasterevin therefore provides an instance not only of incorporation of a pre-existing monastic community but also of continuity of long-established patronage networks.

It remains to be seen whether Berman's reinterpretation of the origins and growth of the Cistercian order gains general acceptance since her supporting charter evidence is drawn primarily from southern France. From an Irish perspective, however, her work usefully draws attention to the possible meaning of *ordo Cisterciensis* as used in the 1150s in Bernard of Clairvaux's *Life of Malachy* and in the Newry charter of 1157. Differentiation of the stages by which a particular monastery was incorporated into the Cistercian order also helps to explain discrepancies between the issue-dates of the charters for Killenny and Monasterevin and their filiation-dates recorded in the Cistercian *tabulae*. On the evidence of the Irish charters, incorporation into the Cistercian order of pre-Cistercian communities was one means that enabled the order's expansion in Ireland.[48] Concomitantly, Cistercian houses were not all located in uncultivated wildernesses. The place-name evidence indicates the incorporation of lands that were already fully under agricultural use and probably tenanted. Diarmait Ua Dimmusaig's charter specified that Tachsartan and Achadadafernan were granted 'cum hominibus easdem terras pertinentibus'. There are references to mills in the Newry, Killenny, and Monasterevin charters, implying established arable cultivation. Cistercian land-reclamation activities may have made an impact in areas of 'new Europe' in the early thirteenth century, but in relation to land exploitation, Ireland, in this aspect at least, falls into the category of 'old Europe'.[49] Incorporated communities brought with them the advantages of accumulated economic wealth, as well as social ties to local families of benefactors and existing patronage ties, as evidenced in the case of Diarmait Ua Dímmusaig and the monastery of Monasterevin.

The Irish charters also highlight the supportive role of royal patronage and the reality of active engagement with lay patrons which is obscured by the Cistercian mythology of the spiritual desert. As indicated in Muirchertach Mac Lochlain's charter, he expected to enjoy an enduring patronal relationship with the monastery of Newry.

Identifying the incorporation of existing communities into the Cistercian order has more general implications for the interpretation of the church reform movement in Ireland. It alters the balance of reformist impulses to take greater account of local initiatives and responses. It places less emphasis on external stimuli and encourages a focus on indigenous currents of reform. It highlights the diversity of monastic practices out of which Cistercian houses may have developed and the slowness with which they may have coalesced into an order in Ireland. The introduction of Cistercian practices has been represented as a confrontation between externally generated reformist institutions and recalcitrant local customs, between Cistercian ideals and Irish divergences which have both suggested the limits of the reform movement in Ireland and highlighted the particularist tendencies in the Irish church. Roger Stalley has argued that 'in Ireland not many years elapsed before the abbeys assumed an Irish identity, as they were absorbed in the local cultural landscape. Ireland in fact presented particular problems to the order, which even the efficient organisation of the Cistercians found difficult to overcome.'[50] Perceived Irish aberration may result, however, at least in part from too early a presumption of articulation of a Cistercian administrative order. This may have implications too for the interpretation of the Mellifont *conspiratio* of 1227–28 during the general visitation of Abbot Stephen of Lexington.[51] That event may perhaps have been caused less by Irish degeneration from the ideals and norms of the Cistercian order, than by the fact that these had not been programmatically adopted in the first instance and that it was the attempt to impose them on houses that had been in existence for decades without experiencing the full weight of the corporate administration of the Cistercian order that occasioned the so-called conspiracy.

There are ramifications too for the architectural evidence relating to Irish Cistercian houses. A perception of architecturally nearly identical early Cistercian churches has contributed to a view of Cistercian institutional unanimity and order. Historians of monastic architecture have become more sensitive to the considerable diversity in detail even in houses often cited as being identical. Mellifont Abbey, for example, did not conform to the so-called Bernardine plan and was unusual in having apsidal chapels flanking a flat-ended chapel in each of its transepts, while Baltinglass—founded by Diarmait Mac Murchada and which, on the evidence of Bernard's letter to that king,[52] almost certainly had monks drawn from Clairvaux—was atypical in having two flat-ended transeptal chapels projecting separately from each other.[53]

It would be unwise to assign too prominent a role to the Cistercians in promoting the use of a particular form of the Latin charter in Ireland. Diarmait Mac Murchada's charter to Abbot Felix of Osraige, 1162×1165, which pre-dates by two decades the recorded filiation-date of *Vallis Dei* to the Cistercian order of 1184, cannot easily be classed as Cistercian beneficiary diplomatic since that house is best described as a pre-Cistercian, or proto-Cistercian, house at the time of issue of the charter. This raises issues about the relative importance of Cistercians in the furtherance of charter use in Ireland. While ecclesiastical beneficiaries undoubtedly played the major role in drafting Irish royal charters, there still remains the question of what models and external influences determined the choice of script and formulae. What was the relative importance of papal diplomatic, in the form of either letters sent to Ireland or documents which were issued by papal legates in Ireland, such as Cardinal John Paparo is known to have issued in 1152,[54] of contacts by correspondence with higher clergy in continental Europe or Britain, such as with the archbishops of Canterbury[55] and with Bernard of Clairvaux,[56] and of the documentary practices of other reformist houses with continental connections such as the Augustinian houses that adopted the customs of Arrouaise? Irish bishops also must have had a series of conscious choices to make in respect of script, formulae, and the iconography of their episcopal seals. Given the paucity both of originals and of transcripts, there can never be sufficient material to trace the relative importance of differing external influences, but it is well at least to be aware of the diverse range of contacts that may have been brought to bear on document production in twelfth-century Ireland. Certain it is that one should allow for influences to have come from a wide spectrum of sources. As the echoes of German imperial diplomatic in the charter of Diarmait Mac Carthaig for the church of St John the Evangelist in Cork demonstrate,[57] the range of continental contacts via Rome and the papacy, the *Schottenklöster*, Cîteaux, Clairvaux, and Arrouaise, not to mention the universities, where at least some Irishmen can be shown to have studied in the twelfth century,[58] must allow for an eclectic diplomatic that should not give preference to the Cistercian order. The closest parallel to the *elongata* script used in Domnall Ua Briain's extant original charter for Holy Cross is with papal documents.[59]

That administrative articulation of the Cistercian order in Ireland more properly belongs to the first half of the thirteenth century is graphically supported by four early thirteenth-century charters issued by Irish kings in favour of the mother-house of Cîteaux, two of which survive as originals.[60] Their most notable feature is the uniformity of their diplomatic which suggests that the initiative lay with Cîteaux for drafting a pro forma text that was nonetheless tailored to reflect local circumstances, as indicated by the uniquely comprehensive holding clause which reflected Irish succession practices.[61] The four charters, ranging in date between 1224 and 1254, record money donations to defray maintenance costs for abbots attending the annual chapter. The Cîteaux archives preserve records of similar donations from other rulers, notably King Richard (1189–99) whose valuable gift of the church of Scarborough was renewed by his successors, John, Henry III, and Edward I. Rents from the French royal demesne were granted by Louis VII (1131–80), Louis IX (1223–26), and other kings.[62] No later than 1219 King Alexander II of Scotland (1214–49) made an endowment that enabled an annual sum of 30 marks sterling to be remitted to Cîteaux via the abbot of Coupar Angus.[63] Rents on royal salt-works were granted by King Alfonso IX of León and confirmed by Ferdinand III of Castile in 1223; King Bela IV of Hungary c.1240 donated a number of royal chapels in Transylvania.[64] At the time of the general chapter a large number of abbots and their attendants would arrive at Cîteaux who had to be housed and fed and it was a heavy burden for the mother-house to supply all that was needed from its own resources. Abbots coming to the general chapter were therefore urged to bring alms with them to help defray expenses. From the early thirteenth century it was the policy of Cîteaux to try and secure regular financial support towards the cost of the general chapter by approaching kings in whose territory Cistercian monasteries were situated. A subvention for specifically the fourth day of the general chapter sought from Irish kings appears to have been determined by the fact that Richard I had donated the church of Scarborough to cover the maintenance costs for the first three days of all abbots attending the chapter. Alexander II of Scotland's grant was in support of the fourth day, so that the Irish kings clearly were approached to augment the grant of the Scottish king. The order of precedence of abbots in the witness lists of the four Irish charters reflects the ranking of houses according to foundation-dates in the Cistercian filiation-tables. These charters testify to the international administrative organization of the general chapter of the Cistercian order and its impact on Ireland by the early thirteenth century. In

Berman's view, however, historians, who have considered the general chapter to have been a legislative institution as early as the 1120s, have projected a later development back into the first half of the twelfth century. For much of the twelfth century a fully functioning Cistercian order may not yet have been elaborated and a time-lag in the transmission of administrative institutions to Irish houses may be expected to have occurred.

Historians have long since learnt to take with a pinch of salt twelfth-century Cistercian polemic in relation to criticism of the Cluniacs. Irish historians not surprisingly have also been wary of Bernard of Clairvaux's description in his *Life of Malachy* of the barbarities of the Irish church and of Irish society. Berman advocates a similarly critical approach to the core Cistercian texts, arguing that layers of accumulated interpretation need to be stripped back to highlight that the Cistercian order's invention was piecemeal and that more attention needs to be paid to its gradual evolution. She warns against facile descriptions of Cistercians as pioneers in wilderness-sites and her insistence on the fact that conventional descriptions of the growth and development of the Cistercian order obscure the importance of the Cistercian take-over of existing houses is borne out by the Irish charter evidence. Incorporation would serve to explain the discrepancies of date and the contradictions with assumed Cistercian practice that are apparent in the twelfth-century Latin charters issued by Irish kings in favour of monastic communities that ought perhaps more accurately to be described not as Cistercian foundations but as pre-existing reformist communities that were incorporated into the Cistercian order. The emphasis in the twelfth-century Irish charters is on the adoption of the Benedictine rule. While the role of the Cistercians in creating a new kind of religious order cannot be gainsaid, it is well to be reminded of the importance of not exaggerating the precocity of Cistercian institution-building.

Notes

1. Flanagan, 'Context and Uses', 113–32. The term 'European Latin charter' is used here to signify broadly the writ-charter, or charter in letter-form of the central Middle Ages. It is not intended to imply that so-called Celtic charters were also not derived from an earlier European tradition.
2. Adamska, 'From Memory to Written Record', 91; Hlaváček, 'Use of Charters', 138.
3. Cf. Wilson, 'Cistercians as "Missionaries of Gothic" '.
4. Tanner, *Decrees*, i, 240–1.
5. Berman, *Cistercian Evolution*. Berman is by no means the first scholar to suggest the gradual evolution of the Cistercian order or to examine in detail the

early Cistercian texts. The particular relevance of her work here, however, is her deployment of charter evidence.

6. Janauschek, *Origines*, pp. xiii–xiv.

7. *Vita Malachiae* in *Sancti Bernardi Opera*, iii, 339, 342 (where Malachy is described leaving some of his company at Clairvaux and in other places 'ad discendam conversationis formam'), 344–5; cf. Bernard's letter to Malachy, c.1141: 'vos autem interim . . . secundum habitudinem locorum quae vidistis apud nos, praevidete et praeparate eis locum a tumultibus saeculi separatum': *Epistola* 341 in *Sancti Bernardi Opera*, viii, 283.

8. 'Quanti sufficerent ad numerum abbatiae' in *Vita Malachiae*, 345, presumably refers to the apostolic number of twelve.

9. Presumably Suir (alias Inislounaght), 1147, Bective 1147, Baltinglass 1148, Monasteranenagh 1148, Boyle 1148. Elsewhere, Bernard mentioned one house by name in passing, that of Suir: See p. 124 [p. 7]. In a letter of confraternity to Malachy dating from 1145×1148, Bernard wrote that although the monks of Mellifont were not from Clairvaux he cherished them as members of a daughter-house of Clairvaux: 'licet enim de domo nostra specialiter nonexstiterint, tamen de filia domus nostrae non minus dilecti, quia omnes et longe et prope unum sumus in Christi': *Epistola* 545 in *Sancti Bernardi Opera*, viii, 513.

10. Berman, *Cistercian Evolution*, 68–79.

11. *Vita Malachiae*, 369. In a letter to Malachy c.1142 Bernard used *ordo* to refer to the house customs of the monastery of Mellifont: *Epistola* 357 in *Sancti Bernardi Opera*, viii, 302.

12. *Epistola* 546 in *Sancti Bernardi Opera*, viii, 514; Meerseman, 'Two Unknown Confraternity Letters', 173–8; Leclercq, 'Deux épîtres de St Bernard', 313–18. The phrase *in ordine nostro* was also used in his letter of confraternity to Malachy: *Epistola* 545 in *Sancti Bernardi Opera*, viii, 513.

13. 'Inspectis consuetudinibus nostris et approbatis, libros nostros et usus ecclesiae transcriptos suam in Hiberniam detulit, et fere omnes clericos in episcopalibus sedibus et in multiis aliis locis per Hiberniam constitutos, ordinem nostrum et habitum et maxime divinum in ecclesiae officium suscipere et observare praecepit': *PL*, ccxvii, col. 67; Dunning, 'Arroasian Order', 300, n. 1; Milis, *L'Ordre des chanoines réguliers*, i, 338–77.

14. Stock, *Implications of Literacy*, 403–54.

15. On the bonds of *caritas* between Bernard and Malachy see *Epistola* 357 in *Sancti Bernardi Opera*, viii, 301. On *caritas* as stronger than death see Bernard's letter of consolation to the *fratres* in Ireland following Malachy's death, *Epistola* 374, ibid., viii, 335. As highlighted by Newman, *Boundaries of Charity*, that bond was existentially as important as administrative conformity. On friendship networks also relevant is McGuire, *Friendship and Community*.

16. *Mon. Ang.*, vi, II, 1133; O'Conor (ed.), *Rerum Hibernicarum Scriptores*, i, II, p. clviii; *Chartularies of St Mary's, Dublin*, ii, pp. cv–cvii; text 5 in my forthcoming edition of *Irish Royal Charters* (where the authenticity of the charters is evaluated in detail). The inclusion of Patrick in the dedication suggests that Newry may have been founded on a church-site or lands associated with that saint, although there is no other evidence to support such a supposition.

17. The data relating to Irish houses in the Cistercian filiation-tables is conveniently tabulated in Mac Niocaill, *Manaigh Liatha*, 1–19.
18. Binns, *Dedications*, 159–60.
19. *Facsimiles of the National Manuscripts of Ireland*, ii, pl. lxii (1); Butler and Bernard, 'Charters of the Cistercian Abbey of Duiske', 5–8; Kissane, *Treasures from the National Library of Ireland*, 136; Howlett, *Sealed from Within*, 81–6; Kenney, *Sources*, no. 656; Lapidge and Sharpe, *Bibliogaphy*, no. 629; text 1 in the forthcoming edition of *Irish Royal Charters*. Its date-limits 1162×1165 are determined by the witnesses Lorcán Ua Tuathail (Laurentius), archbishop of Dublin, an office to which he was consecrated in 1162, and Paidín Ua hÁeda, whose death is recorded in 1165: *AU*, 1165.
20. Mac Niocaill, *Manaigh Liatha*, 4–7.
21. Sheehy, *Pontificia Hibernica*, i, no. 12.
22. This interpretation is supported by the usage in Diarmait Mac Murchada's charter to the Augustinian house of Ferns, where *conventus* is used alongside *domus* and where the former clearly refers to the community: *Mon. Ang.*, vi, II, 1141–42; text 4 in the forthcoming edition of *Irish Royal Charters*. At Cluny *monasterium* was used for the church building: Hunt, *Cluny under St Hugh*, 109. In the account of a prospective monastic foundation by Hervey de Montmorency in Ireland 'omnia nominavit que conferre et assignare disponebat monasterio construendo et conventui monachorum instituendo': Greenway and Watkiss (eds), *Book of the Foundation of Walden Monastery*, 48–9.
23. Mac Niocaill, *Manaigh Liatha*, 6.
24. *Calendar of Patent Rolls, 1358–61*, 488–9; *Mon. Ang.*, vi, II, 1131–2.
25. *ATig; AFM*.
26. Saint Petrán of Cell Lainne occurs among the Dál Messin Corb in the Leinster genealogies and in the genealogies of the saints of Ireland recorded separately within the genealogical corpus: *Book of Leinster*, vi, 1338: 39939, 1554: 47586, O'Brien, *Corpus Genealogiarum Hiberniae*, 41; *Book of Leinster*, ed. Atkinson, 385a52; Ó Riain, *Corpus Genealogiarum Sanctorum Hiberniae*, 30, §181.11. Petrán of Cell Lainne is also named in a litany of Irish saints compiled c.800: *Book of Leinster*, vi, 1699: 52192.
27. *Mon. Ang.*, vi, II, 1137; *Facsimiles of the National Manuscripts of Ireland*, ii, no. lxii (2); Hartry, *Triumphalia*, p. xlviii; text 6 in the forthcoming edition of *Irish Royal Charters*.
28. *Calendar of Documents Relating to Ireland, 1171–1252*, nos 2062, 2063.
29. Mac Niocaill, *Manaigh Liatha*, 6.
30. O'Brien, *Corpus Genealogiarum Hiberniae*, 218. Conlígán's son, Lorcán, became king of Cashel in 922: *AFM*, 920=922; Moody, Martin, Byrne (eds), *New History of Ireland*, ix, 204.
31. *Calendar of Ormond Deeds*, i, no. 4; text 8 in the forthcoming edition of *Irish Royal Charters*.
32. Mac Niocaill, *Manaigh Liatha*, 12.
33. Norman and St Joseph, *Early Development of Irish Society*, pl. 62, 110; Stalley, *Cistercian Monasteries*, pl. 23.
34. *Félire Oengusso*, 165, 173, n. 31; cf. Hogan, *Onomasticon*, 512.
35. *Vitae Sanctorum Hiberniae*, ed. Plummer, ii, 170–1.

36. *AFM.*
37. Nicholls, 'Charter of John, Lord of Ireland', 267–76.
38. Possibly, this is a later addition, as it is the only twelfth-century Irish royal charter to include a Cistercian designation.
39. *Mon. Ang.*, vi, II, 1134; text 11 in the forthcoming edition of *Irish Royal Charters.*
40. As indicated by the attestations of Nehemias, bishop of Kildare, who was consecrated in 1177, and Donatus, bishop of Leighlin (assuming that the latter may be identified with Dúngal Ua Cáellaide, bishop of Leighlin), who died in 1181: Moody, Martin, Byrne (eds), *New History of Ireland*, ix, 314–15.
41. Mac Niocaill, *Manaigh Liatha*, 12.
42. Canivez, *Statuta*, i, 247 (1199: 77).
43. *Miscellaneous Irish Annals*, 1178.1. Éimíne's *bachall* is mentioned in a middle Irish poem on his relics: Poppe, 'Middle Irish Poem on Éimíne's Bell', 64–5.
44. *Félire Oengusso*, 253, 260–1; *Martyrology of Tallaght*, 68, 88, 126; *Félire hÚi Gormáin*, 244, *Martyrology of Donegal*, 344–5.
45. Poppe, 'New Edition of *Cáin Éimíne Báin*', 35–52. See also p. 109.
46. Poppe, 'List of Sureties', 591.
47. Poppe, 'Middle Irish Poem on Éimíne's Bell', 63–6.
48. A long-acknowledged incorporation into the Cistercian order is that of the Savigniac house of St Mary's Abbey, Dublin, traditionally dated to 1147, the foundation-date recorded for that house in the Cistercian filiation-tables. Berman argues, however, that there is no contemporary evidence for what later became described as a general chapter at Cîteaux in 1147 at which a formal incorporation of Savigniac houses was agreed. In her view this is another instance of 'Cistercian mythology', and the incorporation of Savigny occurred at least a decade later and probably not before 1165: Berman, *Cistercian Evolution*, 143–7.
49. The statement in relation to Cistercian foundations that 'with its extensive tracts of waste and forest, Ireland provided plenty of scope for land clearance and new agrarian techniques' requires qualification: Stalley, *Cistercian Monasteries*, 13.
50. Ibid., 7.
51. See Watt, *Church in Ireland*, 52–9.
52. Berman, *Cistercian Evolution*, 68–79.
53. Stalley, *Cistercian Monasteries*, 56–8; O'Keeffe, *Medieval Ireland*, 138; *Romanesque Ireland*, 105–12.
54. *Calendar of Archbishop Alen's Register*, 185.
55. Details in Lapidge and Sharpe, *Bibliography*, nos 617–26.
56. *Epistolae* 341, 356–7, 374, 545–6 in *Sancti Bernardi Opera*, viii, 282–3, 300–2, 335–7, 512–14.
57. Flanagan, 'Context and Uses', 121–2.
58. Hughes, *Early Christian Ireland*, 277–8; Dutton, 'Uncovering of the *glosae super Platonem*', 206–7.
59. I am very grateful to Professor Dr Rudolf Schieffer, president of the *Monumenta Germaniae Historica*, and to Professor Jane Sayers, University College, London, for a considered opinion on the hand of this charter.
60. Arbois de Jubainville, 'Chartes données en Irlande', 81–6; Orpen, 'Some Irish Cistercian Documents', 303–13; texts 12–15 in the forthcoming *Irish Royal Charters.*

61. The donors oblige their heirs 'sive sint filii, cognati, consanginei, proprinqui, sive extranei' to observe the terms of their grant.
62. Dijon, Archives départementales de la Côte d'Or. MS 11 H. 23.
63. Wilson and Lawrie, 'Charter of the Abbot and Convent of Cupar, 1220', 174–5.
64. Dijon, Archives départementales de la Côte d'Or. MS 11 H. 27; brief notices of these grants in Mahn, *L'Ordre cistercien*, 175–6; *Tax Book of the Cistercian Order*, 22–3.

8

Laudabiliter: Text and Context

Michael Haren

For more than a generation, Maurice Sheehy's argument in favour of the authenticity of Adrian IV's letter, *Laudabiliter*,[1] sanctioning Henry II's proposed invasion of Ireland, has served as the main point of reference in Irish historiography on the subject.[2] Sheehy's analysis has been generally successful, if not in utterly allaying the misgivings of historians on the central issue of authenticity, at least in converting energies into an engagement with the significance of *Laudabiliter* considered as a genuine papal response to a royal overture. In important respects, Sheehy's article left diplomatic discussion of the document in as advanced a condition as is possible in dealing with a copy. His general conclusion from study of the formulae of the text was that it contained nothing incongruent with chancery style so as to warrant its rejection on internal grounds. On the other technical criterion, he demonstrated its competent deployment of the cursus, the rythmical prose constructions, at least in final periods, which is a feature of contemporary papal chancery usage and whose non-observance would be deterrent. As regards engagement with the historical context, Sheehy, following in this and on some other points the analysis of J. F. O'Doherty,[3] noted the close association of John of Salisbury (whose account of his part in the issue of a papal letter to Henry II is a crucial piece of evidence in all discussion of *Laudabiliter*) and Archbishop Theobald of Canterbury. Although Sheehy's elaboration of this association was incidental, he may nonetheless be regarded as having lent his authority in pointing the way to what has become the dominant historiographical presentation, that which regards *Laudabiliter* as prompted by Canterbury concern with the issue of its diminished jurisdiction in the aftermath of the establishment of Dublin as a metropolitan see. That case was subsequently stated, with characteristic verve and erudition, by Denis Bethell, in an article that has been hardly less influential for the interpretation of the context of *Laudabiliter* than Sheehy's has been for the formerly vexed question of authenticity. This review focuses on the state of the question under both heads: the solution that Sheehy proposed to the problem of authenticity and the understanding of *Laudabiliter* as a product of Canterbury metropolitan concerns. Although the evidence and arguments concerning authenticity and context are to some extent interrelated, it will be convenient to approach the issues separately. Apart from accepting—in so far as I find it acceptable—the work already done on the technical, diplomatic and legal level, and except in so far as diverted by the need to address specific points of the debate or where conscious of particular indebtedness, I shall focus narrowly on the primary evidence. *Laudabiliter* is so encrusted by historiography that it threatens to burst the confines of a scholarly article. Worse: it is haunted by spirits defiant of exorcism.[4] Pragmatism dictates restriction.

The authenticity of *Laudabiliter*

I referred to the question of the authenticity of *Laudabiliter* as 'formerly vexed'. On the whole, historians after Sheehy—who have been mainly concerned with *Laudabiliter* in Irish context—have been content implicitly to accept *Laudabiliter* as genuine[5] or to express any reservations that they felt on the subject in formally neutral terms (though the issue is so vital and has been so trenchantly examined that 'neutrality' is itself engagement, a position, willy-nilly, as regards the state of the question).[6] In the face of what is at boldest hesitation among Irish historians in demurring from a document that an earlier generation had indicted so confidently, Ian Robinson, writing in continental context, has been relatively forthright.[7] His suspicions of *Laudabiliter* may be summarized as based on the following considerations: that it is accompanied in Gerald of Wales's account by 'a forged letter of Alexander III'[8] (*Quoniam ea*, to be discussed later); that three authentic letters of Alexander III, issued in 1172, following Henry II's invasion, fail to mention *Laudabiliter*; that the *Liber Censuum*'s list of papal financial rights in 1192 fails to record Peter's Pence, an obligation specified by *Laudabiliter*; and arising from the correspondence—long remarked on—between the text of *Laudabiliter* (more fully, in present context, 'Laudabiliter et satis fructuose' or 'Laudabiliter satis et fructuose'),[9] and a letter with the incipit 'Satis laudabiliter et fructuose'[10] issued by Adrian IV over a Spanish crusade contemplated by Louis VII of France and Henry II of England in 1159.[11] To these arguments, Robinson annexed a reference to the diplomatic criticisms of P. Scheffer-Boichorst as not having been taken into account by Sheehy, or by J. A. Watt and W. L. Warren, in their respective considerations of *Laudabiliter*.[12]

In defence of Sheehy's circumspection in reaching his conclusion as to authenticity, a position endorsed by Watt and Warren,[13] it should be observed that Sheehy had in fact noted both Scheffer-Boichorst's contribution[14] and the substantially similar contribution of Scheffer-Boichorst's pupil, O. J. Thatcher,[15] but dismissed their interpretation as not 'particularly convincing',[16] a judgement which may be faulted only for its mildness. Scheffer-Boichorst's approach had already, by the time of Sheehy's study, long since been subjected to judicious examination by A. Eggers.[17] Sheehy, who evidently knew Eggers's work,[18] may well have been influenced by her in formulating his judgement.[19] Her important elaboration of the marked outward distinction between a privilege and a letter[20] anticipated the diplomatic basis of Sheehy's own resolution of the strands of evidence. Eggers's command of the diplomatic argument was indeed generally expert[21] and her application of it was sensitive. As regards Scheffer-Boichorst's concern over the deficiency in the text of *Laudabiliter*, as then known, of the name of the addressee, Eggers was disposed to regard the omission as confirmation of authenticity, since the name might, by curial style, have occurred only as an initial letter, or have been represented by the *gemipunctus*—though it must be said that the latter device would be unexpected in a letter cast in terms so personal as *Laudabiliter*. In this respect, a notable feature of the version of *Laudabiliter* printed for the first time below is that it does contain the addressee's name, written in full in the National Archives (PRO) manuscript (*P*), abbreviated at the first syllable in the Trinity College, Dublin manuscript (*L*). However, Eggers's main departure from Scheffer-Boichorst concerned his elaborate hypothesis that *Laudabiliter* and the purported letter of Alexander III, *Quoniam ea*, were products of rhetorical exercises in the schoolroom and that *Laudabiliter* was modelled on the letter 'Satis laudabiliter et fructuose' to Louis VII. Scheffer-Boichorst had worked towards this hypothesis from his criticisms of what he considered a certain poverty of wording reflected in the repetitions contained in *Laudabiliter*[22]—what Thatcher refers to as 'its general haziness and indefiniteness'.[23] The latter revealed, in Thatcher's judgement, 'the untrained and uncertain hand of a student who is master neither of his materials nor of the proper literary forms'.[24]

It must be accepted that the drafting of *Laudabiliter* is by no means perfect: Eggers, in addition, drew attention to the unexplained use of the subjunctive, 'soleant' (a reading confirmed by *P* and *L*), in the clause, 'eo quod ad bonum exitum semper et finem soleant attingere, quae de ardore fidei et religionis amore principium acceperunt', where the indicative would be expected.[25] However, to allow minor and mainly subjective criticisms of style to outweigh the considerations in favour of taking *Laudabiliter* to be genuine is disproportionate.

As regards the relationship between *Laudabiliter* and 'Satis laudabiliter et fructuose', there is indisputably a dependence.[26] In the Scheffer-Boichorst analysis, as already noted, the letter to Louis VII has been used as the model for the rhetorical exercise which according to him (and Thatcher) resulted in *Laudabiliter*. The Scheffer-Boichorst analysis requires, therefore, that at some juncture between the issue of 'Satis laudabiliter et fructuose' to Louis VII and Gerald of Wales's *Expugnatio*—rather between the actual invasion and the writing of *Expugnatio*, if *Quoniam ea* is to be explained as the counterpart of the same rhetorical exercise, though by a second participant[27]—an unknown student of rhetoric with access to the text of the letter to Louis[28] constructed a piece which Gerald of Wales then obtained as answering to what John of Salisbury had secured in response to Henry II's suit. Evidently finding the conjecture rather too imaginative,[29] Eggers ventured the alternative that Adrian IV's chancery used an earlier letter written to Henry II as the basis of that which it issued to Louis VII.[30]

The silence of the *Liber Censuum* regarding Peter's Pence and the silence of Alexander III's letters, as regards in one case the effect of *Laudabiliter* and in the other its being a point of diplomatic reference, may equally be attributable to another factor: as has been particularly well observed by Robin Frame,[31] Henry II's eventual entry into Ireland was conducted in quite a different spirit and in quite different circumstances from what was envisaged in 1155 or by *Laudabiliter*. Gerald of Wales's account suggests that *Laudabiliter* was deemed eventually to have presentational advantages from Henry's viewpoint but to see it as more than peripheral in context of the actual invasion would be going beyond the evidence. If that is true of Henry's perspective, there are no grounds whatever for thinking that papal policy in the aftermath of the invasion was to insist on *Laudabiliter* as the king's charter of right.

This leaves to be considered, of Robinson's points, the question of *Quoniam ea*, the purported letter of Alexander III confirming *Laudabiliter*, of which Gerald of Wales provides the text together with *Laudabiliter* itself, and which he says was read out at Waterford by William fitz Audelin and Nicholas, prior of Wallingford (in 1173).[32] The only aspect of this letter which is central to my present argument is whether, if it were an actual forgery, it would so contaminate *Laudabiliter* as to counter all the other considerations for accepting the latter. Scheffer-Boichorst was, indeed, forthright on the point. In dismissing *Quoniam ea*, he dismissed also the object of the confirmation.[33] But the issues are separate.[34] Sheehy's point is sound that, in essence, not only can they both not be attributed to Gerald of Wales (or indeed anyone else) but the evidence of circumspection in the textual tradition of Gerald of Wales's works on the subject of *Quoniam ea* encourages reliance in the case of *Laudabiliter*.[35] There is otherwise so large a problem—to which the address can only be speculative—with *Quoniam ea*, that further consideration of it must be deferred until after discussion of the genesis of *Laudabiliter*.

The distinction and authority of Robinson's scholarship on the early medieval papacy would have compelled a re-examination of the question of *Laudabiliter*'s status even if there were no other prompting to embark on it. A re-examination specifically of Sheehy's main conclusion is, however, warranted on quite other grounds than those given by Robinson and from quite a different perspective, that of maintaining the authenticity of *Laudabiliter*.

No one did more in the Irish context than Sheehy, in the course of a long professional commitment, to signal the importance of and contribute to a discipline which as late as 1962 still had an aura of exoticism, a quality captured even by the author's use of the French term *diplomatique* in the title of his article. Nevertheless, his resolution of the problem that he identified cannot be said to have been—to employ the continental disciplinary concept—'scientifically' a happy one. Once the question whether *Laudabiliter* could diplomatically be considered genuine was resolved, the interpreter faced a perplexity— identified by O'Doherty as 'the most serious difficulty which defenders of the *Laudabiliter* have to face'.[36] This was the testimony of John of Salisbury, in an autobiographical passage of the *Metalogicon*.[37] It is so central to the argument over *Laudabiliter* that it is worth quoting in full. Speaking of Adrian IV and recalling the intimacy of their relationship, John of Salisbury continues:

> At my prayers, he granted and gave Ireland to the illustrious king of the English, Henry II, to be possessed in [*or possibly* by] hereditary right, as his letters [*the Latin term may indicate one letter*] witness to the present day. For all islands by ancient law from the donation of Constantine, who founded and endowed the Roman church, are said to belong to it. A golden ring also he sent through me [*apparently, that is, committing it to John*], garnished with a splendid emerald, so

that by it there should [*or* might] be investiture of the right in ruling Ireland, and the same ring still has been ordered to be kept in the public treasury.[38]

On the one hand, the *Metalogicon* establishes a parameter: that Adrian acted in response to a suit and that, as well as a symbol, there was documentation in consequence. The reference to the Roman church's status as regards islands[39] strongly evokes, or at least is recognizably in keeping with the content of, *Laudabiliter*. The reference to possession in or by 'hereditary right', however, is wholly absent from the latter. Sheehy inferred that there had been two documents. Having already[40] set out, perfectly correctly, the contemporary distinction between a solemn papal privilege and a papal letter, he applied it to *Laudabiliter*:

> Giraldus does not appear to have appreciated that what he transcribed from the Winchester archives was in fact a simple letter and not the more solemn grant to which John of Salisbury refers. When, then, was *Laudabiliter* issued? It was probably issued at the same time as, and along with, the solemn privilege. To accompany a privilege with a letter of exhortation, such as *Laudabiliter*, was normal procedure. Pope Innocent III a little later issued a letter of exhortation to accompany a privilege for king John and his heirs. This privilege confirmed John in the kingdoms of England and Ireland as fiefs of the Roman see—and the accompanying letter stressed the obligations and duties of the king which resulted from the *beneficium* granted in the privilege. Even a cursory comparison between *Laudabiliter* and the letter issued to king John in 1213 reveals that both are of the same type, dealing with the duties and responsibilities which must go with the gift or rights specified in a papal *privilegium*. No major difficulty therefore arises because John of Salisbury's description of the privilege which he obtained from Adrian IV does not tally with the text of *Laudabiliter*. Giraldus probably transcribed the wrong document.[41]

On balance, my own judgement is that *Laudabiliter* is indeed not a privilege. I do, however, bear in mind that applying the distinction between the simplified form of the privilege as it developed in the course of the twelfth century and the letter, on the basis of a copy which lacks the important criterion offered by the solemnity of the dating clause, is not wholly without risk.[42] To this complication, the text as preserved by *L* makes an inscrutable addition. Its enigmatic termination, 'Valete', is not characteristic of the simplified form of privilege. It echoes rather the 'Bene Valete' of the solemn privilege from which *Laudabiliter* may safely be differentiated on every internal aspect of its form. The 'Valete' is a puzzling feature of *L* diplomatically. It is critically weakened by its absence from *P* which agrees with the tradition derived through Gerald of Wales. On the current evidence, it is to be judged in all probability a misplaced scribal addition. With Sheehy's subsidiary argument that a privilege might be accompanied by a 'covering' letter, I have no cause to quarrel. For my misgiving in respect of the whole, I have quoted Sheehy's crucial passage in full as well as the source on which it relies, so that the reader may judge how far here one is privileged—if one might so say—to witness the process of creation *de nihilo*, that powerful transition between concept and instantiation so guarded by medieval theologians. John of Salisbury speaks simply of 'litterae' that contain or constitute a grant. It is Gerald of Wales who uses the term *privilege*, both in the *Expugnatio*[43] and in his letter to King John dedicating a new edition of the work.[44] There, referring to what was obtained by Henry II and preserved at Winchester, he gives an admirably precise description of *Laudabiliter* as regards its effect to the king and an only marginally inflated version of its import in ecclesiastical terms.[45] In respect of his original references, one may fairly assess his diplomatic nicety from the fact that his use of 'privilege' is extended to cover not only *Laudabiliter* but *Quoniam ea*, which, whatever it is, is by a consensus with which I fully accord not a product of the papal chancery at all.[46] For such errors as he made on this score Gerald may have had more excuse than is generally allowed, but it is clear that—whatever about the scrupulosity of John of Salisbury's use of 'litterae'—he, at least, was not writing with diplomatists in mind. As for Sheehy's hypothesis, it disturbs not only in the degree of its progressive detachment from the evidence but in the lack of economy by which the deficiency of one original is remedied by the postulation of another, the second lost original not even known in copy nor ever referred to unless as needlessly extrapolated from the *Metalogicon* passage quoted above.

The simplest supposition, to explain the discrepancy between John of Salisbury's account of what Adrian issued and the only document that historians have ever had with a claim to correspond to it, is essentially, as advanced long ago by Kate Norgate,[47] that John construed somewhat amply. Norgate put it as follows: 'John of Salisbury was simply reasoning from analogy when he assumed that Henry's projected lordship over Ireland, if it ever took practical shape at all, would be such as he too might transmit to his descendants to "hold by hereditary right".'[48] To this, one would now have to add the insights derived from Walter Ullmann's elaboration of his contention that John of Salisbury's use of the term *ius hereditarium* referred to an already established right of inheritance: the nuance is quite different from, though not incompatible with, that of Norgate but the fundamental supposition is the same, the economical supposition that John of Salisbury's statement was 'in the nature of a comment or explanatory remark'.[49]

Methodologically, this is in the abstract manifestly preferable to the multiplication of essences. There is, however, an objection. Lodged by O'Doherty, it was probably what constrained Sheehy towards embarking on the extravagant resolution that he preferred. O'Doherty observed of the suggestion made by Norgate—whose work he evidently and rightly esteemed—that her hypothesis was incredible, on the grounds that such reasoning from analogy would have been no longer topical when John wrote, some four years after the circumstances depicted, well after the abandonment of the project to which the 'grant' related and long before there was any new thought of an incursion into Ireland.[50] O'Doherty then made his own suggestion: John's reference was, so to speak, a 'Freudian slip'; what had been in Henry's mind all along was a military conquest; he had been looking for a pretext; John, though sent out to the papal curia nominally in the interests of religion and the church (the focus of *Laudabiliter*), was well aware of the ulterior motive and here betrayed it.

Effectively, O'Doherty's was another, more subtle, version of the hypothesis that John's remarks were explanatory. It is not incompatible with either of its counterparts. In fact, however, the force of O'Doherty's objection against conscious apologetic has been decisively reduced in the interval since he wrote. By close examination of John of Salisbury's correspondence, Giles Constable lucidly established that a period during which John was out of favour with Henry II, indeed had fallen into severe disgrace, should be dated to have begun in the immediate aftermath, 1156, of his return from his sojourn at the papal court at Benevento, during which *Laudabiliter* (or, to keep the two formally distinguished, the document to which the reminiscence in the *Metalogicon* alludes) would have been issued. The correspondence makes clear that the accusations levelled against him were a complex of *lèse majesté* and identification with ecclesiastical interests generally and those of the Roman church in particular ('Quod quis nomen Romanum apud nos invocat, michi imponunt'/'If any one among us invokes the name of Rome, they say it is my doing').[51] Paradoxically, John felt that it all came from his having put too much effort into furthering Henry's affairs and kingly prestige.[52] He had discovered, like Pooh Bear, the risks inherent in trying to be kind to bees.

Constable's interpretation of these references is untendentious and convincing. His conclusion that at least an ingredient in the royal displeasure was the 'clear victory for Adrian'[53] which had emerged from the royal embassy[54] to the papal curia has been too little heeded by those interested in the Irish dimension. Whether John of Salisbury was formally part of the mission to Benevento is unclear, but he was reported on adversely by its most influential member, Arnulf of Lisieux.[55] 'In sending an embassy to discuss the conquest of Ireland with the pope', Constable fairly surmises, 'Henry may have hoped for the declaration of a crusade, such as his great-grandfather had secured, or simply for the pope's blessing and permission to rule Ireland, which Alexander III later granted. Surely he had not looked for the assertion of a theory that threatened the dignity of his own throne.'[56] What that dignity might imply as regards specifically the status of islands is suggested by the Worcester *Altitonantis*, where jurisdiction also over the lesser islands of the British archipelago comes to Edgar directly from God.[57] Whatever about the antiquity of such a notion,[58] it was topical and *Laudabiliter* cut right across it.

Though the old heat has died, there is still a tendency among Irish historians to introduce Adrian IV in context as English. Unexpanded, the information is more apt to mislead than enlighten.[59] Adrian IV was a churchman—and a tough operator at that.[60] He was more than capable of extracting advantage out of his dealing with Henry's envoys: the evidence of *Laudabiliter* is that Adrian did. Even the issuing of a letter at all may have been more than was looked for, as Constable shrewdly allows. William the Conqueror had had ring and standard.[61] Henry got ring and letter—and a ringing letter too. Had the idea been John of Salisbury's egg-headed contribution to the proceedings? He as much as says that it was; and it would have been the more resented if it came from the sidelines. At all events, on Constable's reading, the episode would not have been as remote in John's mind in 1159 as O'Doherty supposed. Rather than mere reminiscence, the passage in the *Metalogicon* may have been forthrightly propagandist, in public as well as in personal terms, in so far as the two need be distinguished. Spin-doctoring is one of the more ancient professions and very well medieval clerks did out of it. Once Adrian's letter had been issued it could not be unwritten: the king (after initial vexation had passed) could only make the best of it by concentrating on what was left inexplicit and the exegetical opportunities that it opened. It is by no means axiomatic that, as maintained by O'Doherty, 'the project of 1155 was not merely postponed, but abandoned',[62] to such effect that preoccupation with the minutiae of it should be thought anachronistic. Medieval civilization is characterized (in a phrase of W. A. Pantin) by zealotry for legal right—fixation with which was part of the dignity as well as of the selfish or, as often, corporate interest of popes, kings, bishops, abbots, and magnates. Possession of it was like the pin in the cliff-face to a rock-climber—a position to be given up only for one higher or more secure. If Henry felt, as in Ullmann's analysis,[63] that he possessed 'hereditary right' as regards Ireland that, to draw on John of Salisbury's suggestive protest, this too was embraced by 'patrum solium' ('the throne of his fathers')[64]—then it is entirely likely that there was a determination in royal circles that *Laudabiliter*, which at least was gratefully silent on the point, should be read as compatible with Henry's claims. John of Salisbury's reminiscence would be a proper deference to that sensitivity. It should not surprise in context that both John's letters during the period of crisis and the battery of accusations publicly flung at him might fall short of identifying explicitly the real nub of contention. Certainly, it is here rather than in the *Metalogicon* that 'verbal economy' might be detected on John's part.[65]

There is indeed a basis for thinking that the original project to invade Ireland was conceived as an assertion of pre-existing lordship. That this was so would explain Henry's early concern with it, which has sometimes been thought unlikely. The evidence most readily falls under what I would loosely call the genesis of *Laudabiliter*: loosely in that the genesis and issues arising in the immediate aftermath of entry into Ireland are not capable of being maintained as altogether discrete.

The understanding of the genesis of *Laudabiliter*

The interpretation of *Laudabiliter* as originating in 'the claims of Canterbury to primatial jurisdiction over the Irish Church, claims which had recently received a serious set-back by the action of the Synod of Kells in 1152', suggested by O'Doherty[66] and patronized by Sheehy, has generally commended itself. Of the foremost contributors to Irish ecclesiastical history more widely and to *Laudabiliter* in particular, only Watt has maintained a position of frank scepticism.[67] The Canterbury connection was dazzlingly canvassed by Bethell.[68] Since then, M. T. Flanagan, while respectful of the sceptical stance of Watt and not without some note of reservation herself,[69] has set the hypothesis of Canterbury interest within a carefully documented and judicious account of the metropolitan question viewed from the Canterbury perspective in the immediately preceding period. The conclusion is clear: the hypothesis could be accommodated within what can be reconstructed of how the Canterbury interest might be conceived. If that question may be regarded as settled, another, more fundamental, remains: how far is the Canterbury hypothesis prompted by or even compatible with the evidence?

The Canterbury hypothesis arose out of John of Salisbury's rôle in the matter. As regards the insinuation loosely derived from John of Salisbury's own Canterbury connections,[70] there is no sign in his self-justification that duty specifically to the church of Canterbury was a point of reference by which he might be excused for whatever his gaffe was.[71] Beyond that insinuation, the evidence for the hypothesis consists of scraps from the chroniclers. First, the more remote and less concrete: a comment in the Winchester Annals on the death of Cardinal John Paparo in 1156. Bethell characterized it, with relish, as 'sulphurous' and it is literally so: 'This year died the Cardinal John. When he was dead, sailors heard a voice under Mount Etna saying "Stoke up the fire".'[72] Paparo was the papal legate who presided over the Synod of Kells in 1152 at which the ecclesiastical provinces of Ireland were constituted in enduring form. As already observed, the major departure in present context was the establishment of Dublin as a metropolitan see. The deduction is that Paparo's activity in Ireland had engendered a lingering resentment in English ecclesiastical circles. The chronicler, Robert of Torigny, specifically noted that what had been done in Ireland under Paparo's legation (though by authority of Pope Eugenius) was a breach of 'the custom of the ancients and the dignity of the church of Canterbury'.[73] If the level of indignation manifest in the Winchester Annal is only by inference evidence of a Canterbury engagement, it may probably be taken as reflecting a general perception among English Benedictines. Whatever their concern for the jurisdictional dimension, they are likely to have associated Paparo's mission in Ireland with the growing influence of their Cistercian rivals.[74] That resentment of some sort was current[75] might just continue to give a slant to a second and more substantive passage—if the content of that passage were indeed what it has been taken to be.

The second piece of information on which the 'Canterbury hypothesis' has relied is directly relevant to understanding the circumstances in which *Laudabiliter* would have been sought out. Supplied by the monk who continued the chronicle of Sigebert of Gembloux at Afflighem in Flanders, it says both more and less than it has been thought to say as bearing on the 'Canterbury hypothesis'. In the context of a campaign embarked on by Henry II, as the anonymous continuator explains, to secure the patrimony of Eleanor of Aquitaine, we are told that the army deployed was that which had been intended for use in Ireland: Henry 'converted against the king of the French the numerous army and great apparatus of war which he had proposed to lead into Ireland, that he might subdue it to his lordship, and, by counsel of bishops and of religious men, constitute his brother king of that island'.[76]

We have other testimony to the deliberations behind this abortive proposal for an Irish expedition. Robert of Torigny states that 'a royal council was held at Winchester in 1155 about the feast of St Michael' (29 September: the campaign would presumably therefore have been contemplated for the following year) when the king 'discussed with his magnates (*cum obtimatibus suis tractavit*)' . . . 'about conquering the realm of Ireland and giving it to his brother William',[77] apparently present at the council.[78] The peculiar value of the Afflighem addition is that it mentions an ecclesiastical lobby and it is this that attracted the attention of the promoters of the 'Canterbury hypothesis': 'The Afflighem continuator of Sigebert of Gembloux tells us that "bishops and certain religious men" wished him to go. These were probably the monks of Canterbury'.[79] Abandoning the nuance of 'certain', which is not in the source, Bethell might well on this count, and to do full justice to his general argument in the paper, have identified the 'religious men' with English monks more widely. Aside from the reference to 'religious men', though, it does not appear that the ecclesiastical lobby of the Afflighem chronicler was so narrow as would necessitate or perhaps even warrant its identification with Canterbury metropolitan concerns. The reference is to 'bishops'[80] in the plural. Beyond that, the entry is explicit on two cardinal points: (1) it was the *king* who had proposed the expedition to Ireland and (2) the contribution of the 'ecclesiastical lobby' was specifically to advocate that Henry's brother be made king there in the aftermath of conquest—an anticipation, it would appear, *mutatis mutandis*, of what was later to be contemplated in the case of Henry's son, John,[81] or of what Gerald of Wales envisaged for one of John's heirs.[82]

Had it stood in isolation, Robert of Torigny's information that this matter had been discussed at all was in some danger of being dismissed as fundamentally implausible.[83] However, the basic fact is put beyond dispute by the dating clause of a charter of John, count of Eu, which was 'given at Winchester in the year in which the proposal was made about conquering Ireland'.[84] The specific detail of the Afflighem chronicler regarding the discussions cannot be confirmed, but the example before us of the danger of discounting a plain statement deters its being ignored. Moreover, an engaging echo is heard of its formulation on one point. The Afflighem chronicle's wording 'ut eam suo dominio subiugaret' ('that he might subdue it [sc. Ireland] to his lordship') recurs suggestively in Alexander III's letters of 20 September 1172 to the Irish bishops ('gentem illam, barbaram, incultam et divine legis ignaram suo dominio subiugavit')[85] and to the king ('ad subiugandam tuo dominio gentem illam').[86] In context of the other promptings[87] towards supposing that Henry II could have entertained from the beginning of his reign the notion that his 'patrum solium' extended to a claim on Ireland, the possibility must be seriously considered that 'suo dominio subiugare' ('subduing to his lordship') is a royal formulation. It might well have been part of the original discussions of an expedition, and by the time of Alexander III in the aftermath of the invasion and the king's 'magnificent triumph'[88] have been accepted into papal terminology in dealing with Henry. Warren thought it unlikely that Henry would have wished to create an appanage for his brother.[89] Just so: and we are given to understand that the project as adumbrated at Winchester had a cold douche from Henry's mother, who must have known about as much as there was to be known of dynastic fission.[90] Possible objections at Winchester and after may have been, variously, the undesirability of Henry's dissipating his own energies in Ireland and the risk of dynastic discord. That would explain the hesitancy in *Laudabiliter* that the king's intention to enter Ireland might not be brought to fruition[91] (the lack of a clear objective in the briefing of the embassy to Benevento might also have provided the greater opportunity for papal axe-grinding).

The 'Canterbury hypothesis' has always had the instability of an inverted pyramid. Founding any hypothesis on the basis of such slight material is hazardous. But if the historian is professionally obliged to maintain reserve, the reserve must be greater over the extended interpretation of the source than over its basic information. The ecclesiastical contribution to the Winchester proceedings, so far as we are ever likely to be able to uncover it, is not associated with the metropolitan issue. In what it is associated with, the project for an Irish kingdom under William, it appears to run directly counter to any scheme—fantastic as that might appear in the aftermath of Kells, and flatly out of keeping as it is with the tenor of *Laudabiliter* itself, which expressly provides that 'the right of the churches of that land' shall be 'preserved whole and unimpaired'—for the reintegration of Ireland, or rather a part of Ireland, into an English metropolitan framework.

There is one last, dubious, piece of evidence which remains to be considered both for its support of the authenticity of *Laudabiliter* and as impinging on the argument concerning Henry's concept of his 'dominion'. This is *Quoniam ea*. As already noted, beyond that it is not a product of the papal chancery, its status is unclear. In summarizing Robinson's objections to the authenticity of *Laudabiliter*, I preserved his description of *Quoniam ea* in quotation marks. I do not, in fact, at all presume that *Quoniam ea* is a forgery, in the formal sense, as well stated by Sheehy, 'that someone drew up this text, wrote it on parchment and attached a papal seal to it'.[92] It is unlikely that the question of what it is can ever be assuredly resolved but, if it is not a mere rhetorical exercise by which Gerald of Wales was in some unexplained manner deluded (the Scheffer-Boichorst thesis), two points of reference offer themselves. The first is that whoever wrote it had a purpose. To the question 'Cui bono?' the answer would seem to be the king. Once it was decided, as Gerald of Wales's account implies that it was, to present *Laudabiliter* for propagandist effect,[93] the text of *Quoniam ea*, while purporting to confirm, glosses its 'predecessor'. In doing so, it adds nothing useful to *Laudabiliter* from the pope's viewpoint, and even were the style congruent with papal usage, one would be disposed to think that it had not emanated from him spontaneously. From a royal viewpoint *Quoniam ea* handles the question of 'lordship' with relative sensitivity: Adrian's letter was a 'grant of the same over the lordship of the realm of Ireland accorded to you'.[94] The formulation here by comparison with *Laudabiliter*—which is hazy on everything outside ecclesiastical rights— is sufficiently fudged to be capable of accommodating divergent perspectives on the issue of lordship (sanctioning Henry's endeavour to make his lordship good in his worldview as suggested above) without venturing too far into the potentially explosive issues of theory. In its other main point of substance from a secular political viewpoint, *Quoniam ea* makes clear that the obligation[95] of Peter's Pence stipulated in *Laudabiliter* as a corollary of the king's entry into Ireland has no more significance in regard to Ireland than his liability to the same tribute has in regard to England: 'saving to blessed Peter and the most holy Roman church *just as in England so also in Ireland* an annual payment of one penny from every household'.[96] The recurrence of the phrase in Gerald of Wales's dedicatory letter to King John of the new edition of his *Expugnatio*[97] might indicate its topicality but it may, of course, be no more than an echo—though a curious one in view of the current understanding of the text's evolution[98]—of *Quoniam ea*. The second point of reference is the important information provided in the tradition of

Gerald's *De Instructione Principum*, where he had returned both to *Laudabiliter* and to *Quoniam ea*.[99] Gerald (or as was previously thought an editor)[100] remarks of this second 'privilege': 'as it is alleged or represented by some to have been impetrated; by others however it is denied that it ever was impetrated'.[101] The doubt was whether the second 'privilege' was ever impetrated: not whether it was read out but whether the pope had actually been asked and had consented to issue it. Taken literally, this is evidence that what we have in *Quoniam ea* is a drafted confirmation that it was intended to impetrate. When impetrated, it would have been redacted in correct papal chancery style, with its substance left unaltered, provided that Alexander III proved co-operative in regard to the points identified. The text in the hands of William fitz Audelin and Nicholas of Wallingford, at a stage at which arrangements were in course for *Quoniam ea*'s being impetrated, need not be thought to have been conveyed to Ireland as a papal letter in physical appearance— no more, it is likely, than *Laudabiliter* itself. Both might more plausibly have been represented by copies of official provenance. (The making of *transumpta* of *Laudabiliter* would have offered ample room for the accumulation of the variants that the tradition affords.) That *Quoniam ea* was, on the evidence that exists, not secured as a papal document may have been due to a sensible decision finally to leave well alone, effectively a yielding of diplomatic to diplomacy.

Notes

The present argument was first delivered to the conference 'In Partibus. Penitentiary, Curia and Local Context' at the Institutum Romanum Finlandiae, 30 November to 1 December 2001. I am grateful for the comments of an audience that comprised a rare assembly of expertise in papal diplomatic. I am no less grateful to the members of the Wiles Colloquium, some of whose contribution is specifically acknowledged.

1. Jaffé, *Regesta*, ii, 109–10, no. 10056.
2. Sheehy, 'Bull *Laudabiliter*'. Though the article was technically published in the journal for the year 1961, a preliminary note makes clear that it was the text of a lecture delivered in 1962.
3. O'Doherty, 'Rome and the Anglo-Norman Invasion', 141.
4. One such ghoul is the O'Neill–MacCarthy letter supposedly testifying to medieval perception of *Laudabiliter*. See most recently, Duggan, 'Totius', 138–9. It might be thought laid peacefully to rest by Ó Murchada, 'Select Documents'. Of the older historiography a valuable review may be had in Weckmann, *Bulas Alejandrinas*, 49–51.
5. As appears, most recently, to be the stance of Lydon, *Making of Ireland*, 51, though the author in referring to *Laudabiliter* as a 'privilege' ignores Sheehy's distinction, which I endorse, while differing from Sheehy in my related hypothesis.

6. So, Duffy, *Ireland in the Middle Ages*, 70: 'In 1155, shortly after his accession to the throne, Henry had discussed plans for an invasion of Ireland. If the papal document *Laudabiliter* is genuine, it was obtained at this point from the English pope, Adrian IV, to provide justification for such an invasion (though Henry may have been acting at the behest of Archbishop Theobald, anxious to re-assert Canterbury's waning influence over the Irish church).' Contrast Richter, 'Giraldiana', 431: 'It is no longer permissible to doubt the authenticity of *Laudabiliter*.'

7. 'The authenticity of this famous letter... has long been a matter of dispute... *Laudabiliter*, is, to say the least, problematical': Robinson, *Papacy*, 311. The author was brought to consider *Laudabiliter* in a review of the political ideas of the early medieval papacy, specifically the papal jurisdiction over islands.

8. Ibid.

9. For the variant see the text as in the appendix.

10. Jaffé, *Regesta*, ii, 142, no. 10546. The letter is printed in *PL*, clxxxviii, cols 1615–17.

11. Robinson, *Papacy*, 311–12.

12. Ibid., 311, n. 67. The references are to Watt, *Church and the Two Nations*, 35–40 and Warren, *Henry II*, 194–7.

13. Warren took his cue as regards authenticity specifically from the arguments of O'Doherty, 'Rome and the Anglo-Norman invasion', which he regarded as putting the issue 'beyond doubt': Warren, *Henry II*, 196, n. 1. O'Doherty had in fact given Sheehy a lead on central points.

14. Scheffer-Boichorst, 'Hat Papst Hadrian IV'; cf. Sheehy, 'Bull *Laudabiliter*', 56, n. 30.

15. Thatcher, *Studies*.

16. Sheehy, 'Bull *Laudabiliter*', 56.

17. Eggers, *Urkunde*.

18. It is listed in Sheehy's bibliography in 'Bull *Laudabiliter*'.

19. Eggers, though critical, was unexceptionably polite towards Scheffer-Boichorst: Eggers, *Urkunde*, 45.

20. Ibid., 18–19.

21. The reader of the sharp reprimand administered to her temerity in challenging Scheffer-Boichorst by the reviewer in *Neues Archiv der Gesellschaft für ältere Geschichtskunde*, 46 (1926), 338, might well be deterred from consulting her. Scheffer-Boichorst evidently elicited strong attachment: Thatcher pronounced his 'arguments... irrefragable, his conclusions final': Thatcher, *Studies*, 6.

22. Scheffer-Boichorst, 'Hat Papst Hadrian IV', 152–4.

23. Thatcher, *Studies*, 26.

24. Ibid.

25. Eggers, *Urkunde*, 25.

26. Ibid., 38–47, offers a comparison.

27. Scheffer-Boichorst, 'Hat Papst Hadrian IV', 154.

28. Thatcher elaborated by postulating an identical version directed to Henry II: *Studies*, 27.

29. Eggers, *Urkunde*, 45.

30. Ibid., 46–7. The same conclusion was proposed independently by O'Doherty, 'Rome and the Anglo-Norman Invasion', 188.

31. Frame, *Colonial Ireland*, 11.
32. Gerald of Wales, *Expugnatio*, 142–7.
33. Scheffer-Boichorst, 'Hat Papst Hadrian IV', 147.
34. Cf. Eggers, *Urkunde*, 75.
35. Sheehy, 'Bull *Laudabiliter*', 65–6.
36. O'Doherty, 'Rome and the Anglo-Norman Invasion', 131.
37. John of Salisbury, *Metalogicon*, ed. Hall, 183.
38. 'Ad preces meas illustri regi Anglorum Henrico secundo concessit et dedit Hiberniam iure hereditario possidendam, sicut litterae ipsius testantur in hodiernum diem. Nam omnes insulae de iure antiquo ex donatione Constantini, qui eam fundavit et dotavit, dicuntur ad Romanam ecclesiam pertinere. Anulum quoque per me transmisit aureum, smaragdo optimo decoratum, quo fieret investitura iuris in regenda Hibernia, idemque adhuc anulus in cimiliarchio publico iussus est custodiri': ibid.
39. It is unnecessary here to consider this aspect. It has been thoroughly explored by Weckmann, *Bulas Alejandrinas*.
40. Sheehy, 'Bull *Laudabiliter*', 60.
41. Ibid., 63. Sheehy's solution to the contrary indications remains influential. Duggan describes it as 'ingenious' though she circumspectly balances the reflection by allowance for exaggeration on John of Salisbury's part: Duggan, 'Totius', 149, n. 211. There seems to be a certain analogous complexity in her own disposition to suppose that *Laudabiliter* might contain 'the essence of Adrian's letter'—presumably, that is, without constituting it: Duggan, 'Totius', 139.
42. The new observations on usage of Hirschmann, *Kanzlei*, 35–7, 55–7 are also pertinent.
43. Gerald of Wales, *Expugnatio*, 142–4.
44. Ibid., 263, l. 104.
45. Ibid., ll. 98–104.
46. O'Doherty, 'Rome and the Anglo-Norman Invasion', 143, and Sheehy, 'Bull *Laudabiliter*', 65, state the diplomatic objections; cf. Gerald of Wales, *Expugnatio*, p. lix. A range of usage in reference to a papal predecessor is recorded in Hirschmann, *Kanzlei*, 29.
47. Norgate, 'Bull *Laudabiliter*'.
48. Ibid., 41–2.
49. Ullmann, 'Alexander III', 377. Prompted by an earlier essay of Ullmann on the subject, Flanagan places a similar construction on John of Salisbury's reference to *ius hereditarium*: Flanagan, *Irish Society*, 51–2. I do not construe that John of Salisbury regarded the 'grant' as a 'confirmation', in view of his formulation and in so far as confirmation has diplomatic overtones, but the fundamental insight of Ullmann's approach remains unaffected. Flanagan herself, if I understand her presentation correctly, is not committed to regarding the 'grant' as a confirmation. Her interest there is in the plausibility of the underlying assumption, which seems to me convincingly demonstrated.
50. O'Doherty, 'Rome and the Anglo-Norman Invasion', 139.
51. The evidence is meticulously presented by Constable, 'Alleged Disgrace', 70–3. For the excerpt quoted, see ibid., 71. Cf. *Letters of John of Salisbury*, 32.
52. 'Si causam quaeritis, ei forte plus iusto faui, promotioni suae ultra quam oportuerit insisti, ad hoc toto desiderio cordis suspirans ut quem fortunae

invidia credebam exulantem, miseratione divina regnantem cernerem in patrum solio, et iura dictantem in populis et nationibus...' ('If you ask the reason, perhaps I favoured him more than was just, and worked for his advancement with greater vigour than I should; for I sighed for this with all my heart's longing, namely that I might behold him whom I deemed to be kept in exile by the malice of Fortune, reigning by God's mercy on the throne of his fathers, and giving laws to peoples and nations...'): Constable, 'Alleged Disgrace', 71; cf. *Letters of John of Salisbury*, 31. Duggan places a different interpretation on the passage but the case for stating that 'it alludes more probably to John's support for the Angevin succession' seems weak against the plausibility of Constable's exposition. Moreover, her statement that the passage quoted above is 'explicitly rejected as the occasion of the king's anger' by John's protestation that 'this is not the fault of which I am accused' misconstrues the train of thought. The fault for which John was not reproved—in this arch sally—was disproportionate effort towards and unphilosophical impatience for the king's advantage (directed and conceived as explained): Duggan, 'Totius', 142–3. On my hypothesis, John's comment in the *Metalogicon* is not merely 'self-regarding' and it would indeed have rung 'distinctly hollow' to those in the know (cf. Duggan, as cited).

53. Constable, 'Alleged Disgrace', 75.
54. For the embassy itself and its main object of obtaining sanction for an invasion there is clear evidence. See Roger of Wendover, *Flores Historiarum*, i, 11; repeated by Matthew Paris, *Chronica Majora*, vii, 2, 210; cf. Matthew Paris, *Historia Anglorum*, i, 304 and Walsingham, *Gesta Abbatum*, i, 125–6, corresponding to a passage in Matthew Paris's *Vitae XXIII Abbatum S. Albani*, as reproduced by Thatcher, *Studies*, 7–8, from the seventeenth-century edition by Wats.
55. Constable, 'Alleged Disgrace', 68, 72, 73.
56. Ibid., 75; cf. Thatcher, *Studies*, 18, and Richter, 'Giraldiana', 431.
57. *Cartulary of Worcester*, 4–7.
58. The evidence is considered by Flanagan, *Irish Society*, 44–7.
59. See the remarks of Richter, 'First Century', 195, 205.
60. Cf. Robinson, *Papacy*, 30–1, 462–72; his record towards English affairs as summarized by Constable, 'Alleged Disgrace', 68–9, and Thatcher, *Studies*, 19–20, for his stiff letter of 23 January 1156 protesting at Archbishop Theobald's supineness as regards the king in the matter of appeals to Rome.
61. The unique source for the ring in the case of William the Conqueror is Wace, *Roman de Rou*. See the remarks of Brown, *Normans*, 128, n. 39.
62. O'Doherty, 'Rome and the Anglo-Norman Invasion', 139.
63. Ullmann, 'Alexander III'.
64. See n. 52. In discussion of my paper at the Wiles Colloquium, I was much interested and stimulated to learn of research currently being conducted by Judith Green on Henry I's outlook, whose result may put my argument here in larger perspective.
65. The phrase is from Duggan, 'Totius', 150.
66. See O'Doherty, 'Rome and the Anglo-Norman Invasion', 140.
67. Watt, *Church and the Two Nations*, 36. Duggan has now added her criticism of the supposition: Duggan, 'Totius', 144–6. While I have to disagree with

much of the detail of her analysis even on this point, I am at one with her in the perception that the motive force for an Irish invasion as adumbrated at the Winchester council was secular political consideration.

68. Bethell, 'English Monks'.
69. 'If it was Canterbury that had proposed a conquest of Ireland in order to associate the king of England with its attempts to re-establish its links with the Irish Church, which had been terminated by the Synod of Kells, then the plan had backfired': this as a judgement, which I heartily endorse, on *Laudabiliter*. Flanagan, *Irish Society*, 53–4. I therefore do not read Flanagan as being so committed to the 'Canterbury hypothesis' as does Duggan, even short of the *reductio ad absurdum* of a 'clerico-papal plot' which is certainly not necessary to Flanagan's exposition. See Duggan, 'Totius', 139.
70. See O'Doherty, 'Rome and the Anglo-Norman Invasion', 140. Cf. above, 140.
71. See the evidence collected in Constable, 'Alleged Disgrace', 70–3. His being subsequently targeted by royal displeasure for defence of ecclesiastical liberties seems, where specified, to be connected with 'celebration of elections' and 'ecclesiastical causes', and to involve other bishops as well as the archbishop and the English church at large: ibid., 71.
72. *Annales Monastici*, ii, 55, as translated in Bethell, 'English Monks', 135. The story is repeated in a slightly variant form in the Worcester Annals: 'Anno MCLVI. Alienora peperit Matildam. Auditur vox sub Ethna monte: "Accendite focum; ecce Johannes cardinalis"' ('In the year 1156 Eleanor gave birth to Matilda. There is heard a voice under Mount Etna: "Stoke up the fire; here comes Cardinal John"'): *Annales Monastici*, iv, 380.
73. Robert of Torigny, *Chronique*, ed. Delisle, i, 262–3; *Cronica*, ed. Bethmann, 500; cf. Bethell, 'English Monks', 135, n. 137.
74. See Gwynn, *Irish Church*, 219–20, 222, on the Cistercian dimension. The Synod of Kells is more accurately the Synod of Kells-Mellifont.
75. Its focus and exact temper is a matter of interpretation. Bethell, whose eye for such detail was acute, even in the course of his own exposition of the case for a Canterbury involvement in *Laudabiliter*, noted a pulse of Canterbury public opinion strongly contrary to the royalist propaganda— endorsed by Alexander III at least as warmly as by Adrian—directed at Ireland: Bethell, 'English Monks', 125. The sentiment at Canterbury might of course have been coloured by the martyr's blood that had flowed meantime. However, Gerald of Wales's stress on the need to justify the Christian carnage involved, both past and future, in conquering Ireland, suggests that such sensitivity was not simply localized. See his *Expugnatio*, 263, ll. 100–2, 112–15. As Bethell observed, the Canterbury manifestation is cautionary indeed.
76. The Latin of the entry as printed in Bethell, 'English Monks', 135, n. 136, is mangled so that the exact implication of the passage is lost. 'Heinricus iunior rex Anglorum, exercitum copiosum et magnum belli apparatum, quem proposuerat ducere in Hiberniam, ut eam suo dominio subiugaret, fratremque suum consilio episcoporum et religiosorum virorum illi insule regem constitueret, convertit contra regem Francorum...': Sigebert of Gembloux, *Chronicon Auctarium Affligemense*, 403.

77. Robert of Torigny, *Chronique*, ed. Delisle, i, 295–6; *Cronica*, ed. Bethmann, 505. See Bethell, 'English Monks', 135, n. 137.
78. He is among the witnesses to the charter for the Knights Hospitallers dated there: Eyton, *Court Household and Itinerary*, 12–13.
79. Bethell, 'English Monks', 135.
80. Flanagan, *Irish Society*, 40, details the episcopal attendance as in the charter evidence.
81. For consideration of what that later arrangement might have meant, see ibid., 277–83.
82. See Gerald of Wales, *Expugnatio*, 262, ll. 59–60.
83. Cf. the remarks of Warren, *Henry II*, 195.
84. See Sheehy, 'Bull *Laudabiliter*', 57, n. 36, and now Flanagan, *Irish Society*, 40, 305–7.
85. Sheehy, *Pontificia Hibernica*, i, 20 ('that race—barbarous, uncivilized and ignorant of divine law—he has subdued to his lordship').
86. Ibid., 22 ('for the subduing of that race to your lordship').
87. Cf. Flanagan, *Irish Society*, 44–7.
88. Sheehy, *Pontificia Hibernica*, i, 21.
89. Warren, *Henry II*, 195. Duggan's suggestion that 'a lordship in Ireland for William, under his own [sc. Henry's] overlordship, would have increased the "family" holdings' sits uneasily with her, to my mind more convincing, case that there was a strong basis for Henry's regarding Ireland as part of his inheritance: Duggan, 'Totius', 146–8. At all events, there is explicit evidence on the origin of the proposal that William be made king of Ireland.
90. Robert of Torigny, *Chronique*, ed. Delisle, i, 295–6; *Cronica*, ed. Bethmann, 505.
91. 'Si ergo quod animo concepisti effectu duxeris prosequente complendum'; to select from the variants in the text see pp. 161, 163.
92. Sheehy, 'Bull *Laudabiliter*', 65.
93. For the motivation, compare the remarks regarding a possible sensitivity, at n. 75.
94. The text as transmitted reads 'indulto' (see Gerald of Wales, *Expugnatio*, 146, l. 71), though 'indultam' could be expected to follow from 'concessionem'. While the translation renders the text as transmitted, it serves to capture the effect were 'indulto' to be the result of attraction to 'dominio'. If such corruption did take place, however, the lack of variants within the transmission imply that it happened at an early stage, perhaps in the copying of the exemplar.
95. Gerald of Wales' remarks, c.1209, imply its non-discharge in effect: *Expugnatio*, 264, ll. 118, 137–9.
96. Ibid., 146.
97. Ibid., 263, ll. 103–4.
98. Ibid., p. lxxiii.
99. *Giraldi Cambrensis opera*, viii, 197.
100. See Gerald of Wales, *Expugnatio*, p. lx.
101. 'Secundi vero privilegii tenor hic, sicut a quibusdam impetratum asseritur aut confingitur, ab aliis autem unquam impetratum fuisse negatur': *Giraldi Cambrensis opera*, viii, 197. *Quoniam ea* is omitted from Gerald's *De rebus a se gestis*, which includes *Laudabiliter*: *Giraldi Cambrensis opera*, i, 60–3.

Appendix: The Text of *Laudabiliter* from the National Archives (PRO), SC 8/177/8818 and Trinity College, Dublin, MS 1339

Introductory note

National Archives (PRO), SC 8/177/8818: a parchment strip 27 cm × 16 cm; written text 25.5 cm × 13.2 cm. The dorse is blank. Hand: late thirteenth-century. Designated below by the siglum *P*.

Trinity College, Dublin, MS 1339. The text of *Laudabiliter* is written on parchment on the verso of a folio of Irish text, being fo. xl in original foliation (fo. 233 in modern foliation). The original folio was reduced by cutting, with loss of text on fo. xlr (original)/233r (modern). The text of *Laudabiliter* is written comfortably if neatly within the dimensions of the resulting parchment strip. There is no basis for deciding whether it was written before or after the reduction of the folio, though if the folio was cut after the writing of the text of *Laudabiliter* care was evidently taken to preserve it intact. Text in a single column, 22.6 cm × 9.5 cm. Hand: late thirteenth-century. (Although my judgement is thus that it is rather earlier, it is proper to record here that William O'Sullivan, whose opinion in these matters commands respect, thought the hand early fourteenth-century. O'Sullivan, 'Notes', 3.) Designated below by the siglum *L*.

Sheehy, *Pontificia Hibernica*, i, 16, noted *P* which he referred to as 'a re-cast version . . . , with a large number of alterations' but, though he had evidently inspected it, he did not present the variants. He failed to note *L*, though it was long signalled in the scholarly literature: see Bémont, 'Bulle', 42–3; Weckmann, *Bulas Alejandrinas*, 54. Richter, 'Giraldiana', 430–1, comments on the import of the variants.

The text below is presented primarily to support diplomatic observations in the preceding study but for comparison variants from the version in Gerald of Wales, *Expugnatio Hibernica*, as presented now in *Expugnatio*, ed. Scott and Martin, 144–6, have been included as designated by the siglum *E*. I am most grateful to Dr Bernard Meehan, Keeper of Manuscripts, Trinity College, Dublin, for his facilitating my use of *L*, my inspection under ultra-violet light of certain obscurities in the text and his discussing with me the interpretation of the same. The judgements presented here on the several points of particular difficulty represent our common conclusions from that examination. For permission to publish the text from *L*, acknowledgement is made to the Board of Trinity College, Dublin; attention is drawn to the National Archives' proprietorship of *P*.

Text

The following version is based on *P* but with a number of readings from *L*, as indicated, admitted to the text. The choice of base text may be briefly justified as follows: *E*'s reading 'tuum cum' is deterred by *L*'s complete omission. The reading 'tuum cum' is probably best judged a scribal elaboration of 'tuum'. To this is added the earlier omission of 'habiturum' in *L* and the agreement of *P* with *E* against *L* in reading 'decursu', which is intrinsically stronger. The preference for *P* is however with discount of, on a substantive point, its reading 'respiciat' and its obvious error in reading 'salvo'. *P*'s reading 'incepisti' is arguably stronger intrinsically but in view of *L*'s agreement with the 'standard' tradition, 'concepisti' has been retained in the text. *L*'s 'solvi', as unquestionably stronger, has been admitted despite the agreement otherwise among the witnesses on 'solvere'.

[a]Adrianus Episcopus servus servorum dei carissimo[b] in Christo filio illustri Regi Anglorum[c] Henrico[d] salutem et apostolicam benedictionem. Laudabiliter et satis[e]/fructuose de glorioso nomine propagando in terris et eterne salutis[f] premio cumulando in celis tua magnificentia cogitat dum ad dilatan/dos[g] ecclesie terminos et[h] ad declarandam indoctis et rudibus populis Christiane fidei veritatem et viciorum plantaria de agro dominico extirpanda[i]/sicut catholicus[j] princeps intendis et ad id conveniencius exequendum consilium apostolicum[k] exigis et favorem. In quo facto quanto/alciori consilio et maiori discrecione procedis tanto in eo feliciorem progressum te prestante domino confidimus habiturum[l] eo quod ad/bonum exitum[m] et finem soleant pertingere[n] que de ardore fidei et religionis amore principium acceperunt. Sane Hiberniam[o] et/omnes insulas quibus sol iusticie Christus illuxit,[p] que documenta fidei[q] perceperunt,[r] ad ius beati Petri apostoli[s] et sacrosancte Romane ecclesie/quod tua[t] voluntas[u] recognoscit non est dubium pertinere. Unde[v] in eis libencius plantacionem fidei[w] et germen gratum Deo inserimus/quanto[x] id a nobis in[y] interno examine districtius prospicimus exigendum. Significasti nobis siquidem[z] fili[aa] in Christo carissime[bb] te Hiber/nie[cc] insulam ad subdendum[dd] populum illum[ee] legibus et inde viciorum plantaria[ff] extirpanda[gg] velle intrare et de singulis domibus annuam/beato Petro unius denarii[hh] solvi[ii] pensionem et iura ecclesiarum illius terre illibata[jj] et integra conservare. Nos itaque pium et/laudabile desiderium tuum[kk] favore congruo prosequentes et peticioni tue benigne[ll] impendentes assensum gratum et acceptum/habemus ut pro dilatandis ecclesie terminis, pro viciorum restringendo decursu,[mm] pro corrigendis moribus et virtutibus inserendis et[nn] pro/Christiane religionis augmento Insulam illam ingrediaris et que ad honorem Dei et salutem terre illius[oo] spectaverint exequaris/et illius terre populus honorifice te recipiat[pp] et sicut dominum veneretur iure nimirum ecclesiarum illibato et integro permanente et/ salva[qq] beato Petro apostolo[rr] et sacrosancte Romane ecclesie de singulis domibus unius denarii annua[ss] pensione. Si ergo quod animo concepisti[tt]/affectu[uu] duxeris prosequente complendum, studeas[vv] gentem illam bonis moribus informare et agas tam per te quam per illos quos ad/hoc fide et[ww] verbo et vita idoneos[xx] esse prospexeris ut decoretur ibi ecclesia, plantetur et crescat fidei Christiane religio et que ad ho/norem Dei et salutem pertinent animarum taliter ordinentur ut a Deo sempiterne mercedis cumulum consequi merearis et in terris gloriosum/ nomen valeas et[yy] in celis[zz] obtinere.[aaa]

[a] Bulla concessa regi Anglie super collacione hybernie in qua nichil derogatur iuri hybernicorum sicut in serie verborum patet *L. An erasure between the heading and the text in L is illegible even under ultraviolet light, apart from its initial letter 'A'. By script and ink, so far as the latter can be judged after the process of partial erasure, it seems to be a piece with the quite extraneous Latin text 'Equore cum gelido zepherus fecit/'[etc.] which appears above the heading for* 'Laudabiliter'.

[b] karissimo *L*.

[c] Regi Anglorum: Anglorum regi *E*.

[d] Henrico: henr' *L; om. E*.

[e] et satis: satis et *E*.

[f] salutis: felicitatis *E*.

[g] *The letters between 'l' and 'd' are obscured in P, though the first and third can be distinguished as 'a'.*

[h] *om.* et *E*.

[i] exstirpanda *L E*.

[j] *The final syllable is lost in P through damage to the parchment.*

[k] apostolicum: apostolice sedis *E*.

[l] habiturum: *om. L. The omission of* habiturum *here represents an evident syntactical deficiency since* progressum *being qualified by* feliciorem *can only be regarded as a noun.*

[m] *add* semper *E*.

[n] pertingere: attingere *E*.

[o] hyberniam *L*.

[p] *add* et *E*.

[q] *add* Christiane *E*.

[r] perceperunt: ceperunt *E*.

[s] *om.* apostoli *E*.

[t] *add* etiam *E*.

[u] *The letters read as 'un' are obscured P.* voluntas: nobilitas *E*.

[v] *add* tanto *E*.

[w] fidei: fidelem *E*.

[x] quanto: quando *P*.

[y] *om.* in *E*.

[z] nobis siquidem: siquidem nobis *E*.

[aa] fili: *inserted above the line P*.

[bb] carissime: karissime *L*.

[cc] hybernie *L*.

[dd] subdendum: *written* su'dendum *L*.

[ee] populum illum: illum populum *E*.

[ff] inde viciorum plantaria: viciorum plantaria inde *E*.

[gg] extirpanda: exstirpanda *L E*.

[hh] beato Petro unius denarii: unius denarii beato Petro velle *E*.

[ii] solvi: solvere *PE*.

[jj] illibata: illabata *P*.

[kk] *om.* tuum *L; add* cum *E*.

[ll] benigne: benignum *E*

[mm] decursu: recursu *L*.

[nn] *om.* et *E*.

[oo] terre illius: illius terre *E*.

[pp] recipiat: respiciat *P*.

[qq] salva: salvo *P*.

[rr] *om.* apostolo *E*.

[ss] unius denarii annua: annua unius denarii *E*.

[tt] concepisti *L*: incepisti *P*; animo concepisti: concepisti animo *E*.

[uu] affectu: effectu *E*.

^{vv} studeas: stude *E.*
^{ww}*om.* et *E.*
^{xx} idoneos: ydoneos *L.*
^{yy} *om.* et *E.*
^{zz} celis: seculis *E.*
^{aaa} obtinere: optinere *L. add.* Valete *L.*

9

The Adoption of Brieves in Scotland

Dauvit Broun

The first half of the twelfth century saw the adoption of new kinds of document within the realm of the king of Scots. Prior to this period property rights may have been the subject of brief written records which lacked a consistent structure beyond the plain information that X had granted Y to Z.[1] It is only from the twelfth century that the extant archives of Scottish beneficiaries begin to yield examples of the written expression of a donor's will in a form that was designed particularly for this purpose. The term 'charter' can usefully be reserved as a generic term for any specialized document of this kind.[2] The earliest charters in the name of a king of Scots belong to the last years of the eleventh century. These, like all Scottish royal charters before about 1120, survive in the muniments of Durham cathedral priory.[3] Durham is the beneficiary or addressee of them all, and almost all were produced by Durham scribes.[4] The earliest extant charters written for (and probably by) a beneficiary within the realm of the king of Scots are those of Alexander I (1107–24) for Scone, datable mostly to the last years of his reign.[5]

English developments and English models

The most common species of charter, taking the twelfth century as a whole, is the prototype of the solemn charter of later centuries.[6] The original habitat of this document-type was in England, evolving out of post-Conquest Latin writs wherein the king communicated information and instructions to key individuals and groups at a local level, or sometimes wider. The simple writ (or 'brieve' in the parlance of Scottish lawyers and historians) also became well established as 'a short document designed to communicate the king's will in the form of positive commands or prohibitions or both'.[7] The earliest extant brieve is one of Alexander I, and survives as an original in Durham.[8] Durham also possesses an original brieve of David before he became king in 1124.[9] The grandest documents, announcing the foundation of a religious house or confirming all its possessions and rights, sometimes took the form of a diploma. None, however, are found in the muniments of reformed Benedictine monasteries (the Cistercians and Tironensians): their grandest documents instead take the form of a distended solemn charter. The two earliest Scottish charters, recording grants in 1094 and 1095, are diplomas; their authenticity has been keenly debated.[10] The diploma almost entirely disappeared after 1150.[11]

The most obvious context for the adoption of this spectrum of documents in Scotland in the early twelfth century is the wider world of English charters that provided the models for these document-types. Crucial stages in the development of charters in England in the 1090s and early 1100s have been identified elsewhere in this book. Richard Sharpe has demonstrated how, before the early years of Henry I's reign, notifications of royal grants or other decisions were addressed to the shire court. Between 1106 and 1110, however, there are several examples where a formulaic general address is used (there is also a lone instance in 1102); the general address became increasingly common thereafter, and the address to the shire court eventually vanished in the 1160s.[12] One possible explanation for this is that documents came to be regarded more as (potentially) enduring witnesses to property rights and privileges: this could even have included later writ-charters addressed to the shire court, even though this form was not originally intended as a title to a perpetuity. The significant increase in extant charters from about 1090, remarked on by David Bates, could also suggest that such documents were increasingly valued.[13] Moreover, as the 'writ-charter' thus began its transformation into the 'solemn charter', so it seems to have colonized the habitat of the diploma and driven it to extinction. The earliest Scottish charters reflect these English developments, particularly in the use of the general address and the emergence of the solemn charter. It is notable that there are no surviving examples of a writ-charter addressed to whatever Scottish equivalent to the shire court that there may have been; neither are there any features which could reasonably be regarded as reflecting an earlier practice of written royal communication or record which may have existed independently, but not been archived.

Developments in England may have made charters more adaptable to a society which lacked shire courts or bookland; there may also have been an increasing consciousness of their value. On their own, however, these factors do not explain the adoption of charters in Scotland. Someone

initiated this. The overwhelming preponderance of ecclesiastical beneficiaries before the reign of William I (1165–1214) points to the church, and
the new monastic foundations, in particular, as providing an immediate
context for the first generation of charters.[14] This is broadly in line with
the pattern which has been identified in the twelfth and thirteenth
centuries elsewhere in Europe in regions previously untouched by such
documents.[15] The first use of charters in Scotland, however, should probably not be envisaged as exclusively determined by ecclesiastical interests.
The huge majority of them are in the king's name and served as expressions of royal authority.[16] There is a strong impression, nevertheless, that
the engine of this process was the church, particularly in the case of grants
or confirmations of perpetuities, which tended in the first half-century
of charters to be produced by ecclesiastical beneficiaries themselves,
albeit with royal approval.[17] In the case of brieves, by contrast, the early
involvement of scribes in the king's service is more apparent: a high
proportion of extant originals of David I (1124–53) and Mael Coluim IV
(1153–65) were written by the best attested royal scribe in each reign.[18]
This is not to deny that many must have been prompted by beneficiaries;
certainly those that survive are, with only a few exceptions, those which
it was in the interests of a religious establishment to keep. The adoption
of brieves, nevertheless, has the potential to offer a different perspective on
the development of writing in the king's name. This chapter is an attempt
to explore this, and thereby to strive for a more complete picture of the
complex relationship between church and secular authority in initiating
the adoption of charters in a society where there were none before.

Problems of definition and survival

The study of brieves in the first decades of their use is seriously hampered
by two fundamental problems. The first is the poor survival rate of
documents, and the need to confront what may generally be termed
'archival issues' before there is any hope of arriving at useful observations
or suggestions: this challenge is almost desperate in the case of brieves,
which by their nature seem much less likely to have been kept and copied.
The second is how to define a brieve in a period when fluidity is much
more apparent than standardization in the drafting and production of
documents. There are only a few cases prior to 1165 where brieves dealing
with the same matter exhibit a notable consistency in structure and phraseology.[19] As in England in this period, there are instances of a notification
of a grant being combined with an instruction for its implementation
(what might, somewhat anachronistically, be regarded as a 'hybrid' form),[20]

and of brieves that are addressed generally.[21] There is, nonetheless, an essential difference between the prototypes of the later more standardized brieves and solemn charters. Brieves—for all that they could be cherished and copied as a form of title or precedent—were created with an eye fixed foremost on a situation in the present, designed to be delivered to officials or other notables for notification and/or implementation.[22] In contrast, the solemn charter is a retrospective record that is meant to endure, and is designed to be retained as evidence of title that could be confirmed in the future. If brieves can be defined by their immediacy rather than by formal diplomatic criteria, however, then what is to be made of the briefest charters?[23] In opting for Barrow's standard definition of brieves in the bulk of this chapter I would not wish to lose sight of the likelihood that other documents were produced in the same spirit. It is simply that the discussion can be launched more effectively by concentrating on clear-cut examples, adhering to Barrow's list of 35 brieves of David I.[24]

Extant brieves before 1165

Barrow's magnificent edition of the charters of David I and his son, Henry, has 149 documents in David's name as king (three jointly with Henry).[25] This represents an average output of two charters in just under five months. There are 164 charters in the name of David's successor, Mael Coluim IV, an average output of about one charter per month.[26] The proportion of charters classifiable as brieves remains fairly similar: David I's 35 out of 149 compares with Mael Coluim's 37 out of 164.[27] (Of 51 charters in Henry's name alone, only 7 are brieves.) If the focus is narrowed to charters surviving as contemporary single sheets until modern times, of which there are 41 for David I and Henry, and 29 for Mael Coluim IV, we find that 6 are brieves of David I or Henry, but as many as 8 are brieves of Mael Coluim IV. Consideration of the survival of 'original' charters in more detail readily reveals how far this depends on the fate of a few archives. No less than 29 documents in the name of David I, Henry, or Mael Coluim IV are preserved in the muniments of the Dean and Chapter of Durham Cathedral. Seven of these (including two brieves) relate to a disputed grant by an earl of Dunbar.[28] The next highest concentration is the 11 which are now, or were in the mid-nineteenth century, in the remains of the archive of Holyrood Abbey owned by Lord Panmure:[29] Nine of these are now in the Dalhousie Muniments, but two have disappeared.[30] In total, 40 out of 70 'originals' owe their survival into the modern era because of two archives. The importance of these archives for the fate of 'original' brieves is even more striking. All 14 extant originals are to be found in either the Dalhousie Muniments or among the charters of the Dean and Chapter of Durham Cathedral.

Widening the focus again to embrace all 35 brieves of David I and 37 of Mael Coluim IV, it is notable that a significant number of these are for English beneficiaries. This includes Durham, although by 16 August 1139 its outpost at Coldingham had been established as a dependent priory and may from that point be considered a Scottish foundation.[31] Brieves for the benefit of English beneficiaries are an important part of the history of documentation in the name of the king of Scots: the collection at Durham, in particular, would benefit from a study of its own. As far as this chapter is concerned, however, these tell us nothing in general terms that we do not know already: that English beneficiaries were familiar with this kind of document, and that the involvement of the scribes in the service of kings of Scots could extend to all aspects of their production. In any event, brieves, along with the diploma and embryonic solemn charter, were not simply prompted by English influence; they also fulfilled a function in Scottish society as channels through which royal authority could be conveyed and preserved. What part did brieves play in the early stages of this process? The answer, if it is to be found at all, must be sought in the remains of the archives of beneficiaries based in the realm of the king of Scots.

The survival of brieves in archives of monasteries founded before 1139

Holyrood, Jedburgh, Melrose

Obviously the muniments of older monastic foundations are the likeliest source for the earliest brieves, taking as an arbitrary cut-off point those established before 1139 (the halfway point in David I's reign). There are six houses in this category:[32] working back in time, there is Jedburgh, an Augustinian priory established in 1138/39; the Cistercian abbey of Melrose, a daughter-house of Rievaulx, founded in 1136; the Augustinian abbey of Holyrood, founded in 1128; the Augustinian priory of Scone, which was established in 1115 with canons from Nostell;[33] the Tironensian abbey of Selkirk in 1113 (which was moved to Kelso in 1128); and finally the Benedictine priory of Dunfermline, founded by St Margaret with three monks sent by Archbishop Lanfranc from Canterbury, augmented by King Edgar, and eventually raised to abbatial status by David I in 1128. Instead of giving a simple list of which of these houses have early brieves, and how many, the scene in each case will be set by a brief account of the materials which survive from their medieval archives. This should give a little depth, albeit sketchy, to the background of the picture of brieve-survival that will emerge. It will begin with those archives whose principal remains are the original charters themselves, and finish with houses whose charters survive only in cartularies. Dunfermline will be treated last, separately from the rest, for reasons that will become apparent. A brief mention will also be made of Glasgow Cathedral, the only other Scottish beneficiary with more than the odd extant charter from this period.

Holyrood's muniments have already been met. When all that survives is gathered together it represents a moderate archive by Scottish standards,[34] with 94 extant originals of all kinds from the twelfth and thirteenth centuries; a further 15 documents are known only from copies,[35] most of which were made by early modern antiquarians.[36] At least 23 originals can be assigned to the period before 1165; only 7 or 8 of these belong to the reign of David I. Unfortunately there is no known cartulary which could reveal some, if not all, of what that archive contained in the middle ages. In the absence of a cartulary, another approach might be to examine general confirmations in which all (or nearly all) of a house's resources and rights were itemized. As a rule I would argue (though Professor Barrow might not agree)[37] that such grand confirmations in this early period need not have been based on individual charters or brieves for each and every item. The only exception is where it appears that the prose of what may have been earlier documents has been reiterated extensively. David I's diploma for Holyrood, datable to sometime in or between 1141 and 1147, was probably composed using at least a lost foundation charter because witnesses from one or more earlier documents have been combined with those of the diploma itself so that the living appear to rub shoulders with the dead.[38] The body of the diploma, moreover, reads almost like a scissors-and-paste production from pre-existing texts, although this can only be demonstrated in the case of the two extant documents which pre-date the diploma.[39] If the diploma was based on earlier texts, then the extent of losses has been severe. These almost certainly included brieves: for example, the instruction embedded in the diploma to royal foresters and officials in Stirlingshire and Clackmannan that Holyrood be allowed to take timber from the king's woods without hindrance. As it is, only two brieves of David I survive as independent texts. The same number survives for Mael Coluim IV.[40]

There is no doubt about the dreadful losses suffered by the Jedburgh archive. Only four royal charters survive for the period before 1165: the original of one of these only came to light as recently as 1966.[41] David I's diploma announcing the foundation of Jedburgh (datable to in or between 1147 and 1151) and the accompanying diploma by Earl Henry survive only in a copy of an inspeximus of Robert I of 12 December 1324.[42]

Much more might be expected of Melrose. More than 250 contemporary single sheets survive relating to its first 150 years.[43] There is also a cartulary from the second half of the thirteenth century which unfortunately has not survived intact, and another cartulary from the fifteenth century.[44] The total harvest of documents from before 1286 is nearly 350. A mere 12, however, have been assigned to the period before 1165. Only one of these is a charter of David I: it is datable to sometime in or between 1143 and 1147, and is a renovation of the lost foundation charter of probably June 1136, together with an additional grant of land perambulated on 29 May 1142.[45] Only one brieve survives from the twelfth century. It is datable to sometime in the mid-1170s, and is of particular interest because it refers to an earlier brieve of David I freeing Cistercian monks from tolls on purchases or sales for their own use in the king's realm.[46] The overall impression is that Melrose's archives were probably not maintained effectively until sometime in the thirteenth century, and that this may be the principal cause of the total loss of brieves of David I and Mael Coluim IV, and the survival of only one William I brieve.

Selkirk/Kelso and Scone

Only a few contemporary single sheets have been preserved from the three remaining pre-1139 foundations (Selkirk/Kelso, Scone, and Dunfermline). There is at least one cartulary for each, however. The most impressive is Kelso, whose cartulary of the mid-fourteenth century contains more than 430 documents from the twelfth and thirteenth centuries.[47] At least 49, and possibly as many as 59, are datable to before 1165; about 20 belong to the reign of David I. The cartulary preserves the texts of eight brieves from the twelfth century, but seven of these are of William I.[48] This at least means that the compiler of the cartulary was not especially ill-disposed to copying this kind of document. It may be significant, then, that the earliest brieve in the cartulary is an administrative brieve of Mael Coluim IV datable to the early 1160s.[49] It appears that whatever the archival practice was, that allowed about 50 documents to survive from the reigns of David I and Mael Coluim IV, the preservation of brieves had not been a priority. This may merely reinforce the general view that brieves were ephemeral. Certainly, the shortage of extant brieves from Kelso is more compelling than a profile of survival like Melrose's, where there is a shortage of early documents. A similar conclusion may be deduced from the *Registrum Vetus* of Glasgow Cathedral.[50] This dates from about the 1220s, and contains a respectable number of charters of David I: six in all,[51] but none of them are brieves. Glasgow Cathedral's archive of original documents, which had been taken to Paris at the time of the Reformation, was almost entirely destroyed during the French Revolution: only eight have so far been recovered.[52]

Scone's two cartularies are neither particularly old nor especially bulky.[53] Both have suffered damage, particularly the earliest (from the second quarter of the fourteenth century), which is a sorry assortment of four gatherings and some loose leaves, and has suffered considerable losses.[54] The second cartulary was created in the fifteenth century: it has 12 charters of Mael Coluim IV as well as the grand confirmation of 1163/4,[55] including a brieve protecting Scone from poinding,[56] and an administrative brieve instructing the mormaer of Angus and sheriff of Forfar not to collect aids from the abbey's lands.[57] There are no charters of any kind in David I's name but there are a few of Alexander I, including the diploma recording Scone's foundation as an Augustinian priory and a brieve of protection addressed to 'all the merchants of England', granting freedom from customs for one ship.[58] These earlier documents have excited suspicion, in part because it was claimed in Mael Coluim's general confirmation that earlier royal charters had been reduced to ashes in a fire, resulting in the need to renew them. Worse still, it is recounted in an original notarial instrument of 1298 that the English wreaked havoc in the abbey, destroying charters and seals, including those of David I and Mael Coluim IV, but without mentioning Alexander I.[59] A. A. M. Duncan has recently undertaken a detailed study of the documents in Alexander I's name, however, and has concluded that they are genuine.[60] This makes the total lack of charters of David I all the more striking. The safest conclusion is that they have perished during Scone's misfortunes. The claim that Mael Coluim IV had to renew instruments that had been lost in a fire may, however, give rise to a slight feeling of unease. Michael Clanchy has commented on how monasteries could experience 'fortunate losses of documents'. He cited two cases where it was alleged that only duplicates survived because the originals had been lost, and how these tragedies furnished the victims with an explanation for any deficiencies in their documents.[61] In Scone's case perhaps it did not have a full portfolio in support of the 13 items attributed to David I's munificence. Be that as it may, the lack of brieves and other documents is, again, unquantifiable.

Preliminary conclusions

So far this brief survey of the muniments of the oldest monastic foundations in the hunt for brieves has arrived at the rather predictable conclusion that very few indeed survive owing largely to a generally poor rate of survival, the result of both the vicissitudes of fortune and, it may be suspected, the lack of effective record-keeping in the early stages by a number of these monasteries. A miserable total of two brieves of David I have been traced from these five houses: both are from Holyrood. Five brieves of Mael Coluim IV have been accounted for: two again from Holyrood, two from Scone, and one from Kelso.[62] There has, moreover, been some indication that brieves were less likely to be kept in this period, in line with the general view that these documents (particularly administrative brieves) were rather 'ephemeral'. By way of contrast, we can turn to the cathedral priory of St Andrews, the next major foundation after my arbitrary terminal date of 1139.[63] Duncan has argued compellingly that the priory was established in 1140, which he maintains is the actual date of Bishop Robert's charter announcing the priory's foundation and listing its possessions. David I's confirmation, which could date to any time in the early or mid-1140s, refers to nine royal benefactions, only two of which were mentioned in Bishop Robert's charter.[64] Individual documents survive for six or seven of these,[65] including the two items which reiterate brieves. A subsequent brieve is also extant for St Andrews Hospital, which belonged to the cathedral priory. It appears, then, that the cathedral priory of St Andrews preserved its muniments quite effectively from the outset, which would help to explain the number of brieves of David I extant in its cartulary. Four brieves survive from the reign of Mael Coluim IV.[66] Effective record-keeping could also account for the significant numbers of brieves of David I surviving in English archives. Durham's four is overtaken by the five preserved in Reading's muniments, relating to its cells on the Isle of May and at Rhynd. Other English houses account for five brieves in total.

Dunfermline's archive

All this is completely overshadowed by Dunfermline. Its cartulary has no fewer than 15 brieves of David I, as well as David's two diplomas confirming all Dunfermline's rights and possessions, and 15 other charters of David I.[67] Dunfermline is less remarkable in its number of brieves of Mael Coluim IV: there are five,[68] which compares with the four for St Andrews Priory and its hospital. Unfortunately, no originals survive, although these were still extant as late as 1612 when an inventory was made.[69] The archive at that time even contained an original writ of King Henry II for Dunfermline.[70] As we shall see, there was no home for this in the cartulary's scheme.

It is Dunfermline's documents of David I which catch the eye and call for closer examination. Is it simply that Dunfermline developed good archival habits earlier than anyone else in Scotland? First, let us look at the cartulary. The original core of this complex codex was created sometime between 4 February 1254 and probably in or not long after 1255.[71] It begins with royal documents arranged by king, then episcopal charters by see, and lay charters. Papal bulls were not part of the original scheme, and were added later in the thirteenth century.[72] Not all the texts in the original cartulary are complete. Only a rubric and opening words are given of some episcopal charters and a few lay ones, although some space has usually been left for the omitted text. This suggests that the cartulary was compiled in some haste. The documents which have suffered this indignity seem on the whole to have been reiterations of earlier deeds; the rubrics reveal, or suggest, that they are either a confirmation of a single transaction, or an agreement to uphold the provisions of a previous charter.

No royal document is so rudely curtailed, however. Indeed, particular care has evidently been taken with them. The collection of each king's charters is arranged so that it concludes with a general confirmation, and the top margin of each page is adorned with the king's name in lombardic capitals, with alternately red and blue letters. The most striking feature of these royal documents is the inclusion of some curious items which suggests that little or nothing was omitted. Foremost among these are two brieves and a charter of David I that could have been of little or no relevance to Dunfermline in the 1250s. One is an instruction to the earls of Orkney and Caithness that they should maintain and protect the *manaig* of the church of Dornoch. This is particularly remarkable because Dunfermline had no known connection with Dornoch. Barrow has suggested that the appearance of this document in the cartulary may have something to do with Andrew, a monk of Dunfermline who was bishop of Caithness (from about 1147 until 1184).[73] Perhaps Bishop Andrew deposited it for safekeeping in Dunfermline's archive. This could also explain a second curiosity, a charter recording David's gift of the upland part of Longforgan to Bishop Andrew.[74] There is no trace of a connection between this land and Dunfermline, so again the presence of this charter in the cartulary is not immediately explicable. Finally, there is a brieve of neyfty obtained not directly for Dunfermline's benefit, but for a certain Leofgifu.[75] Like Bishop Andrew, she had close links with Dunfermline. Barrow has identified her as the person of that name recognized by Dunfermline's mother-church, Canterbury, as a 'sister'.[76] The assumption is that her lands were subsequently acquired by

Dunfermline, and with them this document. It is conceivable, however, that she, like Bishop Andrew, may have placed this document in the abbey for safekeeping. The main point, again, is that this would have been of limited relevance in the 1250s. The abbey had two brieves of neyfty from William I, as well as what might be described as a proto-brieve of neyfty from David I.[77] Two further curiosities in the cartulary are a brieve and a charter of David I relating to two separate grants that disappear completely from view,[78] despite numerous royal and papal confirmations of Dunfermline's rights and possessions. It seems that these two grants were ineffective. They may, of course, have been included in the cartulary because some dim hope was harboured that they might yet be made good (although there is no record of any dispute).[79] Be that as it may, they were of very limited, if any, relevance when they were copied into the cartulary.

It seems, then, that the cartulary was composed with the intention of copying all available Scottish royal documents. This is not to claim that *no* charter was lost in the century or so of the archive's existence prior to the creation of the cartulary. It would not be too rash, however, to suppose that a fairly effective, if indiscriminate, system of record-keeping had been established before the end of David's reign, and that no *significant* losses had been sustained, at least where land, revenue, and rights were involved. If this is accepted, then Dunfermline's archive assumes particular importance as evidence for the adoption of charters in general, and especially brieves. It is certainly the best that is available for assessing this process from the perspective of a Scottish beneficiary.

The adoption of charters at Dunfermline

Looking at Dunfermline's pre-1153 collection overall, some striking patterns can be observed. The most obvious is that, although Dunfermline was about a half-century old when it was promoted to an abbey in 1128, and had been the beneficiary of grants by kings and queens amounting to 19 named settlements or estates, the cartulary has no charter earlier than David I. Our earliest information about these possessions is David I's first general confirmation, which Barrow has argued should probably be dated to 1128, when Dunfermline was granted the status of an abbey.[80] They are repeated in David I's second general confirmation, which Geoffrey Barrow has suggested was probably produced about the time of the dedication of the new abbey church, which probably took place on 11 June 1150.[81] David I's second general confirmation also includes a number of settlements and estates which he had granted previously. These include Carberry and Penick, which are each the subject of charters in their own right, the first datable to the early or mid-1140s, the other to sometime probably in or between 1131 and 1145.[82] There is also the charter recording David's grant of Newburn and Balchrystie on the day of new abbey's dedication, that is probably 11 June 1150.[83] A number of David's grants of land are not, however, the subject of any separate extant record: namely Smeaton, Woolmet, and a carucate called Pitteuchar. A similarly patchy pattern is apparent in other types of grant. For example, there is no separate document(s) relating to the donation after 1128 of the two churches of Stirling or the church of Perth with their pertinents, although all appear in David's final general confirmation of 1150; there is, however, a charter for the grant in the same period of the church of Inveresk after the death of the incumbent.[84] The same is true for tofts in burghs: a single charter from before 17 July 1127 includes grants of dwellings in Dunfermline, Stirling, Perth, and Edinburgh,[85] but no extant charter or charters is concerned specifically with the grant of tofts in Roxburgh, Haddington, and Linlithgow, or the dwellings of Roger, the priest, in Stirling,[86] granted sometime between 1128 and 1150. Mention could also be made of fishings, teinds of specific renders, and money for vestments which are mostly the subject of extant written record for the first time in either the general confirmation of 1128 or that of 1150.

Taken on its own, such a pattern of documentation might simply be explained by uneven survival. It should, however, be viewed in conjunction with the suggestion that Dunfermline's archive of royal documents in the 1250s is exceptionally well represented in the cartulary, and with the indications that the archive at that time was fairly full, including a number of outdated relics from David's reign. It would be extraordinary in these circumstances if the lack of individual charters on this scale was simply due to a failure to include them in the cartulary and/or to an extensive loss of originals before the 1250s. The alternative explanation is that the pattern of extant documents approximates fairly closely to what was actually procured by Dunfermline, at least with regard to the document-types attested there. It should also be recalled that grants to Dunfermline began in a period when there were no charters as such. We should, therefore, expect to find no charters at all for the earliest benefactions, followed by a gradual uptake in their use, until they become almost routine. This is, indeed, the pattern presented to us by Dunfermline's archive as represented by its cartulary. At one end of the spectrum there is nothing at all before David's reign; at the other end of the spectrum we find separate charters for 11 out of 13 grants[87] made between 1150 and King William's first general confirmation, probably soon after his accession in December 1165, the only exceptions being Mael Coluim IV's fresh grant of 23 acres adjacent to the abbey on the occasion of his general confirmation,[88] and William's grant of 100 shillings per annum from the burgh ferme of Edinburgh which 'he gave on the day of the funeral of his brother, King Mael Coluim'.[89] The gradual adoption of charters appears from this evidence to belong, in the case of Dunfermline at least, to the quarter-century before 1150.

Brieves in Dunfermline before 1150

It will be recalled that there are 15 brieves and 15 charters of David I in Dunfermline's cartulary.[90] As might be expected, there is some fluidity between these categories. Eight of the brieves are easily classifiable as instructions of a legal or administrative kind.[91] Five of the seven which remain, however, are grants which have instructions for their implementation attached at the end:[92] for example, a grant of 20 shillings from Elgin was accompanied by a command to the grieves of Elgin that this be paid without impediment.[93] Other brieves of this type relate to the grant of a toft, and to the rendering of teinds of specific renders from named settlements. A starker example is the grant of Penick which has a brieve of protection against poinding tacked on.[94] Finally there is a brieve to the sheriff of Stirling ordering that Dunfermline should have one of the king's saltpans.[95] This could just as well have been expressed as a grant of a saltpan (as in the case of charters for Kelso and Newbattle[96]). A similar freedom in form is found among the 15 charters. Two are grants combined with instructions for their implementation which are similar to what I have called 'hybrid' brieves.[97] Indeed, one is structurally identical to the 'hybrid' brieve granting 20 shillings from the burgh of Elgin; presumably it only escaped from Barrow's list of brieves because it is longer and more solemn than its counterpart: it contains a *pro anima* clause and eight witnesses. A further four charters are exceptionally brief, consisting simply of a short address (David, king of Scots, to all his worthy men, greeting), a brief notification of the grant, and anything from one to three witnesses, and a place-date.[98] Among these terse charters is the only grant of a church by David I and the only grant before 1150 of a settlement to Dunfermline recorded in an individual document. At the other end of the scale are five charters which are recognizably solemn documents: they have, for example, a long address and/or a *pro anima* clause and/or more than half-a-dozen witnesses. Two are datable to 1150 or later.[99] Finally, there are three charters which fall somewhere between the terse and the solemn,[100] and another which is a multiple grant that, unusually, has a named individual (Bishop Robert of St Andrews) in its address, similar to a brieve.[101]

All in all, therefore, there are 20 documents before 1150 (not including general confirmations) in which grants have been recorded. Of these, seven appear in Barrow's list of brieves; a further seven may be recognized as having some of the characteristics of a brieve, either because they include a named individual in their address, or because they incorporate a supplementary instruction that is more elaborate or specific than a simple injunction framed in general terms, or because they are strikingly terse. In contrast, only three have any particularly solemn features. Indeed, when the monks of Dunfermline wanted an especially solemn document, such as a general confirmation of their possessions, revenues and rights, they produced a diploma. For many of their possessions and revenues, moreover, the two diplomas of David I constituted their only written record. It is as if royal power was most readily conceived as operating in the near-present, hence the element of immediacy that features in many records of individual grants, and in the use of the diploma for the grandest occasions.

Dunfermline and the adoption of brieves

How representative is Dunfermline of a broader picture? Perhaps the safest conclusion to draw from this survey is that each monastery had its own approach to documents, particularly in the early stages of charter use. It may be recalled, for example, that diplomas appear not to have been used at all in Melrose and Kelso. In Dunfermline, by contrast, the diploma seems to have been a particular speciality. Barrow has noted that, although it was used in other monasteries during David I's reign, 'only the Dunfermline examples keep strictly to the conventional structure of the diploma'.[102] After 1150 Dunfermline alone continued to frame general confirmations as diplomas: the final example is dated 10 March 1277.[103] It is perfectly feasible, therefore, to imagine that the solemn charter may have been more prevalent in some other monasteries than in Dunfermline, particularly perhaps reformed Benedictine houses like Melrose and Kelso.

Even if it is accepted that Dunfermline may be untypical, it may still be regarded as offering a valuable perspective on the adoption of brieves, and of charters generally, in a Scottish context. All the other monasteries under discussion almost certainly used charters to some extent from the beginning. In their case, this cannot readily be distinguished from the importation of monks or canons from institutions in England, where charters were a regular feature. This distinction can, however, be appreciated in the case of Dunfermline, but only because of its longer history: it appears that neither the original cell established from Canterbury nor the monks sent from Canterbury about 30 years later brought writs and diplomas with them. This also makes Dunfermline particularly well placed to offer a perspective on what may have changed in the Scottish kingdom to encourage the adoption of charters. It alone of all the monasteries under review experienced the transition to documents when already a well-established foundation. Viewed in this light, the prominence of brieves and brieve-like charters in its archive assumes particular interest, especially in situations where other forms could have been deployed. Presumably this reflects the kind of document with which Dunfermline was most familiar at the time when it eventually adopted charters. It is impossible, in the absence of originals, to say how these were produced. Even if they were written in Dunfermline, or at Dunfermline's behest, however, we can still ask from where the immediate experience of documents of this kind is likely to have come.[104]

The earliest Scottish brieves

The most obvious source is the king of Scots himself. As early as the reign of Alexander I the king had at least occasional use for brieves. It can readily be envisaged how Dunfermline, as a key royal centre, would have become aware of this. The likelihood that brieves were a relatively recent innovation would also fit with the apparent chronology of Dunfermline's adoption of documents, which began about a decade later than the earliest extant royal brieve. This points to the king, rather than the church, as the driving force in the initial use of brieves. If so, this would mean that they were first adopted in a Scottish context by the king to communicate his will for his own ends. But do any such documents survive from this period?

Extant brieves tend naturally to be in the interests of the church in whose archive they have been retained. It is unlikely that the king initiated any of these. It is equally unlikely that any brieve written principally for the king's own purpose would survive. Against the odds, however, there are a couple of extraordinary survivals. The earliest known royal brieve, addressed to Durham and its prior, begins with an instruction by Alexander I not to begin proceedings before a particular case is brought before him. The king then added: 'I make known to you, moreover, lord prior, that I have much to say to you in confidence about many things, as soon as it will be possible to do so.'[105] This was obviously not drafted at Durham.[106] An even clearer example of a brieve written ostensibly for the king's own benefit, and no-one else's, owes its preservation to the curious fact that it was copied into Durham's *Liber Vitae*. It is an order by David I, sometime in or before 1136, to replenish the king's log-pile at Berwick with trees from a wood that was in dispute between the addressee and someone else.[107] The existence of these two early examples make it significantly easier to accept that brieves were introduced into Scotland by the king, and that it was as a result of this that Dunfermline, at least, began to seek similar documents as a novel way of using royal authority to safeguard its rights and revenues. It is also at about this time that the first royal chancellor is attested, from the last year-or-so of Alexander I's reign.[108] It is difficult to know precisely what significance may be attached to this. At the very least, however, it may be regarded as another sign of royal interest in documents as a means of conveying the king's will.

According to this scenario, then, the church may not have been the only agency promoting the adoption of charters; it is possible to envisage that in some contexts the king could also have played a crucial role as an initiator of documents in his own right, not just as the authority in whose name the earliest charters were produced. If we ask how the king (apparently Alexander I)[109] came to adopt brieves, however, then we are surely drawn back to the church as a crucial influence, particularly Durham, with which kings of Scots, and Alexander himself, had such close associations.[110]

Acknowledgements

I am very grateful to Profs A. A. M. Duncan and Richard Sharpe for giving me access to forthcoming publications; to Prof. Geoffrey Barrow for reading this piece prior to publication, and alerting me to a 'new' brieve of Mael Coluim IV; to the organizers of the symposium for the invitation to participate; and to Dr Nerys Ann Jones for her constant support.

Notes

1. Broun, *Charters*, 29–37; Barrow, 'Pattern', 131, n. 3. Most relate to transactions in the twelfth century.
2. This has implications for the appropriateness of the term 'Celtic charter': see Broun, *Charters*, 38–44.
3. *ESC*, 10–24, passim.
4. For an exception, see p. 178.
5. See p. 171.
6. For 'solemn charter' see *RRS*, i, 59; Barrow, 'Scots Charter', 97.

7. Barrow, *Charters of King David I*, 9.
8. *ESC*, no. XXVII.
9. Barrow, *Charters of King David I*, no. 11.
10. Duncan, 'Yes, The Earliest Scottish Charters'; Donnelly, 'Earliest Scottish Charters?'; Barrow, 'Kings of Scotland', 315.
11. See p. 177.
12. See p. 46; also Sharpe, 'Use of Writs'.
13. See p. 9.
14. Broun, 'Writing of Charters', 120.
15. Bartlett, *Making of Europe*, 283–5.
16. Broun, 'Writing of Charters', 122.
17. On royal approval see *RRAN*, ed. Bates, 96–109.
18. Barrow, *Charters of King David I*, 27 (and Broun, 'Changing Face of Charter Scholarship', 208–10); *RRS*, i, 86.
19. Standardization is apparent in four brieves of neyfty ordering the return of fugitive serfs in similar terms, each for a different beneficiary; in contrast, a brieve early in the reign of David I, written with the same intent, is more fluid in form and content: Barrow, *Charters of King David I*, nos 20, 142; *RRS*, i, nos 167, 188, 192 (and pp. 62–4).
20. See e.g. *RRAN*, ed. Bates, nos 285, 334 (1086×1087) (*Facsimiles*, ed. Bishop and Chaplais, pl. XXVa; see also ibid., xiv). The injunctive element becomes more substantial in later reigns: e.g. *RRAN*, ii, no. 1493, iii, no. 500 (essentially a repetition of the former) (reproduced in *RRAN*, iv, pl. XVIII), and *RRAN*, iii, no. 800 (iv, pl. VIIIa).
21. See e.g. *RRAN*, iii, no. 346 (iv, pl. XXa).
22. Note, e.g. *RRS*, i, no. 177.
23. See p. 176 for examples.
24. Barrow, *Charters of King David I*, 9, n. 16. As well as comprising documents which feature named individuals or specific officials in their address, and that open with a command, this also includes some notifications which conclude with an instruction; i.e. those which feature a specific command rather than simply an injunction framed in general terms.
25. The figures for total numbers of charters and of originals per donor are Barrow's.
26. This includes the brieves mentioned in note 27, and a charter published in Barrow, *Anglo-Norman Era*, 171.
27. This includes a brieve published in Barrow, *Anglo-Norman Era*, 169–70, and also a brieve for Guisborough priory which has recently been identified in Oxford, Bodleian Library, MS Top. Yorks e.12, fo. 76r–v, a manuscript of John Burton, editor of *Monasticon Eboracense* (York, 1758). I am extremely grateful to Prof. Barrow for this information and for giving me a copy of this document.
28. Barrow, *Charters of King David I*, 44 (and 85 for the dispute); *RRS*, i, 116.
29. *Holyrood Liber*, lxxx and nos 3–6, 12, 15, 18, 20–22, 26.
30. NAS, GD 45/13/216–19, 224, 229, 231–2, 235 (Barrow, *Charters of King David I*, 44; *RRS*, i, 116).
31. Barrow, *Charters of King David I*, no. 68 (comment). All its muniments are to be found in Durham.
32. Barrow, *Kingdom of the Scots*, chs 5 and 6.
33. Duncan, *Kingship of the Scots*, 85.

34. Figures calculated from Cunningham, *Syllabus*.
35. It is not clear whether *Holyrood Liber*, no. 75 was part of the archive; no. 7 was not.
36. *Holyrood Liber*, lxxx.
37. See Barrow, *Charters of King David I*, no. 33 (comment).
38. Ibid., no. 147 (and comment).
39. Ibid., nos 70 and 115.
40. Ibid., nos 115 and 148; *RRS*, i, nos 192, 230.
41. *RRS*, ii, 117–18.
42. Barrow, *Charters of King David I*, nos 147–8.
43. Figures calculated from *Melrose Liber*, i, iii–xviii, in conjunction with the NAS catalogue for GD 55 and BL Cotton Charters XVIII, nos 1–18. *Melrose Liber* is not complete: for example, it does not include the single sheet, BL Additional Charter 76747 (1175×1196).
44. NLS Adv. 34.4.11; BL, MS Harley 3960.
45. Barrow, *Charters of King David I*, no. 120.
46. *RRS*, ii, no. 177 (1173×1177).
47. Figures calculated from Shead, *Syllabus*.
48. *RRS*, ii, nos 64, 68, 95, 123, 239, 248, 289.
49. *RRS*, i, no. 177.
50. NLS, MS Acc. 10301/1.
51. It also contains David's inquest as ruler of 'Cumbria'.
52. Duncan, 'Monk and the Medieval Archives'.
53. NLS, Adv. MSS 34.3.28 and 34.3.29.
54. Its earliest document, of which only a portion at the end survives, is the grand confirmation by Mael Coluim IV in 1163 or 1164 announcing the appointment of an abbot: *RRS*, i, no. 243. This forms the beginning of a gathering of four leaves (fos 9–13) which probably stood at the end of the cartulary.
55. *RRS*, i, nos 215, 244–53, 262.
56. Ibid., i, no. 262.
57. Ibid., i, no. 252. The licence to have three craftsmen (no. 246) is also a brieve.
58. *ESC*, no. XLVIII.
59. Duncan, *Scotland*, 640–1.
60. Duncan, 'Foundation'.
61. Clanchy, *From Memory to Written Record*, 148–9.
62. Scone also has a brieve of Alexander I: *ESC*, no. XLVIII.
63. For what follows see Duncan, 'Foundation'.
64. Barrow, *Charters of King David I*, no. 126.
65. The doubt concerns ibid., no. 173 (1150×1152): Duncan suggests that an earlier charter was lost.
66. *RRS*, i, nos 126, 167, 170, 233.
67. NLS, Adv. 34.1.3a, fos 41ra–44va; see pp. 176–7, for references to Barrow, *Charters of King David I*.
68. *RRS*, i, nos 179, 181, 185, 213, 214.
69. Fyvie Estate Office, bundle 289–97, item 295: see Barrow, *Charters of King David I*, 71. No Scottish royal document before 1250 is mentioned in the inventory that does not appear in the cartulary.
70. Barrow, 'Writ of Henry II'.

71. The original scribe's work is on fos 41r–52v, 57r–61r, 110r–111r, 115r, 117r–124v. His last royal document is dated 4 February 1254 (fo. 52va, *Dunfermline Registrum* no. 84), and is followed (fo. 52va–b, ibid., no. 85) by a document dated 1255 in a contemporary hand. The next document (dated 1278) is in another hand.
72. Fos 135v–143r.
73. Barrow, *Charters of King David I*, no. 155 and comment.
74. Ibid., no. 156.
75. Ibid., no. 142.
76. Barrow, *Kingdom of the Scots*, 196–8.
77. Barrow, *Charters of King David I*, no. 20; *RRS*, ii, 31, 163.
78. Barrow, *Charters of King David I*, nos 99, 137.
79. There is a theoretical possibility that their omission was accidental: David I's grant of a tenth of his gold from Fife and Fothriff (ibid., no. 140) did not appear in a general confirmation until William I's (*RRS*, ii, no. 30, foot of p. 140); William's general confirmation, however, omits the chapel and tofts at Inverkeithing granted by Mael Coluim IV (*RRS*, i, no. 178).
80. Barrow, *Charters of King David I*, no. 33 and comment.
81. Ibid., no. 172 and comment. *Concedo* is used throughout, apart from *do et concedo* for the grant of Newburn and Balchrystie, which was also the subject of a separate charter. Presumably none of the other grants were actually made on this occasion. By implication, the same holds for the earlier general confirmation in which *concede* is used.
82. Ibid., nos 131, 141.
83. Ibid., no. 171.
84. Ibid., no. 21. It does not appear in the confirmation of 1128 (*pace* ibid., 71) and so may be dated 1128×c.1135 (because its royal style has *dei gratia*: see ibid., 11–12), rather than 'probably×1128'.
85. Ibid., no. 19.
86. Unlikely to be Roger Cassus of ibid., no. 137, whom it may be inferred was located in or near Craigmillar.
87. Counting the church of Kellie and chapel of Abercrombie as two gifts, albeit in one charter (*RRS*, i, no. 157); also Walter the Steward's gift of a toft and 20 acres represented by his own charter (*Dunfermline Registrum*, no. 161).
88. Hence *Ego . . . dono* at this point.
89. *RRS*, ii, no. 30 (p. 142).
90. This includes those for Andrew, bishop of Caithness, and Leofgifu, and Dunfermline's cell at Urquhart.
91. Barrow, *Charters of King David I*, nos 17, 20, 50, 142, 152, 155, 189, 190.
92. Ibid., nos 18, 48, 49, 99, 195.
93. Ibid., no. 195.
94. Ibid., no. 131.
95. Ibid., no. 67.
96. Ibid., no. 151 (Kelso), no. 114 (Newbattle).
97. Ibid., nos 38, 44.
98. Ibid., nos 21, 35, 140, 141.
99. Ibid., nos 171, 185. The other three, no. 39 (1124×1136), a grant of a fishery and toft (7 witnesses); and no. 37 (1124×1136), freedom from labour services (*pro anima* clause; 4 witnesses); and no. 137 (1136×1147), a grant of a ploughgate and two dwellings (long address, *pro anima* clause, 5 witnesses).

100. Ibid., nos 36, 138, 156.
101. Ibid., no. 19.
102. Barrow, *Charters of King David I*, 4 (in contrast to the hybrid nature of some other general confirmations).
103. *Dunfermline Registrum*, no. 81. These royal general confirmations, moreover, were confined to benefactions by the king and his predecessors, not to all grants (except for Walter the Steward's gift on the day of Mael Coluim IV's funeral). When Dunfermline wanted a confirmation of all its possessions and rights it obtained this from the pope, not the king, the earliest being a bull of Alexander III dated 7 June 1163 (Somerville, *Scotia Pontificia*, no. 49; *Dunfermline Registrum*, no. 237). The earliest grants not framed as a royal donation are 1153 × 1162.
104. The earliest brieve and charter (Barrow, *Charters of King David I*, nos 17 and 19) definitely pre-date the arrival of a new abbot from Canterbury in 1128.
105. Alexander I regarding a hearing of Durham's right to Swinton, Berwickshire (*ESC*, no. XXVII: Alexander's confirmation of Durham's right is ibid., no. XXVI). Presumably this dates to the same time that Durham's possession of Swinton was the subject of charters of Earl David: Barrow, *Charters of King David I*, nos 9 and 10, dated '1114 × 1118, probably 1116 × 1118'.
106. Note that Barrow, *Charters of King David I*, 25, identifies the scribe as his 'Earl David 1' responsible for 7 out of the 12 extant originals of *acta* of Scottish kings (and Earl David) before 1124, but to my eyes the reproduction in *Facsimiles*, ed. Innes, i, no. IX, suggests otherwise.
107. Barrow, *Charters of King David I*, no. 43.
108. *ESC*, nos 47–9.
109. Aelred of Rievaulx described Alexander as *litteratus* (Aelred, *Genealogia*, col. 736). If this was true, he would have been more familiar with communicating by writing than probably any previous king of Scots.
110. Barrow, 'Kings of Scotland', esp. 316.

10

Culture, Power and the Charters of Welsh Rulers

Huw Pryce

In 1184 the southern Welsh ruler Rhys ap Gruffudd (the Lord Rhys) arrived with an armed force at Rhayader in mid-Wales. At the nearby church of Llansanffraid Cwmteuddwr he issued a charter confirming extensive lands to Strata Florida, a Cistercian abbey situated to the west of Rhayader in Ceredigion whose patronage Rhys had taken over after he captured its founder, Robert fitz Stephen, in 1165.[1] The charter offers some interesting insights into the complex processes of cultural assimilation and adaptation that occurred in the territories under native Welsh control from the mid-twelfth century onwards. It witnesses, not only to support for a reformed religious order of continental origin, but also to the adaptation of the diplomatic of the Anglo-Norman charter; furthermore, the clause that introduces the list of lands granted in the disposition is derived from a papal bull, presumably that issued in favour of Strata Florida by Alexander III.[2] Yet the document also draws on native traditions of charter-writing in its inclusion of lengthy perambulations written in a mixture of Latin and Welsh, and articulates the donor's political aspirations through the use of the styles 'Rhys, prince of Wales' and 'Rhys, proprietary prince of south Wales' in the protocol and notification respectively.

Rhys's charter for Strata Florida is one of almost 200 surviving charter-texts, together with just over 100 further charters known from mentions in other sources, issued in the names of Welsh rulers from the second quarter of the twelfth century to the extinction of native rule following the Edwardian conquest of 1282–83. The nature of this corpus of charters, contained in an edition of Welsh rulers' acts that also comprises letters, letters patent and other documents,[3] is summarized in Tables 10.1 and 10.2. As these tables make clear, the definition of 'Welsh rulers' is deliberately broad, encompassing lords of small territories such as

Table 10.1 Types of documents in *AWR*

	Charters	Letters patent	Letters	Agreements	Petitions	Other	Total
Originals	87	6	67	3	8	6	177
Copies	110	62	39	32	1	11	255
Spuria	6	–	–	–	–	–	6
Dubia	4	–	2	–	–	–	6
Deperdita	104	12	41	6	11	–	174
Total	311	80	149	41	20	17	618

Table 10.2 Total numbers of charters in *AWR* (including mentions but excluding spuria and dubia)

Arwystli	13
Cedewain	3
Deheubarth	46
Elfael and Maelienydd	8
Glamorgan	64
Gwynedd	61
Gwynllŵg	17
Powys	87
Senghennydd	2
Total	301

Arwystli or Gwynllŵg alongside members of the dynasties of the major principalities of Deheubarth (south-west Wales), Gwynedd (north-west Wales) and Powys (north-east Wales). The quantity of charters—both extant texts and those only known from mentions in other sources—is relatively small given the number of years covered, comparing unfavourably with the surviving output of English magnates of this period such as the earls of Chester, for whom 469 charters are extant from c.1071 to 1237.[4] However, irrespective of the extent to which the extant corpus reflects the numbers of documents originally produced,[5] the charters that do survive still have a great deal to contribute to an understanding of twelfth- and thirteenth-century Wales. (The same is also true of other Welsh charters from this period, including those issued by Marcher lords.)

On the whole, historians of Wales have viewed charters as sources for the transfer of property, although some attention has also been given to the styles used in princely documents as evidence for perceptions of power or notions of national identity.[6] By contrast, the diplomatic forms and the language of twelfth- and thirteenth-century Welsh charters have, to a considerable extent, escaped the close scrutiny to which similar documents have been subjected in some other European countries. The need for such scrutiny was recognized over 50 years ago by James Conway Davies, who wrote that 'one of the most clamant needs in Welsh medieval historical research is detailed work on diplomatic forms used in Wales'.[7] Of course, subsequent scholarship has advanced understanding of these forms in several important respects: the work of Wendy Davies on the pre-Norman charters extant in edited form in the Book of Llandaff and that of David Crouch and Julia Barrow on the episcopal acts of Llandaff and St Davids respectively are notable cases in point.[8] Moreover, with respect to the charters issued by twelfth- and thirteenth-century Welsh rulers, several scholars have followed Conway Davies's example and discussed the diplomatic of individual documents or collections of documents.[9] However, the first overview of the diplomatic of charters issued by Welsh rulers of this period only appeared in 2000 in a pioneering paper by Charles Insley.[10]

The following discussion builds on work on the diplomatic of these charters, including that undertaken in editing *The Acts of Welsh Rulers*, in order to highlight the documents' potential as sources for understanding broader developments in both written culture and, more briefly, the articulation of authority in twelfth- and early thirteenth-century Wales. Such an approach will in turn help to clarify the nature and significance of the charters themselves.

Before going any further, three preliminary points about the extant sample need to be made. First, the overwhelming majority of charters (both texts and mentions) are in favour of ecclesiastical beneficiaries, mostly religious houses, notably the Cistercians. This is particularly true of the period from the mid-twelfth century to c.1225 with which this discussion is mainly concerned—that is, the period in which Welsh rulers were particularly active in founding and making benefactions to religious houses (Table 10.3).[11] Second, patterns of archival survival vary considerably. Thus almost half the extant charter-texts are derived from the archives of just two Cistercian monasteries, namely Margam in Glamorgan and Strata Marcella in Powys, while the fifteenth-century cartulary of the Augustinian abbey of Haughmond in Shropshire furnishes texts of a further 21 charters; by contrast, the houses of Whitland and Talley, patronized by rulers of Deheubarth, are represented by only four and five summaries of grants, contained in royal inspeximuses,

Table 10.3 Distribution of charters in *AWR* (excluding spuria and dubia)

Type of beneficiary	301 charters, c.1150–1283	230 charters, c.1150–c.1225	71 charters, c.1225–1283
Ecclesiastical			
Authentic texts	167	145	22
Mentions	88	74	14
Total	255	219	36
Percentage	84.6	95.5	50.7
Lay			
Authentic texts	32	5	27
Mentions	14	6	8
Total	46	11	35
Percentage	15.4	4.5	49.3

respectively. The third point concerns chronology. No charters are known to have been issued by Welsh rulers earlier in the twelfth century than the 1130s, and most are datable to the 1150s onwards. Admittedly, the gap between these and the latest known charter of an eleventh-century Welsh ruler, issued in the 1070s, may be an optical illusion caused by the loss of sources. As David Crouch has argued, Welsh rulers of the late eleventh and early twelfth centuries continued in the main to patronize native ecclesiastical foundations, few of whose archives have survived, rather than the Benedictine houses patronized by Norman lords in Wales.[12] Yet, if native rulers did in fact continue to issue charters for major pre-Anglo-Norman churches after the 1070s, the charters they issued from the 1130s onwards marked a new departure in two related respects, as both the types of ecclesiastical beneficiary and the documents' diplomatic changed.

Of all the surviving charters of twelfth- and thirteenth-century Welsh rulers, only one conforms in its diplomatic with the pre-Norman tradition of charter-writing in Wales identified by Wendy Davies, namely a charter of Madog ap Maredudd, king of Powys, datable to between 1132 and 1151 for a recent native foundation at Trefeglwys in Arwystli—a region in mid-Wales over which Madog claimed overlordship.[13] The most distinctive characteristic of this tradition is the use of the third person, in a past tense; other defining features are 'the consistent inclusion of three constituent parts, disposition, witness list and sanction'.[14] Madog's charter adheres to this form, with a notification incorporating a general address and the grantor's style followed by a disposition whose verb (*dedit*) is in the perfect tense and third-person singular, a blessing and sanction and a witness list. Both the form of the charter and also some of its vocabulary strongly suggest that it was drafted by a Welsh ecclesiastic familiar with an indigenous tradition of diplomatic that differed from both the diploma and the charter of Anglo-Norman England.

Shortly after Madog's charter was issued, the church of Trefeglwys was granted by Hywel ab Ieuaf, local ruler of Arwystli, to the Augustinian abbey of Haughmond. When Hywel and other Welsh rulers confirmed Haughmond's possession of Trefeglwys, they did so in charters whose diplomatic conformed with Anglo-Norman norms—that is, in documents in letter-form which scholars sometimes refer to as writ-charters.[15] This was emblematic of a wider shift in the religious patronage of native rulers towards reformed orders such as the Augustinians and Cistercians, as well as towards Benedictine priories originally established in Wales by Anglo-Norman lords, which led in turn to the use of diplomatic forms with which the beneficiaries were familiar; indeed, it is likely that beneficiaries were usually responsible for drafting the documents. This is not to deny that rulers may also have favoured the writ-charter as a means of appropriating some of the trappings of lordship current in the Anglo-Norman or Angevin worlds, not least through the attachment of the ruler's seal, a form of authentication lacking in Welsh charters of the pre-Norman period.[16] Nevertheless, the variety in the diplomatic of charters issued for different beneficiaries suggests that rulers were not particularly concerned with imposing uniformity on the documents issued in their name, and that their adoption of the writ-charter originated above all in ecclesiastical demand.

In considering some of the characteristics of Welsh rulers' charters from the mid-twelfth to the earlier thirteenth century it may be helpful to draw a distinction between, on the one hand, charters issued in favour of religious houses that previously had a strong tradition of Anglo-Norman patronage and, on the other, charters for houses which native rulers had either founded or of which they were the principal patrons. (As Table 10.3 shows, charters in favour of lay beneficiaries are extremely few in the period up to c.1225, a point to which I shall return.) Broadly speaking, charters for predominantly Anglo-Norman foundations reflect those houses' familiarity with Anglo-Norman diplomatic, whereas charters for houses closely associated with Welsh rulers were more eclectic in their construction, drawing on a variety of models.

Examples of the first category include charters in favour of Goldcliff Priory, some of which are indebted in their phraseology to Robert de Candos's foundation charter for the abbey in 1113, issued by members of the dynasty of Gwynllŵg who held the lordship of Caerleon from

1136 to 1217.[17] It is also notable that the diplomatic of the Lord Rhys's confirmation to Chertsey Abbey of its priory at Cardigan bears suggestive affinities with that of English royal charters, and differs markedly from that of Rhys's only other extant charter-text, in favour of Strata Florida, mentioned at the beginning of this chapter.[18] Likewise, the charters issued from the late 1180s or 1190s by Morgan ap Caradog and other members of the Welsh dynasty of Glamorgan for the Cistercian abbey of Margam, founded by Robert of Gloucester in 1147, are similar in their diplomatic to those of the earls of Gloucester and of Anglo-Norman settlers in Glamorgan—indeed, as Robert Patterson's recent palaeographical study of the Margam charters has made clear, the same scribes not only wrote but also, to judge by the formulae used, drafted charters for both Anglo-Norman and Welsh grantors.[19] Yet even at Margam, whose monastic scribes were almost certainly all of English or French origin, the charters issued by the Welsh lords of Glamorgan contain some distinctive features far less common in the charters of Anglo-Norman grantors, notably a propensity to record the swearing of oaths in support of quitclaims or warranties, and also sometimes the names of pledges who had undertaken to secure the terms of a grant.[20] This bears comparison with Cadell ap Gruffudd's mid-twelfth-century confirmation of the church of Lampeter to Totnes Priory, which refers in its corroboration clause to Cadell's oath as well as his seal although in other respects it adheres to contemporary Anglo-Norman diplomatic.[21]

Given a context of beneficiary production, it is not surprising that Welsh rulers' charters for Anglo-Norman foundations such as Margam were indebted to existing traditions of diplomatic at those houses. But what happened when those rulers themselves founded, or acquired the patronage of, religious houses located within their territories? Of particular importance here is the filiation of Cistercian monasteries descended from Whitland Abbey in Dyfed. Whitland itself had originally been founded in 1140 from Clairvaux by Bernard, the Norman bishop of St Davids, but it is quite likely that by the mid-1160s its patronage had fallen to the Lord Rhys, who also, as we have seen, acquired the patronage of its daughter Strata Florida at about the same time.[22] Other houses affiliated to Whitland were Strata Marcella in southern Powys, Cwm-hir in Maelienydd, Aberconwy and Cymer in Gwynedd, and Valle Crucis in northern Powys. In contrast to Margam, Neath and Basingwerk, the monks of the Whitland filiation of houses were overwhelmingly Welsh and identified themselves with the native dynasties and with native culture.[23] The charters issued in their favour thus show how Welsh rulers assimilated the basic structure of the writ-charter in contexts which arguably offered the greatest room for manoeuvre, largely unconstrained by Anglo-Norman precedents. How much input rulers themselves had in the drafting of these charters is, admittedly, extremely uncertain: it is likely that beneficiary drafting remained the order of the day. The contrasts with charters issued for houses that had strong traditions of Anglo-Norman patronage may, therefore, essentially turn on the models available.

In the case of the Whitland filiation, those models seem to have been predominantly ecclesiastical. This is suggested by some general features, notably a preference for the use of forms of *noscere* rather than *scire* in notifications,[24] but also in some rather surprising details. Consider the charter granted to Whitland by Owain Cyfeiliog, prince of southern Powys, for the foundation of its daughter-house of Strata Marcella near Welshpool c.1170, together with one of the charters issued in favour of Strata Marcella in 1191 by Owain's son, Gwenwynwyn.[25] Both open with a verbal invocation and lack a notification: Owain's charter proceeds immediately to the dispositive clause, Gwenwynwyn's, uniquely among the Strata Marcella charters, contains an arenga or preamble, followed by a dispositive clause introduced by the words *Forma igitur hec est*. Both of these charters appear to be indebted in these respects to the diploma. Although the diploma continued to be used in England until the mid-twelfth century despite the increasing dominance of the writ-charter, it was unusual thereafter.[26] It is possible, therefore, that knowledge of the diploma derived from Whitland, a daughter-house of Clairvaux whose original community presumably included monks from Burgundy. Although no texts of charters for Whitland are extant from before 1170,[27] beneficiary drafting at Whitland, under the influence of continental models, may well explain the unusual features of Owain Cyfeiliog's foundation charter for Strata Marcella, which in turn probably influenced the redaction of Gwenwynwyn's charter. That the monks of Clairvaux were familiar with the diploma is shown by the numerous examples of such documents issued in favour of that monastery by bishops and secular rulers. For instance, several acts of Godfrey, bishop of Langres, open with the same invocation as that in the Strata Marcella charters and likewise omit a notification.[28] Moreover, these, like the Welsh charters under consideration, could have a witness list rather than *signa*.[29] The adoption of aspects of the diploma in Owain Cyfeiliog's charter may also have reflected an assumption, still current on the Continent, that this form was 'peculiarly appropriate for a solemn charter of foundation'.[30]

The dating clause of Gwenwynwyn's charter of 1191 is also unusual and may reflect both continental and English influence. It opens with the phrase *actum pupplice*, a formula that was normal in the dating clauses of acts of Louis VI and Louis VII of France (though it fell into disuse under Philip Augustus).[31] On the other hand, in addition to the year of the incarnation, it gives the regnal year of Richard I of England, echoing the recent innovation of dating English royal charters by regnal year introduced at Richard's accession in 1189.[32] No authentic act of a Welsh ruler includes the ruler's regnal year, and dating by the regnal year of English kings is rare.[33] But perhaps the most remarkable dating clause among the acts of Welsh rulers occurs in the charter issued in May 1212 by Madog ap Maelgwn, who belonged to the dynasty of Maelienydd in mid-Wales, in favour of the Cistercian abbey of Cwm-hir— a charter acquired by the Bibliothèque nationale in Paris c.1886.[34] This reads *Datum litterarum per manum domni Riredi abbatis mense maio*, and is the closest we come among all the charters of Welsh rulers to the form of dating clause that refers to a datary responsible for authorizing the issue of a document. The precise influence at work here is uncertain. The formula *Dat' per manum N. cancellarii* was incorporated in the dating clauses used by the papal chancery by the mid-twelfth century, and this provided at least the ultimate model for its adoption, from Richard I's accession in 1189, by the English royal chancery, whose practice in turn influenced episcopal diplomatic in England, while in France the chancery of Philip Augustus used the same formula in royal diplomas.[35] Yet if the charter for Cwm-hir reflects the influence of such dating clauses, it differs from them in omitting a place-date and in its apparently ungrammatical inclusion of the genitive plural *litterarum* after *Datum*. Possibly what we have here, then, is an inexpert attempt to devise a *per manum* type of dating clause that would emphasize the abbot's role in executing the document. Overall, though, the influence of English royal diplomatic on charters issued for monasteries in the heartlands of native power is conspicuous by its absence—all the more so given that several of these houses received royal confirmations, including Strata Florida in 1182×1183 and Strata Marcella in 1200.[36]

Yet while some of the charters issued by Welsh rulers in favour of houses belonging to the Whitland filiation of Cistercian houses were indebted to a variety of external models (the borrowings from a papal bull in the Lord Rhys's charter for Strata Florida are a further case in point), native influences are evident too. Drafters were often literate in Welsh as well as Latin. Care was taken in the spelling of Welsh place-names and personal names, even to the extent, in some originals, of placing accents to indicate where the stress should fall.[37] For instance, a notable feature of the scribe of Gwenwynwyn's charter of 1191 is his adherence to the Old Welsh orthographical practice of using -*gu*- to render medial /w/.[38] There are also examples of the use of the insular abbreviation ÷ for *est*,[39] though by and large it is difficult to identify palaeographical features in surviving original charters that could be considered distinctively Welsh. As regards diplomatic, though, native influence is clearest in the use of perambulations, which quite often switch back and forth between Latin and Welsh. For example, whereas the papal bull for Strata Florida refers tersely to Rhys's gift of the abbey's site of Ystrad-fflur 'with all its granges and appurtenances', Rhys's 1184 charter for the abbey describes the lands granted by providing two detailed perambulations of their boundaries that include connecting words in Welsh.[40] Perambulations also occur in many of the charters for Strata Marcella, which, like Strata Florida, was a daughter of Whitland Abbey.[41] However, to judge by the extant summaries, they were also a feature of charters issued by the Lord Rhys and his descendants for his Premonstratensian foundation of Talley, and were thus not restricted to Cistercian beneficiaries.[42] In all these cases it is likely that drafters were drawing on earlier Welsh charter-writing practices. Both perambulation and a mixture of Latin and Welsh for the linking words (as well as the use of Welsh alone) occur in the boundary clauses of charters preserved in the early twelfth-century Book of Llandaff (*Liber Landavensis*), and may in some cases have formed integral parts of the texts of the charters from the mid- or late ninth century.[43] Their appearance in twelfth- and thirteenth-century charters is a conservative aspect of Welsh diplomatic by comparison with that of England, where detailed perambulations tended to die out in royal acts with the demise of the Anglo-Saxon diploma, though they continued to be used in private charters, especially in the northern English counties, and were also widespread in twelfth- and thirteenth-century royal charters in Scotland.[44]

The charters issued by Welsh rulers thus witness to a variety of influences which in turn reflected wider political and ecclesiastical changes in Wales. While the almost universal adherence to the writ-charter indicates a readiness to assimilate cultural norms from the Anglo-Norman and Angevin worlds, the process of assimilation was complex and did not entail the slavish imitation of any one particular model. This diversity fits into a bigger picture of cultural adaptation and interaction in Wales at this period.[45] It also probably implies an overwhelming reliance on beneficiary production. Although by no means redundant elsewhere, beneficiary production diminished in importance in the major European kingdoms and principalities during the twelfth and early thirteenth centuries as rulers' chanceries became increasingly responsible for drafting acts according to standardized forms and formulae. This appears not to have happened in Wales, where only the rulers of Gwynedd, the most powerful principality, possessed a writing-office that could be described as a chancery, but probably not before the second quarter of the thirteenth century; and in any case it is uncertain how far this was responsible for drafting rather than simply authenticating charters.[46] In the period up to c.1225, therefore, native rulers seem to have adopted a more *ad hoc* approach to charter production, perhaps because output remained low and resulted mainly from ecclesiastical demand.[47]

What does all this imply, in turn, about the power of the rulers in whose names charters were issued? In other words, what connections may we make between charters as cultural artefacts drawn up, in the main, by ecclesiastical beneficiaries, and charters as expressions of a ruler's will? Two fundamental issues require attention here: first, the light shed by charters on rulers' authority over land; and second, the use of charters to articulate a distinctively regalian or princely status for Welsh rulers superior to that of other lords.

The drafter of a charter clearly recognized the ruler's power over the land and rights whose alienation was recorded in the document. True, it is uncertain how far monks and other ecclesiastical beneficiaries could rely on the written evidence of the charter to uphold the grant if it was challenged in the future. The native legal tradition placed little emphasis on written evidence, although the rule in a legal compilation from early thirteenth-century Gwynedd requiring 'all owners of church land to come to each new king who may come, to declare to him their status and their entitlement' may have envisaged the recitation of a written text, and lawyers in south-west Wales emphasized the written authority of lawbooks in certain circumstances.[48] Records of dispute settlements from this period concerning land in *pura Wallia* are both few and make no mention of reliance on documentary proof.[49] This could suggest that charters were valued essentially as records of, and supplements to, other forms of guarantee that carried greater weight in Welsh society, especially the oath.[50] Consider, for instance, Madog ap Maelgwn's charter for Cwm-hir in 1212, in which both the donor and his *optimates* are recorded as having sworn oaths to maintain the gift, even, remarkably, to the extent of rejecting the lordship of any prince—surely an implicit swipe at the ambitions of Llywelyn ap Iorwerth of Gwynedd.[51] In its attitudes to written evidence, twelfth- and early thirteenth-century *pura Wallia* may have been more similar, say, to Normandy and other regions of northern France a century earlier than to Angevin England.[52] Yet this line of reasoning should not be pushed too far. The very production of charters may have helped to enhance the status of written evidence. Certainly monks and other religious valued them sufficiently to present them for confirmation to subsequent native rulers as well as to bishops and English kings.[53] A comparable literate mentality is also attested in a lay context in 1230, when Llywelyn ap Iorwerth specifically granted the *scriptum* by which he confirmed a purchase of land by his leading official Ednyfed Fychan to Ednyfed and his heirs.[54]

Irrespective of the extent to which the making of a written record formed a crucial part of the process whereby land was transferred to churches or lay recipients (and the issue demands further study), the extant charters reveal that, as elsewhere in Europe, the grantor relinquished valuable rights over the land thus alienated. Charters in favour of religious houses routinely exempt the beneficiary from secular dues and other obligations. Usually these exemptions are phrased in general terms: for example, 'libere et quiete ab omni servitio et consuetudine et exactione seculari', 'liberam et quietam ab omnibus terrenis consuetudinibus et exactionibus' or 'sine aliqua exactione vel consuetudine'.[55] However, some charters articulate the grantor's authority more explicitly by conceding specific privileges. Thus Maelgwn Fychan ap Maelgwn of the Deheubarth dynasty granted the monks of Strata Florida the freedom to buy and sell within all his lands and quitted them of all tolls (1198 × 1227); Llywelyn ap Iorwerth of Gwynedd included wreck and treasure trove among the rights over land granted to Cymer Abbey in 1209; while one of the gifts made by Hywel ap Iorwerth of Caerleon to Goldcliff Priory was explicitly said to be in Hywel's forest of Wentloog.[56] In addition, rulers of Gwynedd and Powys in particular implied that they had the right to control their subjects' alienation of property to religious houses. For example, in the charter just referred to Llywelyn allowed all men under his authority to make a temporary grant of a field or pool to the monks of Cymer; in 1205 Madog ap Gruffudd Maelor of northern Powys permitted the *fideles* of his land to give or sell land to Valle Crucis;[57] and a significant minority of charters issued by Gwenwynwyn ab Owain Cyfeiliog (d. 1216) of southern Powys confirm sales or gifts by freemen (often referred to as *heredes* of the land granted).[58] Likewise, as mentioned above, Ednyfed Fychan obtained a written confirmation of his purchase of lands at Rhosfynaich from Llywelyn ap Iorwerth in 1230.[59]

Ednyfed Fychan was one of only a small number of laity known to have received charters from Welsh rulers. (Strictly speaking, Llywelyn's document for Ednyfed followed the conventions of a letter patent in its diplomatic, but, like a charter, it was intended to convey a right in perpetuity.) The charters in favour of lay beneficiaries that do survive refer to new acquisitions or to special circumstances such as confirmations following conquest or the disposal of estates within the ruler's close kin.[60] True, Welsh lawbooks and other sources show that the thirteenth-century princes of Gwynedd in particular sought to increase their authority over land, notably with respect to the jurisdictional privileges of some native ecclesiastical foundations and the settlement of land disputes.[61] In addition, some legal rules state that patrimonial land should escheat to the king or lord in the event of a failure to render the services due from it or because of treason and other serious offences.[62] Yet neither the law-texts nor the extant charters indicate a systematic attempt, or even desire, to subject the normal patrimonial landholding of freemen to princely confirmation. (When the northern Welsh lawbook known as the Iorwerth Redaction declared that 'A person's coming to land is not valid save by the judgement of the law, or by the investiture of a lord', it clearly had in mind a newcomer to the land rather than one who had inherited it as patrimony from his father.)[63] As far as the obligations of lay grantees were concerned, much no doubt turned on individual circumstances: for example, a few charters reserve the ruler's right to receive military service, but the right is implicitly waived in other documents that exempt the recipient from all services.[64]

Charters offer valuable insights, then, into the rights asserted—and in many cases also exercised—by Welsh rulers over land subject to their authority. The written assertion or recognition of these rights may well, of course, have been intended to make them more effective and have thus served to promote as much as reflect rulers' power. Yet the potential of charters as a means of expressing an ideology of rulership went beyond claims concerning lordship over land, important though that was. It is also necessary to assess how far other aspects of the documents' language, together with the use of seals, served to articulate the status and dignity of rulers.

One important indication of the authority and status claimed by, or attributed to, a ruler was the style adopted in the protocol.[65] Even when it was drafted by a beneficiary, the style was presumably acceptable to the ruler whose name it contained and who authenticated the charter with his seal. Only rulers of Gwynedd, the most powerful principality, are consistently styled in their charters and other documents with a title (usually *rex/princeps Norwallie* in the period up to c.1230), whereas the styles of rulers belonging to other dynasties usually consist simply of a name and patronymic. The same is true of the legends of seals. Admittedly, there were exceptions: thus the Lord Rhys is 'Rhys, prince of Wales' in both of his extant charter-texts, while, in what were probably his latest charters, Hywel ap Iorwerth of Gwynllŵg in the south-east is styled 'Hywel lord (*dominus*) of Caerleon'.[66] The clear tendency, though, is both for *rex* to be replaced by *princeps* as the title for the most powerful Welsh ruler and for *princeps* to be monopolized by the princes of Gwynedd, a development linked to their aspirations to establish over-lordship over the other native rulers. As has been argued elsewhere, the use of *princeps* almost certainly stemmed from a realization that the Welsh kingship expressed by the term *rex* had become devalued by the later twelfth century—after all both Hywel ab Ieuaf of Arwystli and his overlord, Madog ap Maredudd of Powys, incorporated *rex* in their styles in the 1130s or 1140s—and thus a different term was required to convey a superior kind of royalty within Wales.[67]

Yet while there is a broad correlation between styles and the power of rulers, there were clear limits to the extent to which the potential of this and other aspects of the diplomatic of charters was exploited as a means of promoting an ideology of rulership. There are no parallels for the German imperial influence on charters of twelfth-century Irish kings identified by Marie Therese Flanagan.[68] For all that charters recording grants to religious houses proclaimed the piety of rulers, this did not extend to endowing the latter with a sacral dimension: no Welsh ruler is styled in an authentic act as ruling by the grace of God (*Dei gratia*).[69] In addition, only four charters (of which one is of dubious authenticity) enhance the solemnity of the document by including an arenga or preamble.[70] Collective addresses naming all a ruler's subjects, and thus emphasizing his authority over them, are also extremely rare: general addresses remained the norm.[71] Injunctive clauses, ultimately derived from those of English royal writs, are likewise few, and occur only in five charters for the Augustinian abbey of Haughmond in Shropshire and two for Goldcliff Priory, originally a Norman foundation, in Gwent.[72]

The evidence of seals seems to corroborate this picture of attenuated kingship. Until the second quarter of the thirteenth century all native rulers, from lesser lords such as those of upland Glamorgan to the greatest princes, including Llywelyn ap Iorwerth of Gwynedd, usually used single-sided equestrian seals, the largest of which were c.70 mm in diameter (though Llywelyn and his contemporary, Madog ap Gruffudd of northern Powys (d. 1236), each also had a counterseal); they therefore represented themselves in a fashion typical of the aristocracy rather than the kings of major kingdoms.[73] The only example of a Welsh ruler's document bearing a double-sided seal of the type used by royalty is a letter patent issued in 1241 by Dafydd ap Llywelyn of Gwynedd, a document in which, perhaps paradoxically, Dafydd set out demeaning terms of submission to his uncle Henry III.[74] The impression, which unfortunately is damaged, shows a ruler enthroned with an upright sword in his right hand on the front and mounted with a shield on the back; the legend is lost. As no other seal impressions survive for Dafydd and none for his successors, it is possible that the princes of Gwynedd used such a double-sided seal from the 1240s until the extinction of native rule in 1282–83. Indeed, the same may be true of Dafydd's father, Llywelyn ap Iorwerth, for whom no seal impressions survive for the years following his change of style from 'Llywelyn, prince of North Wales' to 'Llywelyn, prince of Aberffraw and lord of Snowdon'—a change, clearly attested in documents from 1 May 1230 onwards, that was designed to proclaim, through its reference to the alleged status of Aberffraw (Anglesey) as the chief court of Wales, the prince's authority over all the other Welsh rulers.[75] At the very least, Llywelyn would have needed a new seal whose legend matched his new style; and, given the assertiveness of that style, he may have adopted a double-sided seal as a further means of enhancing his dignity. If that was the case, though, the tardiness of even the most powerful Welsh rulers in adopting this symbol of royal status is still striking, and stands in telling contrast to the situation in Scotland, whose kings had used double-sided great seals since the reign of Alexander I (1107–24).[76]

These last points have broader implications for our understanding of twelfth- and early thirteenth-century Welsh political culture that can only be touched upon very briefly here by way of conclusion. Was the limited use made of charters as a means of articulating rulers' authority essentially a result of political realism, a recognition that such rulers were, in a wider European perspective, small fry whom it would be absurd to endow with the documentary trappings of the kings of Scots, let alone the Capetians or Plantagenets? Given the relatively small size of Welsh rulers' territories, whose integrity was periodically threatened by both dynastic rivalries and military intervention by Marcher lords or the king of England, this interpretation cannot lightly be dismissed, especially with respect to the period before Llywelyn ap Iorwerth's ascendancy from 1212 onwards.[77] The danger with this approach, though, is that it identifies limitations that may not have been perceived as such by Welsh rulers at the time and may lead us to overlook more positive interpretations. For one thing, charters do not tell the whole story. From at least the 1160s the princes of Gwynedd used diplomatic correspondence to emphasize their aspirations to Wales-wide authority: for example, in a letter to Henry III in 1224 Llywelyn ap Iorwerth claimed to have no less power than the king of Scotland with respect to receiving outlaws from England.[78] In addition, however, it may be that we should regard the types of charter issued as reflecting the values of Welsh society, in which rulers were seen above all as secular warriors, legitimated by their royal pedigrees far more than any sacral charisma, while at the same time articulating the piety and territorial authority of those warriors as benefactors of religious houses.[79] While the validity of this view requires further investigation, there is a strong case for holding that the picture of Welsh rulers' authority presented by charters needs to be compared not only with the uses made of charters by, say, English or Scottish kings, but also with the evidence provided by other kinds of sources for the nature of power within the native principalities and lordships of Wales. At the very least, the charters of Welsh rulers merit close attention in any attempt to understand the political as well as the written culture of twelfth- and thirteenth-century Wales.[80]

Notes

1. *AWR*, no. 28.
2. Cf. Davies, 'Papal Bull'.
3. *AWR*.
4. *Charters of the Anglo-Norman Earls of Chester*, ed. Barraclough; cf. Insley, 'From *Rex Wallie*', 182.
5. An issue addressed in Pryce, 'Welsh Rulers and the Written Word', 77–85; *AWR*, Introduction.
6. See, for example, Cowley, *Monastic Order*, ch. 2; Griffiths, 'Native Society'; Williams, *Welsh Cistercians*, 169–74. Styles: Richter, 'Political and Institutional Background', 42–8; Davies, *Conquest*, 252, 253; Pryce, 'Owain Gwynedd', 20–4; Smith, *Llywelyn*, 145–6, 283–5.
7. Davies, 'Records of the Abbey of Ystrad Marchell', 6.
8. Davies, *Llandaff Charters*; *Llandaff Episcopal Acta*, ed. Crouch, pp. xxxii–xliv; *St Davids Episcopal Acta*, ed. Barrow, 14–27.
9. Davies, 'Grant by David'; *idem*, 'Grant by Llewelyn'; Williams-Jones, 'Llywelyn's Charter', 49–54; Smith, 'Dower', 349–53; *idem*, 'Land Endowments', 153–4; Crouch, 'Earliest Original Charter', 125–31; Pryce, 'Church of Trefeglwys', 25–32; *Charters of the Abbey of Ystrad Marchell*, ed. Thomas, 104–11. For a recent palaeographical study, see Patterson, *Scriptorium of Margam*.
10. Insley, 'From *Rex Wallie*'.
11. For the purposes of this analysis, charters lacking time-dates whose opening terminal dates are no later than 1225 have been assigned to the period up to that date.
12. Crouch, 'Earliest Original Charter', 125–6.
13. *AWR*, no. 480. This analysis is based on Pryce, 'Church of Trefeglwys', 24–7, which follows the criteria set out in Davies, 'Latin Charter-Tradition'.

14. Ibid., 262.
15. *AWR*, nos 2–4, 546; cf. Pryce, 'Church of Trefeglwys', 40–2. For the term 'writ-charter', which I use here as a term of convenience for charters in letter-form, see, for example, Galbraith, 'Monastic Foundation Charters', 205; *RRS*, ii, 69; Hudson, 'Diplomatic and Legal Aspects', 154.
16. Cf. Crouch, 'Earliest Original Charter', 130; *idem*, *Image of Aristocracy*, 138–9, 242–6; and, more generally, Bedos-Rezak, 'Diplomatic Sources', 327–31.
17. *AWR*, nos 463–4, 469–72, 474–5; cf. *Mon. Ang.*, vi, pt II, 1022.
18. *AWR*, nos 26, 28.
19. E.g. *AWR*, nos 122, 127–8, 130–9, 141–6, 148; Patterson, *Scriptorium of Margam*.
20. E.g. *AWR*, nos 131, 137, 142, 154, 158, 166, 168, 183–7, 189–90 (oaths); ibid., nos 167, 185–6 (pledges).
21. Ibid., no. 22; Crouch, 'Earliest Original Charter', 129.
22. Cf. Cowley, *Monastic Order*, 22, 25.
23. Cowley, *Monastic Order*, 24–7, 46–50, 148–9; Williams, *Welsh Cistercians*, 3, 26–32; Huws, *Medieval Welsh Manuscripts*, 52–3.
24. Insley, 'From *Rex Wallie*', 188.
25. *AWR*, nos 539, 544.
26. Galbraith, 'Monastic Foundation Charters', 215–16, notes that the diploma 'still lingered on in documents drawn up in monastic houses' in mid-twelfth-century England, though by then it had been almost entirely displaced by the writ-charter in the royal chancery and in baronial house-holds. In Scotland, by contrast, the diploma continued to be used for royal confirmations in favour of Dunfermline Abbey as late as 1277: see Broun in this volume, p. 177.
27. The earliest surviving charter for the abbey is a confirmation of King John dated 27 December 1214: *Mon. Ang.*, vi, 591.
28. Waquet, *Recueil*, 45–6, 51–2, 62 (nos 19, 27, 41).
29. For example, ibid., 62 (no. 41).
30. Cf. Galbraith, 'Monastic Foundation Charters', 214. I am grateful to David Crouch for emphasizing this point to me.
31. Giry, *Manuel de diplomatique*, 745–6, 754. A more distant echo of this phrase occurs in the preamble to an act of Bishop Guy of Bangor for Haughmond Abbey datable to 1177×c.1190 ('Ne quid a nobis intuitu pietatis et honestatis puplice et solempniter gestum est . . .'): *Cartulary of Haughmond*, ed. Rees, no. 1212.
32. Cf. Chaplais, *English Royal Documents*, 14. For Scottish royal practice in this regard, see Broun, 'Absence of Regnal Years'.
33. The two charters of Llywelyn ap Iorwerth for Aberconwy Abbey that refer to the tenth year of Llywelyn's principate in their dating clauses are spurious: *AWR*, nos 218–19; Insley, 'Fact and Fiction'.
34. *AWR*, no. 113.
35. Cheney, *English Bishops' Chanceries*, 84–9; Chaplais, *English Royal Documents*, 13, 14; Giry, *Manuel de diplomatique*, 755.
36. *Calendar of Various Chancery Rolls*, 300–1; *Charters of the Abbey of Ystrad Marchell*, ed. Thomas, no. 25.
37. *Charters of the Abbey of Ystrad Marchell*, ed. Thomas, 111.

38. *AWR*, no. 544 ('Guenoingven', 'Negued', 'Iegueinc'); cf. Russell, 'Scribal (In)competence', esp. 141.
39. *Charters of the Abbey of Ystrad Marchell*, ed. Thomas, 110–11.
40. Davies, 'Papal Bull', 200; *AWR*, no. 28.
41. *Charters of the Abbey of Ystrad Marchell*, ed. Thomas, 106–7.
42. *AWR*, nos 27, 49, 68, 91.
43. See Davies, *Llandaff Charters*, 142–4 and the examples cited there, most of which are either in Welsh or in a mixture of Welsh and Latin.
44. See, for example, Clanchy, *From Memory to Written Record*, 86; Barrow, *Kingdom of the Scots*, 72–4, 80–2; Neville, 'Charter Writing', 79, 82–3; Hudson, 'Legal Aspects of Scottish Charter Diplomatic', 129–30.
45. Cf. Pryce, 'British or Welsh?', esp. 797; *idem*, 'Frontier Wales', 103–6.
46. A full discussion of the evidence for the production of documents is provided in the Introduction to *AWR*.
47. Cf. pp. 185–7.
48. *Llyfr Iorwerth*, ed. Wiliam, §71/3; translated in Jenkins, *Law of Hywel Dda*, 82; cf. Pryce, *Native Law*, 196. For legal procedures and the lawyers' attitudes towards the written word more generally, see Davies, 'Administration of Law'; Pryce, 'Lawbooks and Literacy'.
49. See, for example, *AWR*, nos 16–17, 336, 342–3, 440, 509, together with discussion of the first two documents in Stephenson, *Thirteenth Century Welsh Law Courts*. By contrast, a judgement recorded in a charter issued jointly in 1234 by Morgan Gam, lord of Afan in upland Glamorgan, and the bishop of Llandaff referred to the evidence of both charters and oral testimony: *AWR*, no. 181.
50. Cf. Pryce, *Native Law*, 39–65.
51. *AWR*, no. 113. For other references to oaths sworn in support of gifts, quitclaims and other obligations such as warranty, most of which occur in charters issued in favour of Margam Abbey by members of the native dynasty of Glamorgan, see *AWR*, nos 11, 22, 131–2, 134, 136–8, 142, 153–5, 166, 168, 175, 177–8, 183–6, 188–90, 317.
52. Cf. Bedos-Rezak, 'Diplomatic Sources', 323–6.
53. For twelfth- and thirteenth-century episcopal confirmations of gifts to Haughmond Abbey in the diocese of Bangor, see *Cartulary of Haughmond*, ed. Rees, nos 791–2, 794–6, 1212, 1219–20.
54. *AWR*, no. 260.
55. Ibid., nos 131, 198, 548.
56. Ibid., nos 63, 229, 472.
57. Ibid., no. 503.
58. Ibid., nos 548–9, 552–3, 565, 575.
59. Ibid., no. 260.
60. Princely grants: *AWR*, nos 84, 318, 322, 423, 441, 457. Confirmations following conquest: *AWR*, nos 124, 130, 239. Wives and other relatives: *AWR*, nos 71, 515–16, 526, 602, 606–7.
61. Davies, *Conquest*, 259–61; Pryce, *Native Law*, 192–8, 205–6, 211–33, 241–51; Smith, *Llywelyn*, 201–18.
62. See, for example, *Llyfr Colan*, ed. Jenkins, §288; *Latin Texts of the Welsh Laws*, ed. Emanuel, 133, 130, 231, 387–8; Pryce, *Native Law*, 66–9.

63. *Llyfr Iorwerth*, ed. Wiliam, §87/7; translated in Jenkins, *Law of Hywel Dda*, 110. I interpret the rule as referring to the *gur dyuot* (incomer), whose rights to land are contrasted with those of the *treftadauc* (patrimonial) earlier in the lawbook: *Llyfr Iorwerth*, ed. Wiliam, §78/4–5; translated in Jenkins, *Law of Hywel Dda*, 92.

64. Reserved: *AWR*, nos 84 (1236×1244), 239 (1217), 318 (1243), 441 (1260), 607 (1277). Laity exempted from all secular service: *AWR*, nos 124 (1189×1203; commuted for one pound of cumin a year), 130 (1189×1208), 260 (1230), 322 (1247), 423 (1281), 457 (1283). Cf. Stephenson, *Governance of Gwynedd*, 89–93.

65. The styles adopted by Welsh rulers are discussed further in the Introduction to *AWR*.

66. *AWR*, nos 26, 28, 473–5.

67. Smith, 'Owain Gwynedd', 16; *idem*, *Llywelyn*, 15–16, 282–4; Pryce, 'Owain Gwynedd', 20–3; *AWR*, nos 1–2 (Hywel), 480 (Madog).

68. Cf. Flanagan, 'Context and Uses', 121.

69. The only possible exception is a letter of Llywelyn ap Iorwerth, datable to 1212, and extant only in early modern copies: *AWR*, no. 234.

70. *AWR*, nos 229, 250, 256 (dubious), 544.

71. As noted by Insley, 'From *Rex Wallie*', 187–8. There are only two examples, both in charters issued by the brothers Morgan and Iorwerth sons of Owain of Gwynllŵg, of collective addresses drafted with respect to territory in Wales: *AWR*, nos 462 ('omnibus hominibus suis Francis et Anglis atque Walensibus', 1147×1157), 464 ('omnibus amicis suis et hominibus Francis, Anglicis et Walensibus', 1154×1158). Charters of Dafydd ab Owain and his wife Emma, both datable to 1186×1194, addressed to 'universis Dei fidelibus Francis et Anglis', refer to the estate of Stockett in Shropshire: *AWR*, nos 200, 202.

72. *AWR*, nos 197–9, 203, 258, 464, 472.

73. Crouch, 'Earliest Original Charter', 130; *idem*, *Image of Aristocracy*, 242; Siddons, 'Welsh Equestrian Seals'. Surviving seal impressions show that the following rulers possessed seals c.70 mm in diameter: Cadell ap Gruffudd of Deheubarth (estimated original size), Gwenwynwyn ab Owain Cyfeiliog of southern Powys, Llywelyn ap Iorwerth of Gwynedd and Madog ap Gruffudd of northern Powys (c.72 mm).

74. *AWR*, no. 304.

75. Earliest certain examples: *AWR*, nos 260–2. The style also occurs in *AWR*, no. 256, dated 1225, but the authenticity of this charter is dubious. See further Pryce, 'Negotiating Anglo-Welsh Relations', 18–20 and references given there.

76. Harvey and McGuinness, *Guide to British Medieval Seals*, 6, 27.

77. For a broader perspective on the contrasting 'political culture zones' represented by the English and the Scottish kingdoms on the one hand and the territories under native Irish and Welsh rule on the other, see Davies, *First English Empire*, ch. 4.

78. *AWR*, no. 255. See further Pryce, 'Owain Gwynedd'; *idem*, 'Negotiating Anglo-Welsh Relations', 17–18.

79. See, for example, the biography of Gruffudd ap Cynan (d. 1137) of Gwynedd: *Historia Gruffud*, ed. Evans. For recent discussion of lawyers' and

poets' views of native kingship, see Charles-Edwards *et al.* (eds), *Welsh King and His Court.*

80. I am grateful to all those who provided feedback on the version of this paper presented at the Wiles Colloquium in Belfast, and also to those who commented on my discussion of some of this material in a paper delivered at the Haskins Society Conference at Cornell University in November 2002.

Works Cited

Primary sources

Alençon, Archives départementales de l'Orne H3333.
Canterbury, Cathedral Library, Register A.
Dijon, Archives départementales de la Côte d'Or, MS 11 H. 23.
Dublin, Trinity College, MS 1339.
Durham, Dean and Chapter Muniments, 1.4 Ebor. 9.
Edinburgh, NAS GD 45; GD 55.
Edinburgh, NLS Adv. MSS 34.1.3a, 34.3.28, 34.3.29, 34.4.11.
Edinburgh, NLS MS Acc. 10301/1.
Evreux, Archives départementales de l'Eure H1438.
Fyvie (Aberdeenshire) Fyvie Estate Office, Bundle 289–97, Item 295.
London, BL, Additional Charter 6039.
London, BL, Additional Charter 76747.
London, BL, Additional MS 15350.
London, BL, Cotton Charters XVIII, nos 1–18.
London, BL, MS Harley 3960.
London, BL, MS Harley 6072.
London, PRO, SC 8/177/8818.
Oxford, Bodleian Library, MS Carte 91 (SC 10537).
Oxford, Bodleian Library, MS Top. Yorks e.12.
Paris, Bibliothèque nationale ms. Dupuy 499, fo. 26v.
Poitiers, Archives départementales de la Vienne, Carton 12 dossier 1 no. 1.

Printed primary sources

Acta of King Henry II, ed. N. Vincent, J. C. Holt and J. Everard (Oxford, forthcoming).
Acta of Henry II and Richard I, ed. J. C. Holt, R. Mortimer and N. Vincent, List and Index Society, Special series, 21 (1986).
Acta of Henry II and Richard I, Part Two: *A Supplementary Handlist of Documents*, ed. N. Vincent, List and Index Society, Special series, 27 (1996).
Aldhelm, *The Poetic Works*, trans. M. Lapidge and J. L. Rosier (Woodbridge, 1985).
Anglo-Saxon Charters III: The Charters of Sherborne, ed. M. A. O'Donovan (Oxford, 1988).
Anglo-Saxon Charters XI: The Charters of Exeter and Crediton, ed. C. L. G. Insley, (Oxford, forthcoming).
Annales Cambriae, ed. J. Williams ab Ithel, RS (London, 1860).
Annales Monastici, ed. H. R. Luard, 5 vols, RS (London, 1864–69).
Anselm, Saint, *S. Anselmi opera omnia*, ed. F. S. Schmitt, 6 vols (Seckau, Edinburgh, 1938–61).
Arbois de Jubainville, H. d', 'Chartes données en Irlande en faveur de l'ordre de Cîteaux', *Revue Celtique*, 7 (1886), 81–6.
Arnoux, M., 'Actes de l'abbaye Notre-Dame-du-Val', *Le Pays Bas-Normand: Société d'Art et d'Histoire* (2000), 5–63.

Barrow, G. W. S., *The Charters of King David I: The Written Acts of David I King of Scots, 1124–53, and of His Son Henry Earl of Northumberland, 1139–52* (Woodbridge, 1999).

Bernard of Clairvaux, *Sancti Bernardi Opera*, ed. J. Leclercq, C. H. Talbot and H.-M. Rochais, 8 vols in 9 (Rome, 1957–77).

Best, R. I., 'An Early Monastic Grant in the Book of Durrow', *Ériu*, 10 (1926–28), 135–42.

Bethada Náem nÉrenn: Lives of Irish Saints, ed. C. Plummer, 2 vols (Oxford, 1922).

Book of Leinster, ed. O. J. Bergin, R. I. Best, M. A. O'Brien and A. O'Sullivan, 6 vols, Dublin Institute for Advanced Studies (Dublin, 1954–83).

Book of Leinster, Sometime Called the Book of Glendalough..., ed. R. Atkinson, Royal Irish Academy (Dublin, 1880).

Book of the Foundation of Walden Monastery, ed. D. Greenway and L. Watkiss (Oxford, 1999).

Boussard, J., 'Trois actes d'Henri II Plantagenêt relatifs à ses possessions françaises', *Bibliothèque de l'Ecole des Chartes*, 118 (1960), 51–7.

Bracton's Note Book, ed. F. W. Maitland, 3 vols (London, 1887).

Brooks, E. St John, 'A Charter of John de Courcy to the Abbey of Navan', *Journal of the Royal Society of Antiquaries of Ireland*, 63 (1933), 38–45.

Butler, C. M. and Bernard, J. H., 'The Charters of the Cistercian Abbey of Duiske in the County of Kilkenny', *Proceedings of the Royal Irish Academy*, 35C (1918), 1–188.

Caithréim Thoirdhealbhaigh, ed. S. H. O'Grady, 2 vols, Irish Texts Society, 26–7, 1924–5 (London, 1929).

Calendar of Archbishop Alen's Register c. 1172–1534, ed. C. McNeill, Royal Society of Antiquaries of Ireland (Dublin, 1950).

Calendar of Charter Rolls Preserved in the Public Record Office, 6 vols, PRO (London, 1903–27).

Calendar of Documents relating to Ireland Preserved in her Majesty's Public Record Office, London, ed. H. S. Sweetman and G. F. Handcock, 5 vols, PRO (London, 1875–86).

Calendar of Ormond Deeds, ed. E. Curtis, 6 vols, Irish Manuscripts Commission (Dublin, 1932–43).

Calendar of Patent Rolls, i–, PRO (London, 1901–).

Calendar of the Liberate Rolls Preserved in the Public Record Office, 6 vols, PRO (London, 1916–64).

Calendar of Various Chancery Rolls, Supplementary Close Rolls, Welsh Rolls, Scutage Rolls, Preserved in the Public Record Office A.D. 1277–1326, PRO (London, 1912).

Canivez, J.-M., *Statuta Capitulorum Generalium Ordinis Cisterciensis ab Anno 1116 ad Annum 1786*, 8 vols (Louvain, 1933–41).

Canterbury Professions, ed. M. Richter, Canterbury and York Society, 67 (Torquay, 1973).

Cartae Antiquae Rolls, ed. L. Landon and J. Conway Davies, 2 vols, Pipe Roll Society, New series, 27, 33 (London, 1939–60).

Cartulaire de l'abbaye Notre-Dame de Chancelade, ed. L. Grillon and B. Reviriego, Archives de Dordogne, 2 (Périgueux, 2000).

Cartulary of Haughmond Abbey, ed. U. Rees (Cardiff, 1985).

Cartulary of Launceston Priory, ed. P. L. Hull, Devon and Cornwall Record Society, New series, 30 (1987).

Cartulary of Worcester Cathedral Priory (Register 1), ed. R. R. Darlington, Pipe Roll Society, New series, 38 (London, 1968).

Charters of the Abbey of Ystrad Marchell, ed. G. C. G. Thomas (Aberystwyth, 1997).

Charters of the Anglo-Norman Earls of Chester c.1071–1237, ed. G. Barraclough, Record Society of Lancashire and Cheshire, 126 (Manchester, 1988).

Charters of the Honour of Mowbray, 1107–1191, ed. D. E. Greenway, British Academy, Records of Social and Economic History, New series, 1 (London, 1972).

Chartularies of St Mary's Abbey, Dublin, 1162–1370, ed. J. T. Gilbert, 2 vols, RS (London, 1884–86).

Chronicle of Battle Abbey, ed. E. Searle (Oxford, 1980).

Chronicles of the Reigns of Stephen, Henry II, and Richard I, ed. R. Howlett, 4 vols, RS (London, 1884–89).

Chronicon Monasterii de Abingdon, ed. J. Stevenson, 2 vols, RS (London, 1858).

Chroniques des comtes d'Anjou, ed. L. Halphen and R. Poupardin (Paris, 1913).

Corpus Inscriptionum Insularum Celticarum, ed. R. A. S. Macalister, 2 vols (Dublin, 1945–49).

Correspondence of Thomas Becket, ed. A. Duggan, 2 vols (Oxford, 2000).

Councils and Synods, with other Documents Relating to the English Church, i, part II, *1066–1154*, ed. D. Whitelock, M. Brett and C. N. L. Brooke (Oxford, 1981).

Coutumiers de Normandie, ed. E.-J. Tardif, 2 vols (Rouen, 1871, 1896).

Curia Regis Rolls of the Reigns of Richard I, John and Henry III preserved in the Public Record Office, 18 vols, PRO (London, 1922–).

Decrees of the Ecumenical Councils, ed. N. P. Tanner, 2 vols (London and Washington, D.C., 1990).

Diplomatic Documents preserved in the Public Record Office, i, *1101–1272*, ed. P. Chaplais, PRO (London, 1964).

Documents of the Baronial Movement of Reform and Rebellion 1258–1267, ed. R. F. Treharne and I. J. Sanders (Oxford, 1973).

Eadmer, *Historia Novorum*, ed. M. Rule, RS (London, 1884).

Early Charters of the Cathedral Church of St Paul's London, ed. M. Gibbs, Camden Society, 3rd series, 57 (London, 1939).

English Episcopal Acta (Oxford, 1980–).

English Lawsuits from William I to Richard I, ed. R. C. Van Caenegem, 2 vols, Selden Society, 106, 107 (London, 1991).

Epistolae Cantuarienses, ed. W. Stubbs, RS (London, 1865).

Facsimiles of Early Charters in Oxford Muniment Rooms, ed. H. E. Salter (Oxford, 1929).

Facsimiles of English Royal Writs to A.D. 1100, Presented to Vivian Hunter Galbraith, ed. T. A. M. Bishop and P. Chaplais (Oxford, 1957).

Facsimiles of the National Manuscripts of Ireland, ed. J. T. Gilbert, 4 vols (Dublin, 1874–84).

Facsimiles of National Manuscripts of Scotland, ed. C. Innes, 3 vols (Southampton, 1867–71).

Félire hÚi Gormáin: The Martyrology of Gorman, ed. W. Stokes, Henry Bradshaw Society, 9 (London, 1895).

Félire Oengusso Céli Dé: The Martyrology of Oengus the Culdee, ed. W. Stokes, Henry Bradshaw Society, 29 (London, 1905).

Foedera, ed. T. Rymer; New edn, i, Part I, ed. A. Clark and F. Holbrooke (London, 1816).

Geoffrey of Burton, *Life and Miracles of St Modwenna*, ed. R. Bartlett (Oxford, 2002).

Gerald of Wales, *Expugnatio Hibernica: The Conquest of Ireland*, ed. A. B. Scott and F. X. Martin (Dublin, 1978).

Gerald of Wales, *Giraldi Cambrensis opera*, ed. D. S. Brewer, J. F. Dimock and G. F. Warner, 8 vols, RS (London, 1861–91).

Gervase of Canterbury, *Historical Works*, ed. W. Stubbs, 2 vols, RS (London, 1879–80).

Die Gesetze der Angelsachsen, ed. F. Liebermann, 3 vols (Halle, 1903–16).

Glossae Divinae Historiae: The Biblical Glosses of John Scottus Eriugena, ed. J. J. Contreni and P. P. Ó Néill (Florence, 1997).

Historia Ecclesia Abbendonensis: The History of the Church of Abingdon, ii, ed. J. Hudson (Oxford, 2002).

Historia Gruffud vab Kenan, ed. D. S. Evans (Cardiff, 1977).

Historians of the Church of York and Its Archbishops, ed. J. Raine, 3 vols, RS (London, 1879–84).

Jaffé, P. (ed.), *Regesta Pontificum Romanorum ad annum 1198*, 2nd edn, 2 vols (Leipzig, 1885–88).

John of Salisbury, *The Letters of John of Salisbury, i, The Early Letters (1153–1161)*, ed. W. J. Millor and H. E. Butler; revised C. N. L. Brooke (Oxford, 1979).

John of Salisbury, *Metalogicon*, ed. J. B. Hall and K. S. B. Keats-Rohan, Corpus Christianorum, Continuatio Medievalis, 98 (Turnhout, 1991).

Keynes, S. D. and Lapidge, M. (eds), *Alfred the Great: Asser's Life of King Alfred and Other Contemporary Sources* (London, 1983).

Kissane, N. (ed.), *Treasures from the National Library of Ireland* ([Drogheda], 1994).

Latin Texts of the Welsh Laws, ed. H. D. Emanuel (Cardiff, 1967).

The Law of Hywel Dda: Law Texts from Medieval Wales, trans. and ed. D. Jenkins (Llandysul, 1986).

Leclercq, J., 'Deux épîtres de St Bernard et de son secrétaire', in J. Leclercq (ed.), *Recueil d'études sur Saint Bernard et ses écrits*, 5 vols (Rome, 1962–93), ii, 313–18.

Lewis, A., 'Six Charters of Henry II and His Family for the Monastery of Dalon', *English Historical Review*, 110 (1995), 651–65.

Liber Ardmachanus: The Book of Armagh, ed. J. Gwynn (Dublin, 1913).

Liber Cartarum Sancte Crucis: Munimenta Ecclesie Sancte Crucis de Edwinesburg, ed. C. Innes, Bannatyne Club (Edinburgh, 1840).

Liber Sancte Marie de Melros: Munimenta Vetustiora Monasterii Cisterciensis de Melros, ed. C. Innes, Bannatyne Club (Edinburgh, 1837).

The Life of King Edward Who Rests at Westminster, ed. and trans. F. Barlow, 2nd edn (Oxford, 1992).

Lives of Saints from the Book of Lismore, ed. W. Stokes (Oxford, 1890).

Llandaff Episcopal Acta 1140–1287, ed. D. Crouch, Publications of the South Wales Record Society, 5 (Cardiff, 1988).

Llyfr Colan, ed. D. Jenkins (Cardiff, 1963).

Llyfr Iorwerth, ed. A. R. Wiliam (Cardiff, 1960).

Mac Niocaill, G., 'The Irish "Charters"', in *The Book of Kells, MS 58, Trinity College Dublin: Commentary*, ed. P. Fox (Lucerne, 1990), 153–65.

——, *Notitiae as Leabhar Cheanannais, 1033–1161* (Dublin, 1961).

Major, K., 'Blyborough Charters', in P. M. Barnes and C. F. Slade (eds), *A Medieval Miscellany for Doris Mary Stenton*, Pipe Roll Society, New series, 36 (London, 1962), 303–9.

Martyrology of Donegal, ed. J. H. Todd and W. Reeves, Irish Archaeological Society (Dublin, 1864).

Martyrology of Tallaght, ed. R. I. Best and H. J. Lawlor, Henry Bradshaw Society, 68 (London, 1931).

Materials for the History of Thomas Becket Archbishop of Canterbury, ed. J. C. Robertson and J. B. Sheppard, 7 vols, RS (London, 1875–85).

Matthew Paris, *Chronica Majora*, ed. H. R. Luard, 7 vols, RS (London, 1872–74).

Matthew Paris, *Historia Anglorum sive ut vulgo dicitur Historia Minor*, ed. F. Madden, 3 vols, RS (London, 1866–69).

Meerseman, G. G., 'Two Unknown Confraternity Letters of St Bernard', *Cîteaux in de Nederlanden, Achel et Westmalle*, 6 (1955), 173–8.

Memoranda Roll for the Michaelmas Term of the First Year of the Reign of King John (1199–1200), ed. H. G. Richardson, Pipe Roll Society, New series, 21 (London, 1943).

Miscellaneous Irish Annals (A.D. 1114–1437), ed. S. Ó hInnse, Dublin Institute for Advanced Studies (Dublin, 1947).

Nicholls, K. W., 'A Charter of John, Lord of Ireland in Favour of Matthew Ua hÉnni, Archbishop of Cashel', *Peritia*, 2 (1983), 267–76.

O'Brien, M. A., *Corpus Genealogiarum Hiberniae*, Dublin Institute for Advanced Studies (Dublin, 1962).

O'Conor, C. (ed.), *Rerum Hibernicarum Scriptores Veteres*, 4 vols (Dublin, 1814–26).

Ó Riain, P., *Corpus Genealogiarum Sanctorum Hiberniae*, Dublin Institute for Advanced Studies (Dublin, 1985).

The Original Acta of St Peter's Abbey, Gloucester, c. 1122 to 1263, ed. R. B. Patterson, Bristol and Gloucestershire Archaeological Society, Gloucestershire Record Series (Gloucester, 1998).

Orpen, G. H., 'Some Irish Cistercian Documents', *English Historical Review*, 28 (1913), 303–13.

Pancartes monastiques des XIe et XIIe siècles, ed. M. Parisse, P. Pégeot and B.-M. Tock (Turnhout, 1999).

The Patrician Texts in the Book of Armagh, ed. L. Bieler, Scriptores Latini Hiberniae, 10 (Dublin, 1979).

Placita de Quo Warranto, ed. W. Illingworth (London, 1818).

Poppe, E., 'A Middle Irish Poem on Éimíne's Bell', *Celtica*, 17 (1986), 59–72.

——, 'A New Edition of *Cáin Éimíne Báin*', *Celtica*, 18 (1987), 35–52.

Ralph of Diceto, *Opera Historica: The Historical Works of Master Ralph de Diceto, Dean of London*, ed. W. Stubbs, 2 vols, RS (London, 1876).

Reading Abbey Cartularies, ed. B. R. Kemp, 2 vols, Camden Society, 4th series, 31, 33 (London, 1986–87).

Recueil des actes des ducs de Normandie (911–1066), ed. M. Fauroux, Mémoires de la Société des Antiquaires de Normandie, 36 (Caen, 1961).

Richard of Hexham, 'De Gestis Regis Stephani et de Bello Standardii', in *Chronicles of the Reigns of Stephen, Henry II, and Richard I*, ed. R. Howlett, 4 vols, RS (London, 1884–89), iii, 139–78.

Robert of Torigny, *Chronique de Robert de Torigni abbé du Mont-Saint-Michel suivie de divers opuscules historiques de cet auteur et de plusieurs religieux de la même abbaye*, ed. L. Delisle, 2 vols (Rouen, 1872–73).

Robert of Torigny, *Cronica*, ed. D. C. L. Bethmann, in *Monumenta Germaniae Historica, Scriptores*, vi (Hanover, 1844).

Robertson, A. J., *Anglo-Saxon Charters*, 2nd edn (Cambridge, 1955).

Roger of Wendover, *Flores Historiarum*, ed. H. G. Hewlett, 3 vols, RS (London, 1886–89).

Rotuli Chartarum, ed. T. D. Hardy (London, 1837).

Rotuli Normanniae, ed. T. D. Hardy (London, 1835).

Rufford Charters, ed. C. J. Holdsworth, 4 vols, Thoroton Society Record series, 29, 30, 32, 34 (Nottingham, 1972–81).

St Benet of Holme 1020–1210: The Eleventh and Twelfth Century Sections of Cott. ms. Galba E ii, ed. J. R. West, 2 vols, Norfolk Record Society, 2, 3 (1932).

St Davids Episcopal Acta, 1085–1280, ed. J. Barrow, Publications of the South Wales Record Society, 13 (Cardiff, 1998).

Sheehy, M. P. (ed.), *Pontificia Hibernica: Medieval Papal Chancery Documents Concerning Ireland, 640–1261*, 2 vols (Dublin, 1962–65).

Sigebert of Gembloux, *Auctarium Affligemense*, ed. D. C. L. Bethmann, in *Monumenta Germaniae Historica, Scriptores*, vi (Hanover, 1844).

Sir Christopher Hatton's Book of Seals, ed. L. C. Loyd and D. M. Stenton (Oxford, 1950).

Somerville, R., *Scotia Pontificia: Papal Letters to Scotland before the Pontificate of Innocent III* (Oxford, 1982).

Stubbs, W. (ed.), *Select Charters*, ed. H. W. C. Davis, 9th edn (Oxford, 1913).

Tax Book of the Cistercian Order, ed. A. O. Johnsen and P. King (Oslo, 1979).

Textus Roffensis, ed. P. H. Sawyer, 2 vols, Early English Manuscripts in Facsimile, 7, 11 (Copenhagen, 1957–62).

Thesaurus Palaeohibernicus, ed. W. Stokes, and J. Strachan, 2 vols (Cambridge, 1901–03).

Treatise on the Laws and Customs of England Commonly Called Glanvill, ed. G. D. G. Hall; 2nd edn, ed. M. Clanchy (Oxford, 1993).

Twelfth-Century English Archidiaconal and Vice-Archidiaconal Acta, ed. B. R. Kemp (Woodbridge, 2001).

Two Cartularies of the Benedictine Abbeys of Muchelney and Athelney in the County of Somerset, ed. E. H. Bates, Somerset Record Society, 14 (London, 1899).

Vita et Passio Waldevi, ed. F. Michel, in *Chroniques Anglo-Normandes*, 3 vols (Rouen, 1836–40), ii, 99–142.

Vitae Sanctorum Hiberniae, ed. C. Plummer, 2 vols (Oxford, 1910).

Vitae Sanctorum Hiberniae ex codice olim Salmanticensi nunc Bruxellensi, ed. W. W. Heist (Brussels, 1965).

Walsingham, Thomas, *Gesta Abbatum Monasterii Sancti Albani a Thoma Walsingham*, ed. H. T. Riley, 3 vols, RS (London, 1867–69).

Waquet, J., *Recueil des chartes de l'abbaye de Clairvaux: XIIe siècle*, fasc. 1 (Troyes, 1950).

Wasserschleben, H., *Die irische Kanonensammlung* (Leipzig, 1885).

William of Malmesbury, *De Antiquitate Glastonie Ecclesie*, ed. J. Scott (Woodbridge, 1991).

William of Malmesbury, *The Deeds of the Bishops of England*, trans. D. Preest (Woodbridge, 2002).

William of Malmesbury, *Gesta Regum Anglorum*, i, ed. and trans. R. A. B. Mynors, R. M. Thompson and M. Winterbottom (Oxford, 1998).

William of Malmesbury, *Gesta Regum Anglorum*, ii, *General Introduction and Commentary*, ed. R. Thompson with M. Winterbottom (Oxford, 1999).

William of Malmesbury, *De Gestis Pontificum Anglorum Libri Quinque*, ed. N. E. S. A. Hamilton, RS (London, 1870).

William of Malmesbury, *De Gestis Regum Anglorum Libri Quinque*, ed. W. Stubbs, 2 vols, RS (London, 1887–89).

Wilson, J. and Lawrie, A. C., 'A Charter of the Abbot and Convent of Cupar, 1220', *Scottish Historical Review*, 8 (1911), 172–7.

Secondary sources

Adamska, A., ' "From Memory to Written Record" in the Periphery of Medieval *Latinitas*: The Case of Poland in the Eleventh and Twelfth Centuries', in K. Heidecker (ed.), *Charters and the Use of the Written Word in Medieval Society*, Utrecht Studies in Medieval Literacy, 5 (Turnhout, 2000), 83–100.

Aird, W. M., *St Cuthbert and the Normans* (Woodbridge, 1998).

Archibald, M. M., 'Coins', in *English Romanesque Art, 1066–1200*, Arts Council (London, 1984), 320–41.

Aurell, M., *L'Empire des Plantagenêt, 1154–1224* (St-Amand-Montrond, 2002).

Bachrach, B. S., 'The Idea of the Angevin Empire', *Albion*, 10 (1978), 293–9.

Baring, F. H., 'The Making of the New Forest', *English Historical Review*, 16 (1901), 427–38.

Barlow, F., *William Rufus* (London, 1983).

Barnes, P. M., 'The Anstey Case', in P. M. Barnes and C. F. Slade (eds), *A Medieval Miscellany for Doris Mary Stenton*, Pipe Roll Society, New series, 36 (London, 1962), 1–24.

Barrow, G. W. S., *The Anglo-Norman Era in Scottish History* (Oxford, 1980).

——, *The Kingdom of the Scots: Government, Church, and Society from the Eleventh to the Fourteenth Century* (London, 1973).

——, 'The Kings of Scotland and Durham', in D. Rollason, M. Harvey and M. Prestwich (eds), *Anglo-Norman Durham, 1093–1193* (Woodbridge, 1994), 311–23.

——, 'The Pattern of Non-literary Manuscript Production and Survival in Scotland, 1200–1330', in R. Britnell (ed.), *Pragmatic Literacy, East and West 1200–1330* (Woodbridge, 1997), 131–45.

——, 'The Scots Charter', in G. W. S. Barrow (ed.), *Scotland and its Neighbours in the Middle Ages* (London and Rio Grande, 1992), 91–104.

——, 'A Writ of Henry II for Dunfermline Abbey', *Scottish Historical Review*, 36 (1957), 138–43.

Barrow, J., 'Chester's Earliest Regatta?', *Early Medieval Europe*, 10 (2001), 81–94.

Barthélemy, D., ' "De la charte à la notice", à Saint-Aubin d'Angers', in D. Barthélemy (ed.), *La Mutation de l'an mil a-t-elle eu lieu?* (Paris, 1997).

——, 'Une crise de l'écrit? Observations sur les actes de Saint-Aubin d'Angers (XIe siècle)', *Bibliothèque de l'Ecole des Chartes*, 155 (1997), 95–117.

Bartlett, R., *Gerald of Wales, 1146–1223* (Oxford, 1982).

——, *The Making of Europe: Conquest, Colonization and Cultural Change 950–1350* (London, 1993).

Bates, D., 'Les Chartes de confirmation et les pancartes Normandes du règne de Guillaume le Conquérant', in M. Parisse, P. Pégeot and B.-M. Tock (eds), *Pancartes monastiques des XIe et XIIe siècles* (Turnhout, 1998), 95–109.

——, 'The Earliest Norman Writs', *English Historical Review*, 100 (1985), 266–84.

——, 'La "mutation documentaire" et le royaume Anglo-Normand (seconde moitié du XIe siècle – début du XIIe siècle)', in M.-J. Gasse-Grandjean and

B.-M. Tock (eds), *Les Actes comme expression du pouvoir au haut moyen âge: actes de la table ronde de Nancy 26–27 novembre 1999* (Turnhout, 2003), 33–49.

——, *Normandy before 1066* (London, 1982).

——, 'The Prosopographical Study of Anglo-Norman Royal Charters', in K. S. B. Keats-Rohan (ed.), *Family Trees and the Roots of Politics: The Prosopography of Britain and France from the Tenth to the Twelfth Century* (Woodbridge, 1997), 89–102.

——, *Re-ordering the Past and Negotiating the Present in Stenton's 'First Century'*, University of Reading, The Stenton Lecture 1999 (Reading, 2000).

Bateson, M., 'The Laws of Breteuil', *English Historical Review*, 15 (1900), 73–8, 302–18, 496–523, 754–7; 16 (1901), 92–110, 332–45.

Bedos-Rezak, B., 'Diplomatic Sources and Medieval Documentary Practices: An Essay in Interpretive Methodology', in J. Van Engen (ed.), *The Past and Future of Medieval Studies* (Notre Dame, IN and London, 1994), 313–43.

Bémont, C., 'La Bulle *Laudabiliter*', in *Mélanges d'histoire du moyen âge offerts à M. Ferdinand Lot par ses amis et ses élèves* (Paris, 1925), 41–53.

Berman, C., *The Cistercian Evolution: The Invention of a Religious Order in Twelfth-Century Europe* (Philadelphia, PA, 2000).

Bethell, D., 'English Monks and Irish Reform in the Eleventh and Twelfth Centuries', *Historical Studies*, 8 (1971), 111–35.

Bianacalana, J., 'Widows at Common Law: The Development of Common Law Dower', *Irish Jurist*, New series, 33 (1988), 255–329.

Bienvenu, J.-M., 'Recherches sur les péages angevins aux XIe et XIIe siècles', *Moyen Âge*, 63 (1957), 209–40, 437–67.

Binns, A., *Dedications of Monastic Houses in England and Wales, 1066–1216* (Woodbridge, 1989).

Bischoff, B., *Latin Palaeography: Antiquity and the Middle Ages*, trans. D. Ó Cróinín and D. Ganz (Cambridge, 1990).

——, *Mittelalterliche Studien: Ausgewählte Aufsätze zur Schriftkunde und Literaturgeschichte*, 3 vols (Stuttgart, 1966–67, 1981).

——, 'Zur Frühgeschichte des mittelalterlichen Chirographum', in *Mittelalterliche Studien: Ausgewählte Aufsätze zur Schriftkunde und Literaturgeschichte*, i (Stuttgart, 1966), 118–22.

Bishop, T. A. M., *Scriptores Regis* (Oxford, 1961).

Bisson, T. N., *Conservation of Coinage: Monetary Exploitation and its Restraint in France, Catalonia, and Aragon, c. 1000–1225 A. D.* (Oxford, 1979).

Boorman, J., 'Nisi feceris under Henry II', *ANS*, 24 (2002), 85–97.

Bouchard, C., 'Organising Eternity', in A. J. Kosto and A. Winroth (eds), *Charters, Cartularies and Archives: Proceedings of a Colloquium of the Commission Internationale de Diplomatique* (Princeton and New York, 16–18 September 1999) (Toronto, 2002), 22–32.

Bouet, P. and Gazeau, V. (eds), *La Normandie et l'Angleterre au moyen âge* (Caen, 2003).

Boussard, J., *Le comté d'Anjou sous Henri Plantagenêt et ses fils, 1151–1204* (Paris, 1938).

——, *Le Gouvernement d'Henri II Plantagenêt* (Paris, 1956).

——, 'Trois actes d'Henri II Plantagenêt relatifs à ses possessions françaises', *Bibliothèque de l'Ecole des Chartes*, 118 (1960), 53–5.

Bowles, C., *A Short Account of the Hundred of Penwith in the County of Cornwall* (Shaftesbury, 1805).

Brand, P., 'Local Custom in the Early Common Law', in P. Stafford, J. L. Nelson and J. Martindale (eds), *Law, Laity and Solidarities: Essays in Honour of Susan Reynolds* (Manchester, 2001).

Breatnach, L., 'Canon Law and Secular Law in Early Ireland: The Significance of *Bretha Nemed*', *Peritia*, 3 (1984), 439–59.

Brett, C., 'A Breton Pilgrim in England in the Reign of King Athelstan: A Letter in British Library Cotton Tiberius A. XV', in D. Dumville and G. Jondorf (eds), *France and the British Isles in the Middle Ages and the Renaissance* (Woodbridge, 1991), 43–70.

Brett, M., *The English Church under Henry I* (Oxford, 1975).

Brooke, C. N. L., with G. Keir, *London 800–1216: The Shaping of a City* (London, 1975).

Brooks, E. St John, 'The Grant of Castleknock to Hugh Tyrel', *Journal of the Royal Society of Antiquaries of Ireland*, 63 (1933), 206–7.

Brooks, N. P., *The Early History of the Church of Canterbury* (Leicester, 1984).

Broun, D., 'The Absence of Regnal Years from the Dating Clause of Charters of Kings of Scots, 1195–1222', *ANS*, 25 (2003), 47–63.

——, 'The Changing Face of Charter Scholarship: A Review Article', *Innes Review*, 52 (2001), 205–11.

——, *The Charters of Gaelic Scotland and Ireland in the Early and Central Middle Ages*, Quiggin Pamphlets on the Sources of Mediaeval Gaelic History, 2 (Cambridge, 1995).

——, 'The Writing of Charters in Scotland and Ireland in the Twelfth Century', in K. Heidecker (ed.), *Charters and the Use of the Written Word in Medieval Society*, Utrecht Studies in Medieval Literacy, 5 (Turnhout, 2000), 113–32.

Brown, R. A., *The Normans and the Norman Conquest*, 2nd edn (Woodbridge, 1985).

Chaplais, P., *English Royal Documents: King John–Henry VI 1199–1461* (Oxford, 1971).

——, *Essays in Medieval Diplomacy and Administration* (London, 1981).

——, 'The Original Charters of Herbert and Gervase, Abbots of Westminster (1121–1157)', in P. M. Barnes and C. F. Slade (eds), *A Medieval Miscellany for Doris Mary Stenton*, Pipe Roll Society, New series, 36 (London, 1962), 89–110; reprinted with an Addendum in P. Chaplais, *Essays in Medieval Diplomacy and Administration* (London, 1981), ch. 17.

——, 'The Seals and Original Charters of Henry I', *English Historical Review*, 75 (1960), 260–75; reprinted with an Addendum in P. Chaplais, *Essays in Medieval Diplomacy and Administration* (London, 1981), ch. 18.

——, 'Une charte originale de Guillaume le Conquérant pour l'abbaye de Fécamp: la donation de Steyning et de Bury', in *L'abbaye bénédictine de Fécamp: Ouvrage scientifique du XIIIe centenaire*, 4 vols (Fécamp, 1959), i, 93–104, 355–7; reprinted with an Addendum, in P. Chaplais, *Essays in Medieval Diplomacy and Administration* (London, 1981), ch. 16.

Charles-Edwards, T. M., 'The Construction of the *Hibernensis*', *Peritia*, 12 (1998), 209–37.

——, 'The Context and Uses of Literacy in Early Christian Ireland', in H. Pryce (ed.), *Literacy in Medieval Celtic Societies* (Cambridge, 1998), 62–82.

——, 'The *Corpus Iuris Hibernici*', *Studia Hibernica*, 20 (1980), 141–62.

——, *The Early Medieval Gaelic Lawyer*, Quiggin Pamphlets on the Sources of Mediaeval Gaelic History, 4 (Cambridge, 1999).

——, Owen, M. E. and Russell, P. (eds), *The Welsh King and His Court* (Cardiff, 2000).

Cheney, C. R., *English Bishops' Chanceries 1100–1250* (Manchester, 1950).

Clanchy, M. T., *From Memory to Written Record: England 1066–1307*, 2nd edn (Oxford, 1993).

Complete Peerage, by G. E. C[okayne], revised edn, V. Gibbs, H. A. Doubleday and G. H. White, 13 vols in 12 (London, 1910–59).

Conner, P. W., *Anglo-Saxon Exeter: A Tenth-Century Cultural History* (Woodbridge, 1993).

Constable, G., 'The Alleged Disgrace of John of Salisbury in 1159', *English Historical Review*, 69 (1954), 67–76.

Cooper, A., 'The Rise and Fall of the Anglo-Saxon Law of the Highway', *Haskins Society Journal*, 12 (2002), 39–69.

Cowley, F. G., *The Monastic Order in South Wales 1066–1349* (Cardiff, 1977).

Crick, J., 'St Albans, Westminster and Some Twelfth-Century Views of the Anglo-Saxon Past', *ANS*, 25 (2003), 65–83.

Cronne, H. A., 'The Office of Local Justiciar in England under the Norman Kings', *University of Birmingham Historical Journal*, 6 (1957), 18–38.

Crouch, D., 'Debate: Bastard Feudalism Revised', *Past and Present*, 131 (1991), 165–77.

——, 'The Earliest Original Charter of a Welsh King', *Bulletin of the Board of Celtic Studies*, 36 (1989), 125–31.

——, *The Image of Aristocracy in Britain, 1000–1300* (London, 1992).

Cunningham, I. C., *Syllabus of Scottish Cartularies: Holyrood*, Colloquium for Scottish Medieval and Renaissance Studies (Edinburgh, 2002).

Davies, J. C., 'A Grant by David ap Gruffydd', *NLWJ*, 3 (1943–44), 29–32.

——, 'A Grant by Llewelyn ap Gruffydd', *NLWJ*, 3 (1943–44), 158–62.

——, 'A Papal Bull of Privileges to the Abbey of Ystrad Fflur', *NLWJ*, 4 (1945–46), 197–203.

——, 'The Records of the Abbey of Ystrad Marchell', *Montgomeryshire Collections*, 51 (1949–50), 3–22.

Davies, R. R., 'The Administration of Law in Medieval Wales: The Role of the *Ynad Cwmwd (Judex Patrie)*', in T. M. Charles-Edwards, M. E. Owen and D. B. Walters (eds), *Lawyers and Laymen: Studies in the History of Law Presented to Professor Dafydd Jenkins* (Cardiff, 1986), 258–73.

——, *Conquest, Coexistence, and Change: Wales, 1063–1415* (Oxford, 1987).

——, *The First English Empire: Power and Identities in the British Isles, 1093–1343* (Oxford, 2000).

Davies, W., 'Charter-writing and its Uses in Early Medieval Celtic Societies', in H. Pryce (ed.), *Literacy in Medieval Celtic Societies* (Cambridge, 1998), 99–112.

——, 'The Latin Charter-Tradition in Western Britain, Brittany and Ireland in the Early Mediaeval Period', in D. Whitelock, R. McKitterick and D. Dumville (eds), *Ireland in Early Mediaeval Europe: Studies in Memory of Kathleen Hughes* (Cambridge, 1982), 258–80.

——, *The Llandaff Charters* (Aberystwyth, 1979).

Declercq, G., 'Originals and Cartularies: The Organisation of Archival Memory (Ninth-Eleventh Centuries)', in K. Heidecker (ed.), *Charters and the Use of the Written Word*, Utrecht Studies in Medieval Literacy (Turnhout, 2000), 147–70.

Doherty, C., 'Some Aspects of Hagiography as a Source for Irish Economic History', *Peritia*, 1 (1982), 300–28.

Dolley, M., *The Norman Conquest and the English Coinage* (London, 1966).

Donnelly, J., 'The Earliest Scottish Charters?', *Scottish Historical Review*, 68 (1989), 1–22.

Duffy, S., *Ireland in the Middle Ages* (London, 1997).

Duggan, A., *'Totius Christianitatis Caput*: The Pope and the Princes', in B. Bolton and A. J. Duggan (eds), *Adrian IV: The English Pope (1154–1159)* (Aldershot, 2003), 105–55.

Duncan, A. A. M., 'The Foundation of St Andrews Cathedral Priory', *Scottish Historical Review*, 84 (2005), 1–37.

——, *The Kingship of the Scots, 842–1292: Succession and Independence* (Edinburgh, 2002).

——, 'The Monk and the Medieval Archives of Glasgow Cathedral', *Innes Review*, 49 (1998), 143–6.

——, *Scotland: The Making of the Kingdom* (Edinburgh, 1975).

——, 'Yes, The Earliest Scottish Charters', *Scottish Historical Review*, 78 (1999), 1–38.

Dunning, P. J., 'The Arroasian Order in Medieval Ireland', *Irish Historical Studies*, 4 (1945), 297–315.

Dutton, P. E., 'The Uncovering of the *Glosae super Platonem* of Bernard of Chartres', *Mediaeval Studies*, 46 (1984), 129–221.

Eggers, A., *Die Urkunde Papst Hadrians IV für König Heinrich II von England über die Besetzung Irlands*, Historische Studien, 151 (Berlin, 1923).

Ellis, P. Berresford, *Celt and Saxon* (London, 1993).

Eyton, R. W., *Court Household and Itinerary of King Henry II* (London, 1878).

Faith, R., *The English Peasantry and the Growth of Lordship* (London, 1997).

Finberg, H. P. R., *Early Charters of Devon and Cornwall* (Leicester, 1954).

——, *Lucerna* (London, 1964).

Flanagan, M. T., 'The Context and Uses of the Latin Charter in Twelfth-Century Ireland', in H. Pryce (ed.), *Literacy in Medieval Celtic Societies* (Cambridge, 1998), 113–32.

——, *Irish Royal Charters: Texts and Contexts* (Oxford, 1995).

——, *Irish Society, Anglo-Norman Settlers, Angevin Kingship: Interactions in Ireland in the Late Twelfth Century* (Oxford, 1989).

Foreville, R., 'Le Régime monocratique en Angleterre au moyen âge', *Recueil de la Société Jean Bodin*, 21 (1969), 151–90.

——, 'Le Sacre des rois Anglo-Normands et angevins et le serment du sacre', *ANS*, 1 (1978), 49–62.

Förster, M., 'Die Freilassungsurkunden des Bodmin-Evangeliars', in N. Bøgholm, A. Brusendorff and C. A. Bodelsen (eds), *A Grammatical Miscellany offered to Otto Jespersen on his 70th Birthday* (Copenhagen and London, 1930), 77–100.

Frame, R., *Colonial Ireland 1169–1369* (Dublin, 1981).

Freeman, E., *Narratives of a New Order: Cistercian Historical Writing in England, 1150–1220* (Turnhout, 2002).

Galbraith, V. H., 'Monastic Foundation Charters of the Eleventh and Twelfth Centuries', *Cambridge Historical Journal*, 4 (1932–34), 205–22.

Garnett, G., *'Franci et Angli*: The Legal Distinction between Peoples after the Conquest', *ANS*, 8 (1985), 109–37.

Gasse-Grandjean, M.-J. and Tock, B.-M. (eds), *Les Actes comme expression du pouvoir au haut moyen âge: actes de la table ronde de Nancy 26–27 novembre 1999* (Turnhout, 2003).

Gillingham, J., *The Angevin Empire*, 2nd edn (London, 2001).

Giry, A., *Manuel de diplomatique* (Paris, 1894).

Green, J. A., 'Aristocratic Women in Early Twelfth-Century England', in C. W. Hollister (ed.), *Anglo-Norman Political Culture and the Twelfth-Century Renaissance* (Woodbridge, 1997), 59–82.

——, *The Aristocracy of Norman England* (Cambridge, 1997).

——, *The Government of England under Henry I*, Cambridge Studies in Medieval Life and Thought, 4th series, 2 (Cambridge, 1986).

Griffiths, M., 'Native Society on the Anglo-Norman Frontier: The Evidence of the Margam Charters', *Welsh History Review*, 14 (1988–89), 179–216.

Guyotjeannin, O., Morelle, L. and Parisse, M. (eds), *Les Cartulaires: actes de la table ronde organisé par l'Ecole Nationale des Chartes* (Paris, 1993).

Guyotjeannin, O., Pycke, J. and Tock, B.-M., *La Diplomatique médiévale*, L'atelier du médiéviste, 2 (Turnhout, 1993).

Gwynn, A., 'The First Synod of Cashel, 1101', in A. Gwynn, *The Irish Church in the Eleventh and Twelfth Centuries*, ed. G. O'Brien (Blackrock, Co. Dublin, 1992).

——, *The Irish Church in the Eleventh and Twelfth Centuries*, ed. G. O'Brien (Blackrock, Co. Dublin, 1992).

——, *The Twelfth Century Reform* (Dublin, 1968).

Hamlin, A., 'Early Irish Stone Carving: Content and Context', in S. Pearce (ed.), *The Early Church in Western Britain and Ireland*, British Archaeological Reports, British series, 102 (Oxford, 1982), 283–96.

Hartry, M., *Triumphalia Chronologica Monasterii Sanctae Crucis in Hibernia*, ed. D. Murphy (Dublin, 1891).

Harvey, P. D. A. and McGuinness, A., *A Guide to British Medieval Seals* (London, 1996).

Harvey, S., 'The Knight and the Knight's Fee in England', *Past and Present*, 45 (1970), 3–43.

Haskins, C. H., *Norman Institutions* (Cambridge, Mass., 1918).

Heidecker, K. (ed.), *Charters and the Use of the Written Word in Medieval Society*, Utrecht Studies in Medieval Literacy, 5 (Turnhout, 2000).

Herbert, M., 'Charter Material from Kells', in F. O'Mahony (ed.), *The Book of Kells: Proceedings of a Conference at Trinity College, Dublin* (Aldershot, 1994), 60–77.

——, 'Crossing Historical and Literary Boundaries: Irish Written Culture Around the Year 1000', in *Proceedings of the Twelfth International Congress of Celtic Studies*, ed. P. Sims-Williams (forthcoming).

——, *Iona, Kells and Derry: The History and Hagiography of the Monastic Familia of Columba* (Oxford, 1988).

——, 'Latin and Vernacular Hagiography of Ireland from the Origins to the Sixteenth Century', in G. Phillipart (ed.), *Hagiographies*, iii (Turnhout, 2001), 327–60.

Hirschmann, S., *Die päpstliche Kanzlei und ihre Urkundenproduktion (1141–1159)* (Frankfurt am Main, 2001).

Hlavácek, I., 'The Use of Charters and other Documents in Premyslide Bohemia', in K. Heidecker (ed.), *Charters and the Use of the Written Word in Medieval Society*, Utrecht Studies in Medieval Literacy, 5 (Turnhout, 2000).

Hogan, E., *Onomasticon Goedelicum Locorum et Tribuum Hiberniae et Scotiae: An Index, with Identifications, to the Gaelic Names of Places and Tribes* (Dublin, 1910).

Hollister, C. W., 'Normandy, France and the Anglo-Norman Realm', in C. W. Hollister, *Monarchy, Magnates and Institutions in the Anglo-Norman World* (London, 1986), 17–57.

Hollister, C. W. and Keefe, T. K., 'The Making of the Angevin Empire', *Journal of British Studies*, 12 (1973), 1–25; reprinted in C. W. Hollister, *Monarchy, Magnates and Institutions in the Anglo-Norman World* (London, 1986).

Holt, J. C., '1153: The Treaty of Winchester', in E. King (ed.), *The Anarchy of King Stephen's Reign* (Oxford, 1994), 291–316.

——, 'Feudal Society and the Family in Early Medieval England', IV: 'The Heiress and the Alien', *Transactions of the Royal Historical Society*, 5th series, 35 (1985), 1–28.

——, *Magna Carta*, 2nd edn (Cambridge, 1992).

——, 'The Origins of the Constitutional Tradition in England', in J. C. Holt, *Magna Carta and Medieval Government* (London, 1985), 1–22.

Hooke, D., *Pre-Conquest Charter-Bounds of Devon and Cornwall* (Woodbridge, 1994).

Hoskins, W. G., *The Westward Expansion of Wessex* (Leicester, 1960).

Howell, M. E., *Regalian Right in Medieval England* (London, 1962).

Howlett, D., *Sealed from Within: Self-authenticating Insular Charters* (Dublin, 1999).

Hoyt, R. S., *The Royal Demesne in English Constitutional History* (Ithaca, NY, 1950).

Hudson, J. G. H., 'Diplomatic and Legal Aspects of the Charters', in A. T. Thacker (ed.), *The Earldom of Chester and Its Charters: A Tribute to Geoffrey Barraclough*, *Journal of the Chester Archaeological Society*, 71 (Chester, 1991), 153–78.

——, *Land, Law and Lordship in Anglo-Norman England* (Oxford, 1994).

——, 'Legal Aspects of Scottish Charter Diplomatic in the Twelfth Century: A Comparative Approach', *ANS*, 25 (2003), 121–38.

Hughes, K., *Early Christian Ireland: Introduction to the Sources* (London, 1972).

Hunt, N., *Cluny under St Hugh, 1049–1109* (London, 1967).

Hurnard, N. D., *The King's Pardon for Homicide Before A.D. 1307* (Oxford, 1969).

Huws, D., *Medieval Welsh Manuscripts* (Cardiff, 2000).

Hyams, P. R., 'The Charter as a Source for the Early Common Law', *Journal of Legal History*, 12 (1991), 173–89.

——, 'The Common Law and the French Connection', *ANS*, 4 (1981), 77–92, 196–202.

Iogna-Prat, D., 'La confection des cartulaires et l'historiographie à Cluny (XIe–XIIe siècles)', in O. Guyotjeannin, L. Morelle and M. Parisse (eds), *Les Cartulaires: Actes de la table ronde organisé par l'Ecole Nationale des Chartes* (Paris, 1993), 27–44.

Insley, C. L. G., 'Fact and Fiction in Thirteenth-Century Gwynedd: The Aberconwy Charters', *Studia Celtica*, 33 (1999), 235–50.

——, 'From *Rex Wallie* to *Princeps Wallie*: Charters and State Formation in Thirteenth-Century Wales', in J. R. Maddicott and D. M. Palliser (eds), *The Medieval State: Essays Presented to James Campbell* (London, 2000), 179–96.

——, 'Where Did All the Charters Go? Anglo-Saxon Charters and the New Politics of the Eleventh Century', *ANS*, 24 (2002), 109–27.

Janauschek, L., *Origines Cisterciensium* (Vienna, 1877).

Jankulak, K., *The Medieval Cult and Relics of St Petroc* (Woodbridge, 2001).

Jared, L. H., 'English Ecclesiastical Vacancies during the Reigns of William II and Henry I', *Journal of Ecclesiastical History*, 42 (1991), 362–93.

Jenkins, D., 'From Wales to Weltenburg? Some considerations on the Origin and Use of Sacred books for the Preservation of Secular Records', in N. Brieskorn *et al.* (eds), *Vom mittelalterlichen Recht zur neuzeitlichen Rechtswissenschaft: Bedingungen, Wege und Probleme der europäischen Rechtsgeschichte* (Paderborn, 1994), 75–88.

Jenkins, D. and Owen, M. E., 'The Welsh Marginalia in the Lichfield Gospels (Part 1)', *Cambridge Medieval Celtic Studies*, no. 5 (Summer, 1983), 37–66.

Johns, S. M., *Noblewomen, Aristocracy and Power in the Twelfth-Century Anglo-Norman Realm* (Manchester, 2003).

Keats-Rohan, K. S. B., 'Portrait of a People: Norman Barons Revisited', in E. Hallam and D. Bates (eds), *Domesday Book* (Stroud, 2001), 121–40.

Kelly, F., *A Guide to Early Irish law*, Early Irish Law Series, 3 (Dublin, 1988).

Kelly, S., 'Anglo-Saxon Lay Society and the Written Word', in R. McKitterick (ed.), *The Uses of Literacy in Early Medieval Europe* (Cambridge, 1990), 36–62.

Kenney, J. F., *Sources for the Early History of Ireland: Ecclesiastical* (New York, 1929).

Keynes, S., 'The West Saxon Charters of King Æthelwulf and his Sons', *English Historical Review*, 108 (1994), 1109–49.

Lapidge, M., 'The Cult of St. Indract at Glastonbury', in D. Whitelock, R. McKitterick and D. Dumville (eds), *Ireland in Early Medieval Europe: Studies in Memory of Kathleen Hughes* (Cambridge, 1982), 179–212.

——, 'Some Latin Poems as Evidence for the Reign of Athelstan', *Anglo-Saxon England*, 9 (1980), 61–98.

Lapidge, M. and Sharpe, R., *Bibliography of Celtic-Latin Literature, 400–1200* (Dublin, 1986).

Lawson, M. K., 'Archbishop Wulfstan and the Homiletic Element in the Laws of Aethelred II and Cnut', *English Historical Review*, 107 (1992), 565–86; reprinted in A. R. Rumble (ed.), *The Reign of Cnut: King of England, Denmark and Norway* (Leicester, 1994).

Liebermann, F., 'The Text of Henry I's Coronation Charter', *Transactions of the Royal Historical Society*, New series, 8 (1894), 21–48.

Lowe, K., 'Lay Literacy in Anglo-Saxon England and the Development of the Chirograph', in P. Pulsiano and E. M. Traherne (eds), *Anglo-Saxon Manuscripts and their Heritage* (Aldershot, 1998), 161–203.

Lydon, J., *The Making of Ireland from Ancient Times to the Present* (London, 1998).

McGuire, B. P., *Friendship and Community: The Monastic Experience, 350–1250* (Kalamazoo, MI, 1988).

McLeod, N., *Early Irish Contract Law*, Sydney series in Celtic Studies, 1 (Sydney, [1992]).

McManus, D., *A Guide to Ogam* (Maynooth, 1991).

Mac Niocaill, G., 'Admissible and Inadmissible Evidence in Early Irish Law', *The Irish Jurist*, New series, 4 (1969), 332–7.

——, *Na Manaigh Liatha in Éirinn, 1142–c. 1600* (Dublin, 1959).

Maddicott, J., 'Edward the Confessor's Return to England in 1041', *English Historical Review*, 119 (2004), 650–66.

Mahn, J., *L'Ordre cistercien et son gouvernement des origines au milieu du xiiiᵉ siècle* (Paris, 1951).

Marritt, S., 'King Stephen and the Bishops', *ANS*, 24 (2002), 129–44.

Maund, K. L., *Handlist of the Acts of Native Welsh Rulers* (Cardiff, 1996).

Metcalf, D. M., 'The Taxation of Moneyers under Edward the Confessor and in 1086', in J. C. Holt (ed.), *Domesday Studies* (Woodbridge, 1987), 279–93.

Milis, L., *L'ordre des chanoines réguliers d'Arrouaise*, 2 vols (Bruges, 1969).

Milsom, S. F. C., 'Inheritance by Women in the Twelfth and Thirteenth Centuries', in M. S. Arnold *et al.* (eds), *On the Laws and Customs of England: Essays in Honour of S. E. Thorne* (Chapel Hill, 1981), 60–89.

Moody, T. W., Martin, F. X. and Byrne, F. J. (eds), *A New History of Ireland*, ix, Maps, Genealogies, Lists (Oxford, 1984).

Morelle, L., 'The Metamorphosis of Three Monastic Charter Collections in the Eleventh Century (Saint-Amand, Saint-Riquier, Montier-en-Der)', in K. Heidecker (ed.), *Charters and the Use of the Written Word*, Utrecht Studies in Medieval Literacy, 5 (Turnhout, 2000), 171–204.

Mortimer, R., 'Anglo-Norman Lay Charters, 1066–c. 1100: A Diplomatic Approach', *ANS*, 25 (2003), 153–75.

——, 'The Charters of Henry II: What are the Criteria for Authenticity?', *ANS*, 12 (1990), 119–34.

Musset, L., 'Le problème des chartes de franchises en Normandie (XIe–XIVe siècles)', in *La charte de Beaumont et les franchises municipales entre Loire et Rhin: Actes du colloque organisé par l'Institut de recherches régionales de l'Université de Nancy II (Nancy 22–25 Septembre 1982)* (Nancy, 1988), 43–57.

——, 'Que peut-on savoir de la fiscalité publique en Normandie à l'époque ducale?', *Revue Historique de Droit Français et Étranger*, 4th series, 38 (1960), 483–4.

——, 'Recherches sur le tonlieu en Normandie à l'époque ducale', *Autour du pouvoir ducal Normand Xe–XIIe siècles*, Cahiers des Annales de Normandie, 17 (Caen, 1985), 61–76.

Neville, C. J., 'Charter Writing and the Exercise of Lordship in Thirteenth-Century Celtic Scotland', in A. Musson (ed.), *Expectations of the Law in the Middle Ages* (Woodbridge, 2001), 67–89.

Newman, M., *The Boundaries of Charity: Cistercian Culture and Ecclesiastical Reform, 1098–1180* (Palo Alto, CA, 1996).

Nightingale, P., 'Some London Moneyers, and Reflections on the Organization of English Mints in the Eleventh and Twelfth Centuries', *Numismatic Chronicle*, 142 (1982), 34–50.

Norgate, K., 'The Bull *Laudabiliter*', *English Historical Review*, 8 (1893), 18–52.

Norman, E. R. and St Joseph, J. K., *The Early Development of Irish Society* (Cambridge, 1969).

O'Brien, B., 'From *Morðor* to *Murdrum*: The Pre-Conquest Origin and Norman Revival of the Murder Fine', *Speculum*, 71 (1996), 74–110.

——, *God's Peace and King's Peace: The Laws of Edward the Confessor* (Philadelphia, 1999).

Ó Corráin, D., 'Nationality and Kingship in Pre-Norman Ireland', in T. W. Moody (ed.), *Nationality and the Pursuit of National Independence*, Historical Studies, 11 (Belfast, 1978), 1–35.

——, Breatnach, L. and Breen, A., 'The Laws of the Irish', *Peritia*, 3 (1984), 382–438.

O'Doherty, J. F., 'Rome and the Anglo-Norman Invasion of Ireland', *Irish Ecclesiastical Record*, 5th series, 42 (1933), 131–45.

O'Donovan, M. A., 'An Interim Revision of Episcopal Dates for the Province of Canterbury', *Anglo-Saxon England*, 1 (1972), 23–44; 2 (1973), 91–113.

O'Keeffe, T., *Medieval Ireland: An Archaeology* (Stroud, 2000).

——, *Romanesque Ireland: Architecture and Ideology in the Twelfth Century* (Dublin, 2003).

Olson, B. L., *Early Monasteries in Cornwall* (Woodbridge, 1989).

Olson B. L. and Padel, O. J., 'A Tenth-Century List of Cornish Parochial Saints', *Cambridge Medieval Celtic Studies*, 12 (1986), 33–71.

Ó Murchada, D., 'Select Documents XXXVI: Is the O'Neill–MacCarthy Letter of 1317 a Forgery?', *Irish Historical Studies*, 23 (1982), 61–7.

Orme, N., *The Saints of Cornwall* (Oxford, 2002).

——, *Unity and Variety: A History of the Church in Devon and Cornwall*, Exeter Studies in History, 29 (Exeter, 1991).

O'Sullivan, W., 'Notes on the Scripts and Make-up of the Book of Leinster', *Celtica*, 7 (1966), 1–31.

Padel, O. J., 'The Cornish Background to the Tristan Stories', *Cambridge Medieval Celtic Studies*, 1 (1981), 53–81.

——, *Cornish Place-Name Elements*, English Place-Name Society, 56–7 (Cambridge, 1985).

——, 'Some South-Western Sites with Arthurian Associations', in R. Bromwich *et al.* (eds), *Arthur of the Welsh* (Cardiff, 1991), 229–48.

——, 'Two New Pre-Conquest Charters for Cornwall', *Journal of Cornish Studies*, 6 (1978), 20–27.

Palmer, R. C., *The County Courts of Medieval England 1150–1350* (Princeton, 1982).

Parisse, M., 'Écriture et réécriture des chartes: les pancartes aux XIe et XIIe siècles', *Bibliothèque de l'Ecole des Chartes*, 155 (1997), 247–65.

——, 'Les Pancartes: étude d'un type d'acte diplomatique', in M. Parisse, P. Pégeot and B.-M. Tock (eds), *Pancartes monastiques des XIᵉ et XIIᵉ siècles* (Turnhout, 1999), 11–62.

Patterson, R. B., *The Scriptorium of Margam and the Scribes of Early Angevin Glamorgan: Secretarial Administration in a Welsh Marcher Barony, c. 1150–c. 1225* (Woodbridge, 2001).

Pearce, S., *The Early Church in Western Britain and Ireland*, British Archaeological Reports, British series, 102 (Oxford, 1982).

Pelteret, D. A. E., *Slavery in Early Medieval England* (Woodbridge, 1995).

Picken, W. M. M., 'Bishop Wulfsige: An Unrecognised Tenth-Century Gloss in the Bodmin Gospels', *Journal of Cornish Studies*, 14 (1986), 34–8.

Poppe, E., 'The List of Sureties in *Cáin Éimíne*', *Celtica*, 21 (1990), 588–92.

Powicke, F. M., *The Loss of Normandy*, revised edn (Manchester, 1960).

Pryce, H., 'British or Welsh? National Identity in Twelfth-Century Wales', *English Historical Review*, 116 (2001), 775–801.

——, 'The Church of Trefeglwys and the End of the "Celtic" Charter Tradition in Twelfth-Century Wales', *Cambridge Medieval Celtic Studies*, 25 (1993), 15–54.

——, 'Frontier Wales c. 1063–1282', in P. Morgan (ed.), *The Tempus History of Wales, 25,000 B.C.–A.D. 2000* (Stroud, 2001), 77–106.

——, 'Lawbooks and Literacy in Medieval Wales', *Speculum*, 75 (2000), 29–67.

—— (ed.), *Literacy in Medieval Celtic Societies* (Cambridge, 1998).

——, *Native Law and the Church in Medieval Wales* (Oxford, 1993).

——, 'Negotiating Anglo-Welsh Relations: Llywelyn the Great and Henry III', in B. K. U. Weiler with I. W. Rowlands (eds), *England and Europe in the Reign of Henry III (1216–1272)* (Aldershot, 2002), 13–29.

——, 'Owain Gwynedd and Louis VII: The Franco-Welsh Diplomacy of the First Prince of Wales', *Welsh History Review*, 19 (1998–99), 1–28.

——, 'Welsh Rulers and the Written Word, 1120–1283', in P. Thorau *et al.* (eds), *Regionen Europas—Europa der Regionen: Festschrift für Kurt-Ulrich Jäschke zum 65. Geburtstag* (Cologne, 2003), 75–88.

Pulsiano, P. and Traherne, E. M. (eds), *Anglo-Saxon Manuscripts and their Heritage* Traherne (Aldershot, 1998).

Raine, J., *The History and Antiquities of North Durham* (London, 1852).

Richardson, H. G. and Sayles, G. O., *Law and Legislation from Aethelberht to Magna Carta* (Edinburgh, 1966).

Richter, M., 'The First Century of Anglo-Irish Relations', *History*, 59 (1974), 195–210.
——, 'The Political and Institutional Background to National Consciousness in Medieval Wales', in T. W. Moody (ed.), *Nationality and the Pursuit of National Independence*, Historical Studies, 11 (Belfast, 1978), 37–55.
——, 'Giraldiana', *Irish Historical Studies*, 21 (1978–79), 422–37.
Riess, L., 'The Reissue of Henry I's Coronation Charter', *English Historical Review*, 41 (1926), 321–31.
Robinson, I. S., *The Papacy 1073–1198: Continuity and Innovation* (Cambridge, 1990).
Rollason, D., 'Relic-cults as an Instrument of Royal Policy *c. 900–c. 1050*', *Anglo-Saxon England*, 15 (1986), 91–103.
Roquelet, A., *La Vie de la forêt Normande à la fin du moyen âge: le coutumier d'Hector de Chartres*, 2 vols (Rouen, 1984–95).
Round, J. H., *Geoffrey de Mandeville* (London, 1892).
Russell, P., 'Scribal (In)competence in Thirteenth-Century North Wales: The Orthography of the Black Book of Chirk (Peniarth MS 29)', *NLWJ*, 29 (1995–96), 129–76.
Scheffer-Boichorst, P., 'Hat Papst Hadrian IV zu Gunsten des englischen Königs über Irland verfügt?', *Mitteilungen des Instituts für österreichische Geschichtsforschung*, Ergänzungsband 4 (1893); reprinted in *Gesammelte Schriften von Paul Scheffer-Boichorst*, *Historische Studien*, 42 (Berlin, 1903), 132–57.
Sharpe, R., 'Dispute Settlement in Medieval Ireland: A Preliminary Inquiry', in W. Davies and P. Fouracre (eds), *The Settlement of Disputes in Early Medieval Europe* (Cambridge, 1986), 169–89.
——, *Medieval Irish Saints' Lives: An Introduction to Vitae Sanctorum Hiberniae* (Oxford, 1991).
——, 'Palaeographical Considerations in the Study of the Patrician Documents in the Book of Armagh', *Scriptorium*, 36 (1982), 3–28.
——, 'The Use of Writs in the Eleventh Century', *Anglo-Saxon England*, 32 (2004), 247–91.
Shead, N. F., *Syllabus of Scottish Cartularies: Kelso*, Colloquium for Scottish Medieval and Renaissance Studies (Edinburgh, 2002).
Sheehan, M. M., *The Will in Medieval England* (Toronto, 1963).
Sheehy, M. P., 'The Bull *Laudabiliter*: A Problem in Medieval *Diplomatique* and History', *Journal of the Galway Archaeological and Historical Society*, 29 (1961), 53–70.
Short, I., ' "Tam Angli quam Franci": Self-definition in Anglo-Norman England', *ANS* 18 (1996), 153–75.
Siddons, M., 'Welsh Equestrian Seals', *NLWJ*, 23 (1983–84), 292–318.
Smith, J. B., 'Dower in Thirteenth-Century Wales: A Grant of the Commote of Anhuniog', *Bulletin of the Board of Celtic Studies*, 30 (1982–83), 348–55.
——, 'Land Endowments of the Period of Llywelyn ap Gruffudd', *Bulletin of the Board of Celtic Studies*, 34 (1987), 150–64.
——, *Llywelyn ap Gruffudd, Prince of Wales* (Cardiff, 1998).
——, 'Owain Gwynedd', *Transactions of the Caernarvonshire Historical Society*, 32 (1971), 8–17.
Smyth, A. P., *Alfred the Great* (Oxford, 1995).
Stafford, P., 'The Laws of Cnut and the History of Anglo-Saxon Royal Promises', *Anglo-Saxon England*, 10 (1981), 173–90.

——, 'Political Ideas in Late Tenth-Century England: Charters as Evidence', in P. Stafford, J. L. Nelson and J. Martindale (eds), *Law, Laity and Solidarities: Essays in Honour of Susan Reynolds* (Manchester, 2001), 68–82.

——, 'Women and the Norman Conquest', *Transactions of the Royal Historical Society*, 6th series, 4 (1994), 221–49.

Stalley, R., *The Cistercian Monasteries of Ireland* (London, 1987).

Stenton, D. M., *English Justice Between the Norman Conquest and the Great Charter 1066–1215* (Philadelphia, 1964).

——, 'Frank Merry Stenton, 1880–1967', *Proceedings of the British Academy*, 54 (1968), 315–423.

Stephenson, D., *Thirteenth Century Welsh Law Courts* (Aberystwyth, 1980).

——, *The Governance of Gwynedd* (Cardiff, 1984).

Stevenson, J., 'The Beginnings of Literacy in Ireland', *Proceedings of the Royal Irish Academy*, 89C (1989), 127–65.

——, 'Literacy in Ireland: The Evidence of the Patrick Dossier in the Book of Armagh', in R. McKitterick (ed.), *The Uses of Literacy in Early Mediaeval Europe* (Cambridge, 1990), 11–35.

Stock, B., *The Implications of Literacy: Written Language and Models of Interpretation in the Eleventh and Twelfth Centuries* (Princeton, 1983).

Thatcher, O. J., *Studies Concerning Adrian IV*, University of Chicago Decennial Publications, 1st series, 4 (Chicago, 1903).

Thomas, G., *Les Comtes de la Marche de la maison de Charroux (Xe siècle–1177)* (Paris, 1928).

Thomas, H. M., *The English and the Normans: Ethnic Hostility, Assimilation and Identity, 1066–c. 1220* (Oxford, 2003).

Thompson, K., 'Family and Influence to the South of Normandy in the Eleventh Century: The Lordship of Bellême', *Journal of Medieval History*, 11 (1985), 215–26.

Thornton, D., 'Edgar and the Eight Kings, A.D. 973: *Textus et Dramatis Personae*', *Early Medieval Europe*, 10 (2001), 49–80.

Thurneysen, R., 'Aus dem irischen Recht V', *Zeitschrift fur Celtische Philologie*, 18 (1930), 353–408.

Tinti, F., 'From Episcopal Conception to Monastic Compilation: Hemming's Cartulary in Context', *Early Medieval Europe*, 11 (2002), 233–61.

Todd, M., *The South-West to AD 1000* (London, 1984).

Tout, T. F. T., *Chapters in the Administrative History of Medieval England: The Wardrobe, the Chamber and the Small Seals*, 6 vols (Manchester, 1920–33).

Tsurushima, H., 'The Fraternity of Rochester Cathedral Priory about 1100', *ANS*, 14 (1991), 313–37.

Turner, R. V., 'The Problem of Survival for the Angevin "Empire": Henry II's and his Sons' Vision versus Late Twelfth-Century Realities', *American Historical Review*, 100 (1995), 78–96.

Ullmann, W., 'Alexander III and the Conquest of Ireland: A Note on the Background', in F. Liotta (ed.), *Miscellanea Rolando Bandinelli Papa Alessandro III* (Siena, 1986); reprinted in W. Ullmann, *Law and Jurisdiction in the Middle Ages* (London, 1988), 371–87.

Van Caenegem, R. C., *Royal Writs in England from the Conquest to Glanvill*, Selden Society, 77 (London, 1959).

Van Houts, E. M. C., 'The Anglo-Flemish Treaty of 1101', *ANS*, 21 (1998), 169–74.

Vincent, N., 'The Charters of King Henry II: The Introduction of the Royal Inspeximus Revisited', in M. Gervers (ed.), *Dating Undated Medieval Charters* (Woodbridge, 2000), 97–120.

——, 'King Henry II and the Monks of Battle: The Battle Chronicle Unmasked', in R. Gameson and H. Leyser (eds), *Belief and Culture in the Middle Ages: Studies Presented to Henry Mayr-Harting* (Oxford, 2001), 264–86.

——, 'King Henry II and the Poitevins', in M. Aurell (ed.), *La Cour Plantagenêt (1154–1204): Actes du colloque tenu à Thouars du 30 avril au 2 mai 1999* (Poitiers, 2000), 103–35.

——, 'Les Normands de l'entourage de Henri II Plantagenêt', in P. Bouet and V. Gazeau (eds), *La Normandie et l'Angleterre au moyen âge* (Caen, 2003), 75–88.

——, 'Why 1199? Enrolment in the Chanceries of John and his Contemporaries', in A. Jobson (ed.), *The Birth of Red Tape* (Woodbridge, 2004), 17–48.

——, 'William Marshal, King Henry II and the Honour of Châteauroux', *Archives*, 25 (2000), 1–15.

Walker, R. F., 'Henry II's Charter to Pembroke', *Bulletin of the Board of Celtic Studies*, 36 (1989), 132–46.

Warren, W. L., *Henry II* (London, 1973).

Watt, J., *The Church and the Two Nations in Medieval Ireland* (Cambridge, 1970).

——, *The Church in Medieval Ireland*, 2nd edn (Dublin, 1998).

Webber, M. J. T., 'The Scribes and Handwriting of the Original Charters', in A. T. Thacker (ed.), *The Earldom of Chester and its Charters: A Tribute to Geoffrey Barraclough, Journal of the Chester Archaeological Society*, 71 (Chester, 1991), 137–51.

Weckmann, L., *Las Bulas Alejandrinas de 1493 y la Teoria Politica del Papado Medieval: Estudio de la Supremacia Papal sobre Islas 1091–1493* (Mexico City, 1949).

Williams, D. H., *The Welsh Cistercians* (Leominster, 2001).

Williams-Jones, K., 'Llywelyn's Charter to Cymer Abbey in 1209', *Journal of the Merioneth Historical and Record Society*, 3 (1957–60), 45–78.

Wilson, C., 'The Cistercians as "Missionaries of Gothic" in Northern England', in C. Norton and D. Park (eds), *Cistercian Art and Architecture in the British Isles* (Cambridge, 1986), 86–116.

Wood, M., 'The Lost Life of King Athelstan', in M. Wood, *In Search of England* (London, 1999), 149–68.

——, 'The Making of King Athelstan's Empire: An English Charlemagne?', in P. Wormald, D. Bullough and R. Collins (eds), *Ideal and Reality in Frankish and Anglo-Saxon Society: Studies Presented to J. M. Wallace-Hadrill* (Oxford, 1983), 250–72.

Wormald, P., '*Laga Eadwardi*: The *Textus Roffensis* and its Context', *ANS*, 17 (1994), 243–66.

——, *The Making of English Law: King Alfred to the Twelfth Century, I Legislation and Lawsuits* (Oxford, 1999).

——, 'Quadripartitus', in G. Garnett and J. Hudson (eds), *Law and Legislation in Medieval England and Normandy* (Cambridge, 1994), 111–47.

Young, C. R., *The Royal Forests of Medieval England* (Philadelphia, 1979).

Index

The following abbreviations have been used: abp (archbishop); bp (bishop); bpric (bishopric); kg (king); qn (queen)